INTO THE STORM

INTO THE
STORM

Chronicle of a Year in Crisis

Christopher R. Altieri

TAN Books
Gastonia, North Carolina

Cover design by Caroline Green

Cover image: Storm Surrounding the Vatican, photo by TT Studios / Shutterstock.

Library of Congress Control Number: 2019957045

ISBN: 978-1-5051-1521-5

Published in the United States by
TAN Books
PO Box 269
Gastonia, NC 28053
www.TANBooks.com

Printed in the United States of America

For Joseph and Rachel

CONTENTS

CONTENTS ix

FOREWORD

The task of the Catholic journalist is to inform, explain, encourage, inspire, and elucidate the events of the Church and the world through the lens of an authentically Catholic perspective.

Often, the task of a journalist is to understand and then to explain the context, history, and background that give meaning to unfolding events. To set the scene and lay out the stakes. To know what matters and what doesn't. To make choices in service to the truth. Journalism, done well, requires wisdom.

Catholic journalism requires something more than that. Because for the Catholic, writing about the Church requires understanding who she really is. Understanding that the Church is more than a sociological phenomenon—that she is, instead, the divinely instituted sacrament of salvation founded by Christ himself.

The Catholic journalist has an odd task. He must, on the one hand, approach his subject using the tools of his profession: seeking objectivity and fairness in his work. He must be willing to recognize the Church's successes and failures on a human level and the abilities and deficiencies of its leaders. On the other hand, he has to remember that the tools of his profession cannot, by themselves, tell the whole story of the Church—that they cannot unpack the movement of the Holy Spirit, the manifestation of Divine Providence.

The Catholic journalist must be at once reporter and believer, and he must balance those things knowing that his work might impact the communion of the Church itself, the salvation of those who read him.

This task is challenging at any time. In the scandal that enveloped the Church in 2018 and 2019, it has been far more difficult. To do it well—to be the kind of Catholic journalist who might actually serve the cause of truth intelligently and faithfully—requires a foundation of life in Jesus Christ, a foundation of prayer, and study, and formation. To be a Catholic journalist, one must first be a disciple of Jesus Christ, and to understand what's really happening, one must understand the spiritual dimension of the Church's life and ministry.

In short, the faithful Catholic journalist must accept and embrace the prophetic dimension of the Christian vocation to holiness, and he must approach his work with the humility that entails. He must be a servant of Jesus Christ by serving the truth, in its entirety, as best as he can grasp it.

Christopher Altieri is a journalist who approaches his work in precisely that way. His analysis and insight are borne of his experience working for and covering the Church, but his practical expertise is complemented by his life as a faithful Catholic: as a husband and father, as a scholar, as a man of prayer.

I do not always agree with Altieri's conclusions, or even, at times, with his premises. The reader might find the same.

But journalism is the first draft of history, not the final version, and this text, and the work it represents, is meant to contribute to a conversation about what has happened in the life of the Church and about how we might best conform ourselves, our structures, and our processes to the Gospel that we proclaim. The strength of this text is that it offers an informed viewpoint that takes into account the reality of the Church as she truly is: an institution both human and divine—the Mystical Body of Christ, comprised of often-miserable sinners. To understand this Catholic moment, we must see both of those things, as Altieri does.

The Church is always need of renewal and reform, and she needs especially for her faithful sons and daughters to call for that reform and to aid in that renewal in the confidence of their wisdom, their expertise, and their vocation. Christopher Altieri has done just that. May his work bear fruit for the kingdom.

J. D. Flynn

PREFACE

When I left what was then styled the Secretariat for Communication of the Holy See, after two years with the new dicastery and a decade before that with its predecessor, Vatican Radio, I wrote, "Friends, today [October 26, 2017] I submitted my letter of resignation to the Secretariat for Communication of the Holy See, effective December 31, 2017. It is always an honor to be in the service of the Holy Father, one I have borne for a dozen years, and do not put down lightly. Said quite simply: it is time to move on." I meant it then, and I stand by it now.

I went on to say, "In addition to the time with my wife and children my liberation from the constraints of a 24/7 news cycle will hopefully afford, I look forward especially to writing, teaching, and growing Vocaris Media, the little production and consulting project I started earlier this year." That part did not happen exactly as I had envisioned.

The end of January 2018 brought worldwide scandal, and intense media scrutiny of Pope Francis's leadership record, especially with respect to the clerical sexual abuse of minors, precipitated by some ill-chosen remarks to a press gaggle outside the stadium in Iquique, Chile, where he was going to say Mass. The *scintilla* was the so-called "Barros Affair"—about which you will be able to refresh your memory shortly—but one inexplicable decision after another caused the scandal to spiral, while new revelations emerged, manifesting deep cultural crisis and systemic rot in the clerical and hierarchical leadership of the Church, reaching all the way to the Apostolic Palace.

The pieces contained in this volume are one journalist's attempt to make sense of the crisis as it was unfolding. A few sentences that appear here have been recast to remedy ambiguities of expression with respect to matters of fact and, on rare occasion, to ameliorate gross infelicities of style. Otherwise, the pieces appear as they did when they were published. They are, as we say in the trade, a "first draft" of history, in fine copy.

They represent roughly half my total output for the year, February 2018 to February 2019. I would not belabor you with a detailed explanation of the criteria by which I chose which entries to keep and which to omit. Suffice it to say my object was to offer a selection that would avoid as much redundancy as possible—some is inevitable as one goes over facts and events in an effort to discover the logic of action—and still together constitute, as the title I have chosen suggests, a sort of chronicle of a year in crisis, by which I mean to convey that these essays are one man's attempt to make sense of especially appalling and often bewildering circumstances.

Here, then, is how I saw the rough twelvemonth running from late January 2018 to the end of February 2019, with an afterword on how I see things in the rough present. I am grateful to everyone reading this collection, and encourage critical engagement. In this line of work, one calls them as one sees them, and takes the hits as they come.

> CRA
> Rome, October 16, 2019
> Vigil of the Feast of St. Ignatius of Antioch

ACKNOWLEDGMENTS

To Damian Thompson, Luke Coppen, Dan Hitchens, Mark Greaves, and Nick Hallett go great gratitude. Andy Leisinger was a constant support (and occasionally a lightning rod), for which I am likewise grateful. Carl E. Olson at the *Catholic World Report* took a chance on me when I was still rusty, while Cate Harmon patiently helped me see stories more clearly and write them better. To them, I am likewise grateful. I lost count of the times my editors at the *Catholic Herald* and the *Catholic World Report* saved me from myself, and am impossibly indebted to them all.

John Moorehouse at TAN Books welcomed the idea of this project and shepherded it to a very happy completion, while Nick Vari's careful and discreet copyediting improved the manuscript in keeping with the ethos of the endeavor. Caroline Green's cover design captured the spirit of the thing perfectly. Thanks to everyone at TAN.

JD Flynn wrote a foreword describing the journalist I'd like to be, and work I'd very much like to do.

Ester Rita is my go-to canonical consultant. She is also my wife. Her steadfast encouragement all through a grueling year that was supposed to be one of rest, decompression, recuperation and reacclimating to "normal" life, kept me sane and hopeful, while her intellectual support was merely indispensable.

CHAPTER 1

FROM CHILE TO ROME

January 2018

For the Catholic World Report: January 23, 2018

"The Pope's misuse of 'calumny' distracts from deeper, more troubling questions"

On Thursday of last week, Pope Francis accused Chilean victims of clerical sexual abuse and their supporters in the Church of "calumny." It isn't that the Pope doesn't believe their accusations of abuse. After the Vatican found their accusations credible, and sentenced their abuser, Fr. Fernando Karadima, to a life of prayer and penance—this was in 2011, under Benedict XVI—Pope Francis decided in 2015 to put one of the criminal cleric's protégés, Bishop Juan Barros, on the See of Osorno, over the objections of the victims, at least one of whom, Mr. Juan Carlos Cruz, says Bishop Barros knew of his mentor's crimes and even witnessed them.

Things took an ugly turn, when, later in the same year of Barros's election to the See of Osorno, Francis insulted the people protesting Barros's appointment. "The Osorno community is suffering because it's dumb," the Pope told a group of pilgrims on the sidelines of a General Audience in May of 2015. The story made the rounds in the worldwide press at the time, and then disappeared.

When a Chilean journalist, who was part of a press gaggle at the gate of the venue in Iquique, where the Holy Father was to celebrate Mass on Thursday of last week, asked Pope Francis about Bishop Barros, the Pope replied, "The day they bring me proof against Bishop Barros, I'll speak." Then he doubled down. "There is not one shred of proof against [Barros]," he said. "It's all calumny, is that clear?" On the plane home from Perú—the second and final leg of his South American voyage—Pope Francis revised and extended his remarks, saying, "[If] anyone says with obstinacy, without evidence, that [so-and-so] did [such-and-such], it is calumny." He then said that Barros's accusers have brought him no evidence, and concluded, "One that accuses without evidence, with obstinacy, this is calumny."

The first thing to note is the Pope's problematic use of the term "calumny," which is not the leveling of accusations in the absence of evidence, but the leveling of accusations for the purpose of damaging another person's reputation, and/ or the repetition of such accusations for the same malicious purpose, without respect to the truth of the accusations. A person who claims to have seen someone commit a crime, however, is not accusing without evidence. The evidence he brings is essentially co-extensive with his own credibility as a witness. In the case of Bishop Juan Barros, his principal accuser is a witness, whose testimony a Vatican court found credible enough to use against Barros's mentor, Fr. Fernando Karadima.

This would not be the first time Pope Francis's lexical idiosyncrasies were cause for confusion. I still have not met anyone trained in the sacred sciences who can tell me what Francis means when he speaks of "casuistry"—or "abstract casuistry"—though it is clear he does not mean what is generally meant by the term, i.e. the resolution of moral problems by investigation into the specifics of the case and careful application of the general principles of moral science to the specific case, from within the specifics of the case, themselves. In this case, the trouble is that no one is asking the right questions.

Why is Pope Francis taking a series of maxims lifted from criminal law, and applying them to a personnel decision? Also during the course of the in-flight presser, in explaining his analysis of the Barros case, Pope Francis said, "I am waiting for evidence to change position [on Barros], but I apply the judicial principle basic in any tribunal: *nemo malus nisi probetur*—no one is guilty until it is proven [so]." At the risk of belaboring the obvious: the "presumption of innocence" applies to criminal procedure; the only protection it can afford Bishop Barros is found on the other side of a criminal indictment. The other maxim, *in dubio pro reo*, which Pope Francis invoked in defense of his decision to reduce the sentence against the convicted pedophile, Fr. Mauro Inzoli— over and against the recommendation of the Vatican's own tribunal—applies principally to the determination of guilt, which in the case of Inzoli was never in doubt, and in any case would have been well known to the legal professionals and trained jurists who handled the case and gave the sentence.

The problem here is not that the Pope has a poor grasp of technical legal terminology. The problem is not even that he keeps using those words, even though they do not mean what he thinks they mean. The former is merely a fact; he is not a lawyer, after all. The latter is symptomatic of an unfortunate quirk of character, which might be overcome or overlooked. The real problem is that he thinks he knows better, and refuses to listen to the people who do. While that quality of character will be frustrating in a parish priest, consternating in a religious superior, and genuinely difficult to manage in a local Ordinary, it will always—always—prove disastrous in anyone who attains to a position of high leadership.

There is another, prior question, though, which no one is asking: Why is Barros a bishop in the first place? During the presser, Pope Francis gave a summary of the matter, saying, "When the scandal with Karadima was discovered—we all know this scandal—we began to see many priests who were formed by Karadima, who were either abused or who were abusers." That is what abusers do. They insinuate themselves and their favorites—some of whom are also their victims— into the formation process and then into the leadership structures of the Church, and use their advantages of place and position to protect and promote one another.

"In Chile," Pope Francis went on to say, "there are four bishops, whom Karadima invited to the seminary." Barros is one of the four. He was consecrated in June of 1995, when Pope St. John Paul II was in Rome and Archbishop Piero Biggio was Nuncio in Chile. Barros served first as an auxiliary in Valparaiso, then moved to the See of Iquique, then to the Diocese for Military Services. When the See of Osorno became vacant, Francis tapped Barros, even though he was known to have advanced under the aegis of a notorious pedophile, and faced allegations of aiding and abetting his mentor's abuse, allegations that came from at least one victim, whose testimony a Vatican court had deemed credible.

The bishops of Chile had written to Pope Francis, expressing their concern over Barros's appointment. Francis responded with a lengthy letter, explaining that he had asked Barros to resign as bishop of the forces and take a year's sabbatical, only after which he might have been considered for another post. The AP reports that Francis's Nuncio in Chile, Archbishop Ivo Scapolo, conveyed the request, and explained to Barros that similar arrangements were being made for two of the other bishops who came up under Karadima. Scapolo reportedly asked Barros to keep the plan quiet, but Barros named the two others in the letter he wrote announcing his resignation from the military see. So, Francis decided that the way to handle this tainted and insubordinate prelate was to give him care of the souls of Osorno.

"When [Barros] was appointed [to Osorno]," Pope Francis said, again during the in-flight presser, "and all this protest took place, he gave me his resignation for the second time. I said, 'No, you go.' I spoke with him for a long time, others spoke at length with him. 'You go [back to your See]'," Pope Francis told reporters he told Barros. The Holy Father went on to say, "They continued to investigate Barros, but there is no evidence—and this is what I wanted to say," in the remarks outside the venue in Iquique. "I cannot condemn him because I don't have the evidence," Pope Francis repeated, "and this is what I wanted to say. I cannot condemn him because I do not have the evidence. But I am also convinced that he is innocent." In short, Pope Francis feels he has to leave Barros in place, because he does not have enough evidence to convict him in open court, and because he is personally convinced of Barros's innocence.

Speaking in Santiago de Chile in 2011, after the Vatican court came back with the guilty verdict against Karadima, Fr. Antonio Delfau, SJ, of the Chilean province—currently serving as Assistant to the General Treasurer of the Society—is quoted in a *New York Times* report on the story as saying, "[The conviction] is going to mark a before and after in the way the Chilean Catholic Church proceeds in cases like these, or at least it should." Delfau went on to say, "From now on, every case of sexual abuse must be treated with meticulous care and not be based on the gut feeling of a given Church official."

For the Catholic World Report, January 26, 2018

"Observers remain 'mystified' over Pope's remarks on clerical sex abuse, and call for bishop accountability"

Pope Francis has faced a great deal of criticism since he leveled accusations of calumny against victims of clerical sex abuse last week. Those victims claim that Bishop Juan Barros, whom Pope Francis appointed to the Diocese of Osorno, Chile, on January 10, 2015, had first-hand knowledge of their abuser's crimes and was an active participant in their cover-up. The highest-ranking churchman to respond has been Cardinal Sean O'Malley of Boston, who is also a member of the C9 Council of Cardinal Advisors and the man the Holy Father personally chose to head the Pontifical Commission for the Protection of Minors (an organization for which people within and without the Church had high hopes when it was launched in 2014, but which quickly proved both toothless and dysfunctional, and now exists in a sort of juridical limbo, its members' appointments having expired late last year without renewal or replacement).

"It is understandable that Pope Francis's statements yesterday in Santiago, Chile were a source of great pain for survivors of sexual abuse by clergy or any other perpetrator,"

Cardinal O'Malley's January 20 statement begins. It goes on to say, "Words that convey the message 'if you cannot prove your claims then you will not be believed' abandon those who have suffered reprehensible criminal violations of their human dignity and relegate survivors to discredited exile."

Another prominent US churchman with ties to the Vatican, Father James Martin, SJ—who serves as a consultor to the Holy See's Secretariat for Communications—is expressing disappointment over Pope Francis's comments. "Like many of Pope Francis's admirers," Father Martin told *CWR* when contacted about the story, "I was disappointed in the Pope's comments regarding Bishop Barros's accusers, and found Cardinal Sean O'Malley's insights a much-needed contribution to the discussion." Father Martin recognized that Pope Francis made an effort to ease the hurt his words have caused. "To that end, I was also grateful to see the Pope's apology," Father Martin said. Nevertheless, he remains perplexed at the broader situation.

"In general, what mystifies me is that there is rarely, if ever, any hard and fast evidence in clergy sex abuse cases, because of the nature of the crimes ([viz.] someone preying on a child in private)," Father Martin said. "Consequently, we must take what the victims say very seriously, because, needless to say, there are not going to be photographs or records of any kind. Moreover, some of these same victims were believed in the case of Bishop Barros's mentor, Father Karadima, so I'm not sure why we would suddenly disbelieve them now. As I said, it's mystifying to me."

Father Martin also said the Church must implement systems capable of holding the Church's hierarchical leadership accountable. "Until we see real accountability for bishops, we will not be able to get past the abuse crisis," he said. "The papal commission, then, really needs teeth. In particular, bishops who have offended must be removed, and when they are removed it must be said that this is why they are being removed."

Martin is not the only prominent US Jesuit to make such a call. Writing for Religion News Service, Father Thomas J. Reese argued, "The fundamental problem is that the Church has no process for judging bishops that is transparent and has legitimacy with the public."

Pope Francis maintains that he has chosen to leave Bishop Barros in place, because, "There is not one shred of proof against him." Pressed on the plane trip home from South America, the Pope explained, "The word 'proof' wasn't the best [word to use] in order to be near to a sorrowful heart. I would say evidence. The case of Barros was studied, it was re-studied, and there is no evidence. That is what I wanted to say. I have no evidence to condemn. And if I were to condemn without evidence or without moral certainty, I would commit the crime of a bad judge."

The Pope does have the claims of the three victims, though. Not to put too fine a point on it: that is evidence, in the form of witness testimony; witnesses a Vatican criminal tribunal believed when they said Father Fernando Karadima abused them. Barros, moreover, is one of four Karadima protégés to have been made bishops before their mentor's crimes came to light. The accusations against Barros have been in the Chilean press at least since 2012. So, it simply is not true that Pope Francis has no evidence. Pope Francis does not believe the witnesses.

Why the Pope would choose not to believe the victims' witness against Bishop Barros now, when his own court has found them credible, is, as Father Martin says, "mystifying." It also raises a serious question about the Holy Father's governance of the Universal Church. The presumption of innocence, in its strict juridical sense, is the explicit basis on which the Holy Father has justified his behavior in the Barros case. Even if the Holy Father is correctly applying the principle—and there are strong reasons to believe he is not—it is not the standard a prudent leader employs in making personnel decisions.

"Will the Pope's project result in real reform—or turn Rome into a Buenos Aires-on-Tiber?"

The first month of 2018 has not been smooth sailing for Pope Francis. Within the space of four weeks, he has brought his record of leadership in the ongoing fight against clerical sexual abuse of minors under intense (and frankly overdue) scrutiny, and drawn the ire of a man universally recognized as a hero of the faith over his China policy. In addition to these major crises, he has faced increasing criticism on a whole host of issues, ranging from the controversy over the proper interpretation and implementation of the post-Synodal Apostolic Exhortation, *Amoris laetitia*, to the "rethinking" of the teachings articulated in the encyclical letter *Humanae vitae*, on the regulation of birth. It is not too much to say that Pope Francis's ability to respond to the major crises will determine in large part his ability to address himself to the work of reform he was elected to undertake and oversee.

All of that followed a dust-up over remarks by the Cardinal Secretary of State, Pietro Parolin, that appeared during a broad-ranging interview with Vatican Media at the start of the year—an interview deserving of attention, insofar as it lays out the programmatic vision of a major Vatican official for the work of Pope Francis in 2018. In particular, Cardinal Parolin drew the attention of critics for his talk of a "new paradigm" in the Church.

The talk of a new paradigm is telling, though probably not in the way that most of the commentary has suggested. To parse the language fairly, the first thing to note is that the Secretary of State deployed it only after laying out the terms controlling its deployment, namely, the shift of emphasis for which Francis is calling in relation to young people. "I believe that the most innovative aspect of this approach," Parolin said in response to a prompt from interviewer Alessandro Gisotti regarding the expectations of the Church from the youth of the world, "is the search for a new relationship between the Church and young people, based on a paradigm of responsibility exempt from all paternalism."

It would be easy (too easy) to impugn the language as the "smoking gun" that proves the Pope is a Marxist (he's not) or dismiss it as boilerplate. The more difficult, and more useful project is to put the best possible construction on it and see what there is to see in it.

Cardinal Parolin went on to quote the famous line from U.S. President John F. Kennedy's inaugural, "Ask not what your country can do for you. Ask what you can do for your country." Parolin continued, saying, "I believe that this is, at bottom, also the [essence of the] innovative approach: that is, the Church asks young people—the Pope, the Church—both ask young people what they can do for the Church, what contribution they can give to the Gospel, to the spread of the Gospel, today—and I believe that young people will be able to respond to this invitation with their generosity and also with their enthusiasm."

There really is nothing wrong with that, and just about everything right. The desire for means of diversion completely severed from the responsibility from which we might need to be diverted—in essence, for fully-funded and perpetual adolescence—is a capital feature of our sick and possibly moribund culture. Pope St. John Paul II saw this coming, and started early and often to tell young people to grow up. Pope Benedict followed him, and Francis has been arguably more fervent in his appeals and stark in his warnings than were his predecessors. Listen to him in 2016:

> [W]hen we opt for ease and convenience, for confusing happiness with consumption, then we end up paying a high price indeed: we lose our freedom. We are not free to leave a mark. We lose our freedom. This is the high price we pay. There are so many people who do not want the young to be free; there are so many people who do not wish you well, who want you to be drowsy and dull, and never free! No, this must not be so! We must defend our freedom!

Francis follows with this:

> My friends, Jesus is the Lord of risk, he is the Lord of the eternal "more". Jesus is not the Lord of comfort, security and ease. Following Jesus demands a good dose of courage, a readiness to trade in the sofa for a pair of walking shoes and to set out on new and uncharted paths. To blaze trails that open up new

horizons capable of spreading joy, the joy that is born of God's love and wells up in your hearts with every act of mercy. To take the path of the "craziness" of our God, who teaches us to encounter him in the hungry, the thirsty, the naked, the sick, the friend in trouble, the prisoner, the refugee and the migrant, and our neighbors who feel abandoned. To take the path of our God, who encourages us to be politicians, thinkers, social activists. The God who encourages us to devise an economy marked by greater solidarity than our own. In all the settings in which you find yourselves, God's love invites you to bring the Good News, making of your own lives a gift to him and to others. This means being courageous, this means being free!

Whatever else one may say about Pope Francis, no candid observer can deny that he understands the ecclesiastical, political, and cultural—let us call them civilizational—stakes are as high as they can be, that the window for effective action to correct the civilizational course is rapidly closing, and that the Church needs to lead the effort of renewal if she is going to be a credible witness to the saving Gospel of Our Lord, Jesus Christ.

We ought therefore to construe the language of the "new paradigm" to refer to the shift in emphasis toward greater responsibility on the part of the faithful and an abandonment of paternalism on the part of the Church's pastoral and hierarchical leadership. We ought further to construe Cardinal Parolin's remarks as expressive of the Holy Father's desire to see that shift in emphasis applied to the whole Church.

We may also understand the use of the language as Cardinal Parolin's more-or-less conscious and deliberate borrowing of a play from the boss's Jesuit playbook. St. Ignatius famously counseled early Jesuit missionaries:

> Whenever we wish to win someone over and engage him in the greater service of God our Lord, we should use the same strategy for good that the enemy employs to draw a good soul to evil. The enemy enters through the other's door and comes out his own. He enters with the other, not by opposing his ways but by praising them. He acts familiarly with the soul, suggesting good and holy thoughts that bring peace to the good soul. Then, little by little, he tries to come out his own door, always portraying some error or illusion under the appearance of something good, but which will always be evil. So, we may lead others to good by praying or agreeing with them on a certain good point, leaving aside whatever else may be wrong. Thus, after gaining his confidence, we shall meet with better success. In this sense we enter his door with him, but we come out our own.

Francis, in other words, may well be perfectly happy to use the institutional language of the people he sees as the "hip and with it" modern crowd, who don't believe in things like dogma, or hell, or the devil, who maybe want to "sing a new Church into being," and so get in through their door, only to lead them out by "his" door (the path through which he constantly tells us is Divine judgment—which will be perfectly merciful if we ask for it, but must be judgment nonetheless—on the wrong side of which hell does await). As far as his pastoral approach is concerned, this seems to be the long and the short of it. I continue to find it personally challenging and in the main highly effective.

In any case, most of the hay that got made out of Cardinal Parolin's remarks, got made over the appearance of his turn-of-phrase in connection with *Amoris laetitia*. A few commenters, whose clarity of vision I generally admire, have seen the phrase as a red flag. It is as though Francis, the heretofore cagey Modernist, is now showing his true colors. That is, to say the least, highly unlikely. For one thing, he keeps at it, even though he is so far "in the door" with the NuChurch and Social Justice crowds by now, that they have tried to put his name on it.

(Just so we are abundantly clear on this point: The Pope's clarion calls for tireless practice of the works of mercy is a great strength of his pontificate. God is just, and He shall judge us on the basis of what we shall have done for the least of His children. We ought to tremble when we reflect on this, and dedicate ourselves with increased devotion to the works He prescribes for our salvation.)

The mainstream media portrait of Francis as a smiling, friendly old grandpa has always been at the very best a gross caricature, and more often a poorly executed grotesque in the service of an incredible narrative of Francis as darling of the mainstream media's favorite pet causes. The cantankerous old man who steadfastly refuses to prepare his *fervorini* for the 7am Mass in Santa Marta is far closer to the genuine article.

For another, his aforementioned willingness to cajole and harangue—especially in his extemporaneous remarks—is not recently discovered, nor is it the stuff of which successful cons are made. In fact, he seems as often as not to be preaching to himself when he goes on his grumpy avuncular jags. Therein lies the risk. Francis tells us he likes frankness and forthrightness, a free spirit in counsel. He is also confessedly headstrong and more than a little prickly, with tendencies toward micromanagement that have proven persistent.

He is right to warn us, as he often does, against legalism and especially against Pharisaism, by which he means the use of the law to bind and to trap and to lord it over the small and the weak. The opposite extreme is a sort of antinomian libertinism, the effect of which is at least as deleterious as that of Pharisaism, and arguably more corrosive. Laws can be changed (except when they cannot be changed). Occasionally, they need to be changed. Everyone knows that those responsible for upholding the law injure society especially gravely when they break the law.

They do greater injury to society, however, when, being unable or unwilling to change the law, they wink at it. A thing of great worth may be cracked by mishandling, or smashed to smithereens in a moment of frustration. Then the precious thing may be repaired or recast. We wink at trifles, and pass them by without another thought. Pope Francis, in luffing the sails of Pharisaism, has let wind into those of antinomianism. Whether he has the strength to keep the barque right, with the antinomian sails full of wind, is an open question and a legitimate concern.

The controversy over *Amoris laetitia*, which is a chapter in
a greater controversy over the right response of the Church
to the crisis in society over marriage—a crisis that does not
touch only the decadent West—has poisoned our counsels.
We are all—on every side of the issue—increasingly unable
to see and unwilling to look for the good in the other(s).
The two great camps, let us call them *Amoris* enthusiasts and
Amoris skeptics for short, cannot hear one another, and have
stopped trying to hear one another, if ever they did. There
are serious problems with the document itself, and more
serious ones with its "implementation" by local Ordinaries
and conferences around the world. Seeking a good faith
discussion of those problems is not dissent, but *parrhesia*.
By the same token, recognizing that contemporary society—
its membership, ourselves included—is broken in ways that
were only dimly discernible in 1980, and that we need serious, profound, pastorally informed and sensitive theological
reflection on how to use the gifts of grace Our Lord has
given us for healing, restoration, and renewal, is also true.

Law ought to follow theology. It ought also to be controlled by immutable Divine law, which is at once the bridge
between theology and the Church's legal apparatus, and the
Church's tether to the truth. Pope Francis has encouraged
theological reflection, and invited the voices of all the faithful to participate in a Church-wide effort of discernment in
these regards. Certain bishops have seen fit to skip the process of discernment, and/or arrogate it to themselves. Their
behavior is premature and irresponsible. Saying so does not
make one disloyal, and noting the confusion caused by the

Pope's at least tacit (though not always merely tacit) approval of those bishops' behavior is not dissent.

The in-flight wedding at which Pope Francis officiated is a case-in-point. Was it a great gesture of pro-active pastoral *premura* for a couple in irregular circumstances, or was it an ill-considered publicity stunt? It could be both. What is certain is that Mr. and Mrs. Ciuffardi were in a canonically irregular situation, and now they are not. They asked the Church for marriage, and the Church responded. To anyone concerned over the validity of the marriage as performed, I would say that the Pope has universal, supreme, and immediate jurisdiction over all the Churches and all the faithful.

To those with concerns over the prudence of the Pope's action, I would point out that there is no *sed*—no "but"— after the maxim, *Salus animarum suprema lex*. The words Pope Francis is reported to have said to the couple are also telling. "This—the Sacrament of Marriage—is the Sacrament that is missing in the world," Ciuffardi reports the Holy Father as saying. The Pope reportedly added, "I hope this motivates couples around the world to marry." I hope so, too.

It was a teachable moment in many ways. While having the Vicar of Christ on Earth receive your consent will compensate for a lack of flowers, dresses, friends and family (not to mention sacred space), the episode does show quite clearly what the essence of the thing really is.

There is no Sacrament of Matrimony that exists apart from a valid marriage contract. Marriage, said simply, is a contract. Marriage is the law. Marriage is also the natural state: it requires no special maturity beyond that, which

is strictly necessary in order that the contracting parties—
when they attempt marriage—understand what it is they
are attempting, i.e. marriage. When two baptized Christians
validly contract marriage, or when two people with a valid
marriage contract are both baptized, they have the Sacrament. That's it, and, that's all of it.

Nor do marriage tribunals conduct theological investigations into the question whether there are the prerequisites
for some phantom category called "sacramentality." They
rather conduct legal investigations apt to determine whether
a legal contract was validly executed. If it was, then the couple joined by it have the Sacrament. Once the union thus
made is consummated, it binds them until death do them
part. If not, not.

The Romans have an expression: *Le parole del Santo Padre
vanno misurate con contagocce*, i.e. "The words of the Holy
Father are to be measured with a medicine dropper." If his
recent predecessors occasionally honored this pearl of wisdom in the breach, Pope Francis has not only rejected it out
of hand, but extended his rejection to his conduct in office.
Almost from Day One, Pope Francis has insisted he will not
change his attitude, his habit(s), or his behavior to suit his
new office and environs. That is, as they say, "his business,"
but it is also ours.

"The Pope goes as the pastor of the universal Church, to
meet with local Churches," Cardinal Parolin said in response
to the final question in the interview with Vatican Media,
regarding the then-imminent trip to Latin America. The
thing is, the Church's universal pastor is also her universal
governor. He was elected because he was known to be an

independent-minded (fairly headstrong) and deeply committed religious priest, who was an excellent Archbishop of Buenos Aires. As Bishop of Rome, he still is.

2018 is likely to be the year in which Pope Francis will have to decide whether he will use his immense talents, charisma, and strength of personality to harness and direct the energies of the Curia and the Church in a manner consistent with the best angels of her tradition, or whether he will continue to channel his efforts into a project that appears to have as its only overarching vision the remaking of Rome into a sort of Buenos Aires-on-Tiber. What is certain is that he will need our prayers.

CHAPTER 2

THE WIND PICKS UP

February – March 2018

"A crisis of leadership? Francis's defenders call for reform on sex abuse"

During his nearly five-year pontificate, Pope Francis has been profoundly challenging to Christians of all stripes, issuing calls for a radical commitment to the Gospel that have earned him respect and admiration across social and cultural divides, even as they have made him a polarizing figure among persons on different ends of the political spectrum.

From a media perspective, Francis has also been good for a story: unpredictable, often quotable, given to gestures that generate sympathetic "buzz." His recent accusations of calumny against victims of disgraced Chilean priest Fernando Karadima, however, have provoked scrutiny from mainstream media outlets, and have precipitated what even some of the Pontiff's greatest defenders consider a crisis of leadership.

Francis has said many of the right things about clerical sex abuse scandals. In a letter dated February 2, 2015, addressed to the world's bishops and religious superiors and explaining the rationale behind his decision to create a Pontifical Commission for the Protection of Minors, Pope Francis wrote, "[E]verything possible must be done to rid the Church of the scourge of the sexual abuse of minors and to open pathways of reconciliation and healing for those who were abused." He went on to say, "Families need to know that the Church is making every effort to protect their children. They should also know that they have every right to turn to the Church with full confidence, for it is a safe and secure home."

The Holy Father explained that the protection of children must be the capital concern of pastors, everywhere and at all times. "Priority must not be given to any other kind of concern, whatever its nature, such as the desire to avoid scandal, since there is absolutely no place in ministry for those who abuse minors," Francis said. The man who made such a call has shown so much sensitivity to victims as well in his many personal encounters with them. He has also repeatedly accused of slander certain victims who allege misconduct by Bishop Barros of Osorno. That has been a cause of disappointment, grief, and consternation, even and especially among persons who take a generally favorable view of the Holy Father and his record of leadership.

"It is stunning," Professor Charles Camosy of Fordham University told *Catholic World Report*, "and seemingly so unlike him." Camosy—a theologian who is at present writing a book on Pope Francis—went on to say, "Normally, [Pope Francis] is quite good about being concerned with the most vulnerable in a particular context. Here, however, there seems to be something else at work." Asked for his estimation of the gravity of the crisis, Camosy responded, "If something is not done soon, his leadership is in serious trouble. And I say this as a lover of Pope Francis. Given what we know now, and having learned from our past mistakes, one cannot have this kind of reaction to sex abuse allegations and maintain moral authority. At least in the US context." Camosy said he thinks at the very least "an immediate retraction and even deeper apology" are in order. "Then a commitment to meet with the victims and their families personally."

Rome-based theologian and ecumenist A.J. Boyd takes a somewhat different view. "My impression of Pope Francis's leadership is not generally affected by news media, but by his words and actions, his welcome efforts to both continue reforms started by Pope Benedict (such as financial reforms in the Vatican) and more broadly reforms of the Curia and the episcopate in continuity with the direction of the [Second Vatican] Council," Boyd told *CWR*. "In that respect, he has improved upon his immediate predecessor's response to the abuse crisis in that he has addressed one of the core, systemic issues head on: clericalism."

"Just as Pope Benedict far surpassed John Paul II in addressing [the clerical sex abuse crisis] by taking tough action on the abuser priests, Francis has continued and surpassed Benedict," Boyd said. "Where all three have thus far failed is in demonstrating clearly, transparently, and publicly that it is above all the bishops who must be held accountable; that the cover-up of abuse is as bad if not worse than the abuse itself; and that the systems that allowed abuser priests to continue—rooted in clericalism that they are—are being dismantled."

"The light I have seen in recent days has been that Francis acted quickly and decisively in admitting the possibility of his error and sending [Archbishop Charles] Scicluna to investigate," Boyd went on to say. "It shows he is listening now, at least, and willing to act to correct mistakes, and has no problem admitting them when shown that he has made them. I strongly suspect a public admission of his mistakes in this affair will not be long in coming, a *metanoia*, turning away from mistaken accusations of calumny."

Günther Simmermacher, editor-in-chief of South Africa's leading Catholic weekly, *The Southern Cross*, told *CWR* the Bishop Barros story has left him disappointed and perplexed, with several questions that need answering. "I'm disappointed that the good game the Pope has talked about the abuse crisis has not translated into sufficiently concrete or, indeed, wise action," Simmermacher said. "I don't think that Pope Francis has been duplicitous or dishonest, but he certainly made a big error in judgment." Simmermacher went on to say the sense of uncertainty and disorientation at the developments is understandable and too familiar.

"I suppose anybody who has had contact with clergy is familiar with those feelings of doubt and denial when a priest we like and respect is embroiled in scandal," he said. "I expect that, rather than indifference to the victims of abuse, this is the source of Pope Francis's gross misjudgment—and perhaps a bit of pride as well. That's where I see the source of the intemperate language he used. I don't think he was acting in bad faith. But for the world to see, it looks like he was."

Asked how the developments will affect Pope Francis's ability to provide moral leadership, Simmermacher said, "The Barros case will feature in Pope Francis's obituary, but it won't define his papacy. I don't think that incident, in itself, discredits or otherwise undermines Francis's moral leadership of the Church any more than St. John Paul II's friendship with the truly depraved Marcial Maciel stains the treasures of that pope's legacy."

Simmermacher went on to say he is concerned the Barros case may be exploited to derail Pope Francis's broader reform efforts. "My concern is that the critics of Pope Francis might use the Barros case as a proxy to undermine the Holy Father and his program of reform," he said. "To do so would be reckless and dishonest. And it would be immensely disrespectful to those affected by clerical abuse to do so. If the crisis is used to deepen divisions, then that is a dangerous game."

The crisis has also affected perceptions in the broader Christian community. Father Jonathan Jong is a priest of the Anglican Diocese of Oxford. He is also a research fellow in psychology at Coventry University, and research associate in anthropology at Oxford University. He told *Catholic World Report* his view—from the outside looking in, as it were— is one of disappointment, but not surprise. "Pope Francis has been consistently disappointing on this issue, promising strong action and zero tolerance, with little evidence of fulfilling them." He went on to say, "More telling than public outrage over any given case are the recent resignations of Marie Collins and Peter Saunders from the Pontifical Commission for the Protection of Minors: these two abuse survivors had hoped to work with a repentant Church willing to reform, and were met instead with defensiveness and denial."

At bottom, the question for Fr. Jong is one of the ability of all Christians to give credible witness to the Gospel. "This issue, above others, threatens any shred of the Church's moral witness in the world," he said. "Unless there is proof—to echo the Pope's own words—that the Church is repentant and reforming, it is not just the Pope's ability to provide moral leadership that is at stake, it is the whole Church's."

He said there are lessons to be learned from broader society with regard to the disastrous effects of denial, and the painful but necessary processes that must accompany the effort of learning how to listen. "Whatever one makes of the #metoo campaign, the Church must at least learn from it that victims and survivors are to be listened to, not with a hermeneutic of suspicion, but with one of mercy."

For the Catholic Herald, February 10, 2018

"The Bishop Barros crisis: How bad is it?"

"**H**ow bad is it?" That was the question a friend put to me, à propos the leadership crisis in the Catholic Church. Pope Francis precipitated the crisis by levelling repeated accusations of calumny against survivors of sexual abuse perpetrated by a prominent Chilean cleric, Fernando Karadima, who was convicted of his crimes by a Vatican court in 2011. Karadima's victims claim one of their abuser's protégés, Juan Barros—ordained bishop in 1995 and appointed by Pope Francis to head the diocese of Osorno, Chile, in 2015—witnessed the abuse they suffered at Karadima's hands, covered for his mentor and enabled his abusive behavior. Put just like that, it is bad enough. It gets worse.

Pope Francis first accused the victims of calumny in a heat-of-the-moment exchange with a reporter in a press gaggle at the gate of the Iquique venue where he was heading to say Mass on the last day of his recent visit to Chile. News of the Pope's "hot takes" overshadowed the final, Peruvian leg of his South American tour. The Pope then used his in-flight press conference—days later—on the return trip to Rome, to double down on his accusations of calumny, saying he has not received any evidence of Barros's alleged wrongdoing, and that the victims had never brought their case to him. "You [reporters], in all good will, tell me that there are victims, but I haven't seen any, because they haven't come forward," Pope Francis said. Even at the time Pope Francis made it—again, during the in-flight presser *en route* to Rome from Perú, days after his impromptu response had garnered the attention of the press—the assertion was, to say the very least, problematic.

The accusations against Barros have been before the public since at least 2012. Victims have given testimony to Chilean prosecutors regarding the matter. It appears, therefore, that the Pope's assertion can save itself only if it rests on a hyper-technicality: that he had no direct, personal acquaintance with the accusations. Upon hearing the Pope's claim, however, the abuse survivor and former member of the Pontifical Commission for the Protection of Minors, Marie Collins, made it known that she had delivered an 8-page letter to the Pope describing life in the Chilean institute where their abuse took place and detailing Barros's alleged role in their abuse. The letter, Collins explained to AP, was from Juan Carlos Cruz, a victim of Karadima and Barros's most outspoken accuser. Collins claims she delivered the letter in 2015, through the Pope's own chief adviser on sexual abuse matters (and president of the Commission for the Protection of Minors), Cardinal Seán O'Malley of Boston.

About the letter and its delivery, Marie Collins told the *Catholic Herald*: "It was at the time a private letter [written in Spanish] from Juan Carlos Cruz to the Holy Father." Collins went on to explain: "As well as I can recollect it was sealed when given to Cardinal O'Malley. It was in a simple plain envelope. I did have a general idea of its content as

[Mr. Cruz] had also sent a detailed explanation of events in English." Asked specifically about Cardinal O'Malley's confirmation of delivery, Collins told the Herald: "He said he had given the letter directly to the Holy Father and that at the same time he had discussed our concerns about Bishop Barros with him."

At this point, there are four possibilities: Collins and Cruz are both lying about the letter; Cardinal O'Malley gravely misrepresented the diligence with which he discharged his promise to deliver it directly to Pope Francis (though Collins has expressed full confidence in him on several occasions); Pope Francis received the letter and did not read it; Pope Francis received it and read it, only to forget about it.

If Cardinal O'Malley did not deliver the letter directly into the hands of the Pope, he needs to say so. If Pope Francis did receive the letter, only to put it aside without reading it, he needs to say so, and explain why he did not read it. If the Pope did receive it, and read it, then the only way to save him from an accusation of deliberate untruthfulness is to admit he is relying on another hyper-technicality: that he received nothing submitted specifically and explicitly as evidence in an open judicial process, or that he received no new evidence—i.e. evidence about which he had no prior knowledge of any kind in any capacity—or that he received no evidence of Barros's wrongdoing as a bishop, such as would warrant investigation and possibly trial under pertinent law.

As Fr. Robert Gahl, who teaches ethics at Rome's Pontifical University of the Holy Cross, told Catholic News Agency in a story that ran earlier this week, "[Barros's] alleged failure to report did not constitute episcopal negligence and yet his

being somehow an accessory, at least insofar as he is accused
of not having stopped a crime from taking place, would constitute the negligence of someone who is now a bishop." The
accusations against Barros arguably come to more than failure to report abuse. In any case, the point is that Pope Francis appointed Barros to the See of Osorno in 2015, years
after the accusations against Barros were public knowledge.

The appointment of Barros was also over and against
the objections of the bishops of Chile, who wrote to Pope
Francis about the matter. The Holy Father responded to the
Chilean bishops with his own letter, in which he explained
that he had in fact asked Barros to resign the post in which
he found himself at the time (when Barros was appointed
to Osorno he was bishop of the Chilean forces). The Pope
also asked Barros to take a year's sabbatical, before being
considered for any other post. The AP story detailing the
exchanges reports that the Apostolic Nuncio to Chile, Archbishop Ivo Scapolo, who acted as go-between, also told Barros that two other bishops who came up under Karadima
were being given similar requests, and reportedly also told
Barros to keep the news to himself. Barros, however, decided
to give the names of the two other bishops in a letter he
wrote announcing his renunciation of the military see. At
that point, instead of sending Barros into retirement as damaged goods, or rejecting him as insubordinate, Pope Francis
decided to make Barros the head of the Church in Osorno.

Quite apart from the legal cavils, the question is: what
was Pope Francis thinking?

In various public and private conversations about the crisis, a few people have suggested that Pope Francis may have

read and then forgotten about the letter. The details of the published excerpts alone make that highly unlikely. An AP story published last Sunday contains lurid particulars. "[W]e were in Karadima's room," the story quotes Cruz's letter, "and Juan Barros—if he wasn't kissing Karadima—would watch when Karadima would touch us—the minors—and make us kiss him, saying: 'Put your mouth near mine and stick out your tongue.' He would stick his out and kiss us with his tongue." If Pope Francis could read those sentences and forget he had, then there is reason to suspect that he is not in full possession of his faculties.

If the letter was intercepted after Cardinal O'Malley delivered it, and before Pope Francis had a chance to read it, then the Holy Father is a victim of a grave and likely criminal disservice that has damaged his credibility. If he is a victim of such a disservice, he must nevertheless own his dismissal of the general public claims registered in the letter, and account for his part in the creation of a working environment in which such miscarriage was possible. He must also apologize to the persons whose names and reputations he has injured.

Even if the outstanding questions regarding Pope Francis's handling of the Barros affair are clarified—as they must be—the crisis of leadership in the Church will nevertheless remain. The known facts of this case and others constitutive of Pope Francis's record in these regards bespeak a style of governance in which the man at the top is more inclined to listen to fellow clerics, than to victims: to believe bishops—ones with skin in the game, to boot—over laity who bring credible allegations of clerical misbehavior; to trust his own "gut instinct" even when it is informed by the opinion of interested parties, and to compound this imprudence with the self-delusion of self-reliance in these regards; to believe he can manage the crisis of clerical sexual abuse by way of gimmicks like the powerless Commission for the Protection of Minors he set up between 2014 and 2015 before ignoring it and allowing it to expire; to blame underlings and hide behind cavils of law, rather than face the filth in the Church squarely and fight it without ruth or stint.

How bad is it? It is very bad indeed. If the manner in which the crisis as it has heretofore unfolded in the world-wide Church, and especially in the US and Ireland, is any lesson, then a candid mind would not be incapable of concluding that Pope Francis is not only part of the problem, but that he is the problem.

"Five years on: a Vatican reporter remembers Benedict XVI's resignation"

February 28, 2013, was a blur. I'm pretty sure I was in the newsroom at Vatican Radio for some of the day, but I can't recall whether I was there, or at home, or in a bar watching the chopper take off and carry the soon-to-be Pope Emeritus Benedict XVI to his retirement at Castel Gandolfo. I can talk a little about my feelings that day—they are with me still—as the reality of the situation pressed itself upon me. My thoughts were clear, and have not only stayed with me, but sharpened over the past five years.

To be perfectly frank, I thought the resignation was bad for the Church and for the Petrine office. I understand the arguments for it, but I did not then and do not now agree with them. A lot has changed in the world over the last fifty or one hundred years, and people do generally live longer, but human nature has remained the same. As Karr said, *Plus ça change, plus c'est la même chose.*

Bishops in general are said to be the spouses of their dioceses, and last time I checked, "…until death do us part," was still in the Catholic marriage vows, however often the promise is honored in reality. The See of Rome is supposed to be exemplary in this and every other regard. The idea that the world has made exemplary witness impossible—that we ought therefore to abandon the standard and give up even trying to meet it—struck me then and continues to strike me as an attitude arising from jadedness if not despair.

If a man like Benedict XVI did not feel himself equal to the task of governance, let alone of reform, then he nevertheless might have done his best with what he had for as long as he had breath in his body, and taken a page from Pope St. John XXIII's book, saying at the end of every long and trying day, "It's your Church, Lord. I'm going to bed." There is a whole system in place, designed to be a buttress for weak Popes, who would reign but not rule, as the saying goes. If that system—the Roman Curia—is broken, then the thing to do is to fix it.

To be sure, the crisis of governance in the Curia did not begin on Benedict's watch, and was not ever going to end on his watch either, even if he had the vigor of a man of forty, and unlimited resources at his disposal. Nevertheless, things in the Curia did get worse on his watch, largely because he simply did not govern it. Even as his teaching and leadership of the universal Church were strong.

He put an ill-equipped and incapable man at the head of the Secretariat of State (Cardinal Bertone), because that man had been for him a competent lieutenant and was an old and trusted friend. Then he refused to pull the trigger on his man—for friendship's sake?—and preferred to throw in the towel (or the Pallium, if you will). Retiring oneself when one is unable or unwilling to send troublesome underlings into retirement is perhaps the necessary and even praiseworthy thing. Still, here we are.

Benedict was not always a weak or ineffective governor, though. This is perhaps why his weakness in dealing with particular issues during the course of his reign stood out so prominently. His weakness in handling the Legion of Christ, for example, was in stark contrast to his handling of the Legion's notorious founder, and gave the impression that, if only folks kept their heads down, the moment would pass, and it would be back to business as usual. That has largely proven to be right.

People were already praising Benedict XVI's courage and humility—not wrongly, I hasten to add—but that never struck me as the story, then or now. All the words I could muster that evening were, "I can think of nothing to say, except: let us pray for Bishop Benedict, emeritus of Rome. God only knows how I love him." I also remember feeling what I imagine sons feel when their fathers abandon them. It looks absurd to me as I write it on the page, but I confess I wondered if it was somehow my fault, and what I might have done differently, and how I might have served him better. What if I'd prayed more for him?

In any case, I knew the job he'd left for his successor would be hard, and I knew he'd made it harder. His successor would have all his problems, and the new ones, and he would have the specter of resignation as an option. I can and do believe that the resignation of Pope Benedict XVI was, in the ways and respects most everyone says, to the good. It was not unalloyed, however, and while everyone else is focusing on the good, I can't help but see the rest. There's a lot to see, if you look.

For the Catholic Herald, March 2, 2018

"How US cardinals faced a donor uprising at the Papal Foundation"

Adispute between US cardinals and wealthy supporters of a major Catholic philanthropic organization emerged publicly last week. Leaked documents published by *Life Site News* showed the prelates pushed through an extraordinary $25 million in financial assistance to a scandal-ridden and failing Roman hospital, at Pope Francis's behest and over the objections of laymen on the board of the organization giving the assistance.

That organization is the Philadelphia-based Papal Foundation, founded in 1988 as a fundraising engine to meet the financial needs of the Holy See in the wake of the Banco Ambrosiano scandal. The foundation relies on the support of wealthy donors, who each pledge no less than $1 million over 10 years, in doing so becoming "stewards" of the foundation.

When a measure of financial stability returned to the Holy See, the Papal Foundation's primary activity became the support of charitable initiatives dear to the Holy Father, in grants given upon request by the Vatican in amounts usually not in excess of $200,000. The Papal Foundation has done great good, especially for Catholic organizations working in the world's poorest nations. But something went wrong this time around.

Late last year and in early January, the Papal Foundation approved initial assistance packages of $8 million and $5 million for the *Istituto Dermopatico dell'Immacolata*, a Rome-based outfit wrapped up in scandals involving alleged money laundering and reeling from a roughly $1 billion siphoning scheme. (A four-year investigation led to 24 separate indictments last year.) The Vatican named new hospital leadership in 2017.

An unofficial summary prepared by James Longon, the chairman of the Papal Foundation's audit committee, declares: "[B]oth the process by which the grant was given [and] the grant itself are disturbing. In my opinion … these recent actions will make it virtually impossible to recruit new stewards, or to retain the membership of many current stewards. In many respects, the decision to grant $25 million to a dermatology hospital in Rome without proper due diligence is a disaster for the Papal Foundation."

The board maintains that due diligence was conducted, but Longon resigned from the committee and as a trustee. The clerical leadership of the Papal Foundation—including Cardinal Donald Wuerl of Washington DC—wrote a letter to the stewards, insisting that the money went to the Vatican. "[W]e did not send money to a hospital," the board's letter to stewards reads, "[w]e sent money to the Holy See."

Longon's summary says: "This is a badly run business venture, not a helping of our Church or a helping of the poor. Cardinal Wuerl stated that the Holy Father is simply turning to the Papal Foundation for assistance to get through that bridge time while the hospital gets back on its feet. Sounds like a business loan to me." In the wake of the row, the cardinals walked back their promise of assistance. Cardinal Wuerl has requested that the Vatican not accept the outstanding $12 million. The cardinals have also promised increased lay involvement to approve requests greater than $1 million. That's all fine, but when a group of successful business leaders raise issues over the prudence of a measure involving the money they earned, one tends to think it wise to heed them.

So, how did this happen?

The answer is, in a word, clericalism. The stewards upon whose generosity the Papal Foundation depends are businessmen of great acumen, long years' experience and extraordinary accomplishment. More to the point, they are stewards—at least they are styled so—and do not take kindly to being treated as cash cows. "It felt like irresponsible and immoral stewardship," Longon told the *Wall Street Journal*. "I'm 73," he added, "and getting close to Judgment Day."

Frankly, when churchmen who have spent their entire careers playing with house money hear such objections and reply to the effect that there's nothing to see here, one tends to think that perhaps there is. "The Papal Foundation has bylaws that put the ultimate control of the organization in the hands of the US-domiciled cardinals," the board's letter reminds the stewards who have given their time and treasure. "No one," the letter continues, "has ever represented that this organization is controlled by the laity." For all their talk about the need for informed and dedicated lay leadership in areas of Church life in which lay persons have particular expertise in virtue of their experience and vocation, the old maxim sometimes still applies: "Pray, pay, obey."

For the Catholic World Report, March 9, 2018

"Pope Francis and clericalism"

Pope Francis is a popular and powerfully charismatic leader. He has received his share of criticism in the five years he has been in office, but then, popular and powerfully charismatic leaders are lightning rods for criticism. Frankly, much of it is undeserved. Even more of it is either misplaced or poorly articulated, even when it is reasonably well founded. Often, criticism of the Pope is expressed in unreasonable terms, even when the complaint itself is legitimate. This is generally true of criticism leveled at leaders at every level, and especially true of that leveled against people in positions of high leadership. Sitting in the big chair means courting controversy.

"Heretic!" is a favorite aspersion of the Pope's detractors. "Modernist!" is a common permutation of the charge. To see that Pope Francis is not a Modernist, one need look no further than his warnings against the dangers of hell, which are certainly more frequent than those of his two predecessors in the office, and could already be more numerous than all of his two most recent predecessors' similar admonitions, combined. His certainty with regard to the inevitable Divine judgment is pronounced, his constant exhortations to frequent the Sacrament of Penance are passionate to the point

of enthusiasm, and his desire for reform in continuity with
tradition—epitomized in his praise for the enduring importance of the Council of Trent in the life of the Church—as
eloquent as it is overlooked.

In more general terms, Pope Francis seems neither to
know nor to care enough about doctrine to be a real heretic.
In this, he is like most Bishops of Rome since St. Peter. Like
them, he has people for that sort of thing. One might wish
to see Pope Francis make more, or better use of the people
he does have for that sort of thing, but that is another matter—and one on which there have been some encouraging
signs of late. Even when the charges leveled against him have
been badly placed, ill-suited, or poorly couched, they often
have been a genuine expression of the sense that something
is wrong. What, though?

There is a rather pedestrian answer: Pope Francis suffers
from a sort of constantly creeping tendency toward clericalism, which colors more of his thought and behavior than
anyone—especially Francis himself, who rightly sees clericalism as a disease in the body of the Church—would care
to admit. Some of this tendency is discernible in remarks
regarding specific kinds or categories of lay people, e.g.
women, or the elderly.

From his unfortunate descriptions of women as "strawberries on the cake" of the Church's theological effort—
in fairness, he did say we need more strawberries—to his
employment of frankly ageist and sexist language to describe
the ills of the Church and of society, viz., "a general impression of weariness and aging, of a Europe which is now a
'grandmother', no longer fertile and vibrant," to his slights

at religious women who are more like "spinsters" or "old maids" than the "mothers" they are supposed to be, to his tactless wisecracks about pastors of parishes being under the thumb of their housekeepers (who are obviously women), the Pope has cut a poor figure.

Sure, he has spoken in defense of the elderly: of the store of civilizational wisdom and memory of which they are the keepers—though that talk is often frankly reductive and patronizing; and he has spoken of the need for increased involvement of women in Church leadership and decision-making. In the main, however, he has not put his money where his mouth is. He appointed two women to positions touted as "key" roles in the new Dicastery for Laity, Family and Life. Bioethicist Prof. Gabriella Gambino and canon lawyer Dr. Linda Ghisoni became Undersecretaries to the Dicastery in 2017. For all the ballyhoo, they are essentially glorified desk jockeys in a department without a well-defined mission.

Despite his repeated and vehement denunciations of clericalism, Francis's more general remarks about the laity sometimes nevertheless exhibit a sort of clerical chauvinism. If this is surprising, perhaps it ought not be. Francis often gives the impression he is preaching to himself when he dips into his bag of signature aspersions and condemnations.

His talk of an "ideal" of Christian marriage, for example, which it is impossible to uphold in practice, bespeaks an attitude of clerical sufficiency, if not superiority. "A lukewarm attitude, any kind of relativism, or an undue reticence in proposing that ideal, would be a lack of fidelity to the Gospel and also of love on the part of the Church," Pope

Francis writes in paragraph 307 of his post-Synodal Apostolic Exhortation, *Amoris laetitia*. "To show understanding in the face of exceptional situations," he continues there, "never implies dimming the light of the fuller ideal, or proposing less than what Jesus offers to the human being."

The problem here is not that what the Pope says is not true as far as it goes. The problem is that the promises that are constitutive of marriage as such are not the ideal or even a dim picture of it: they are the baseline and bare minimum to which one publicly commits oneself in contracting marriage. In fact, Pope Francis often seems to think lay persons incapable of even the most basic acts of faith—the public faith on which the giving and taking of vows is entirely based, not the supernatural faith that gives Christians to glimpse the inner life of the Trinity and work under the impetus of charity to emulate it in their lives.

"[T]he culture of the provisional," Pope Francis told the participants in the ecclesial convention of the Rome diocese, in one of his unguarded moments, on June 16, 2016, "is why a large majority of our sacramental marriages are null: because they say, 'Yes, all my life,' but they do not know what it is they are saying, because they have another culture." In order that the specific kind of misunderstanding Pope Francis adduced should vitiate marital consent, one of the contracting parties would either have to be completely ignorant of the very notion of permanence, or exclude permanence by a positive act of the will: either not only not understand what "permanent" means existentially, but have no idea what the word "permanent" even means; or really and positively mean not to contract a permanent obligation, even though one mouthed the words by which one contracts one. Said bluntly, if Pope Francis does understand the mechanics of consent, then he believes the majority of Christians in putatively valid marriages are either idiots, or liars. One would rather believe he misspoke even more gravely than the Orwelled official transcript of the event would have it, which replaces "majority" with "a part," or that he simply misunderstands the mechanics.

He went on in those same off-the-cuff remarks to say, in regard to people he has met, who are cohabiting or at least living in canonically irregular situations, "[R]eally, I say that I have seen a great deal of fidelity in these cohabiting couples, a great deal of fidelity; and I am certain that this is a true marriage, they have the grace of matrimony, precisely because of the fidelity that they have."

The part about the vast majority of putatively "sacramental" unions being null was worth a double-take, but it ought not have been deeply shocking to learn that a grunt cleric in the pastoral trenches was fuzzy on the point, even if the grunt cleric in question was the Bishop of Rome. One might even say, "Especially if the cleric in question was the Bishop of Rome." Marriage, however, is not so much a matter of doctrine, as it is a practical matter—a matter of law—created by public promises, the effective enactment of which requires no special knowledge or training, but only the ability to give one's word.

Pope Francis seems to think most lay folk are mostly incapable of this. That is, again, disappointing. It is not surprising. It was galling, however, to hear Pope Francis say that cohabiting couples have the grace of matrimony. People living in concubinage are neither better nor worse than other people, and the Lord no doubt pours out abundant graces on them, though they are not the graces of Matrimony. According to Pope Francis, however, my wife is probably not my wife, but my concubine; while another man's concubine is really his wife.

Then there is Pope Francis's willingness to believe bishops over laity in matters regarding child safety and justice: a willingness epitomized in his own words to pilgrims on the sidelines of the weekly General Audience in May 2015. "[The Church in Osorno] has lost her freedom," said Pope Francis, "by letting her head be filled with [words of] politicians, blaming a bishop without any proof, after 20 years of being a bishop." Francis specified, saying, "[The Church in] Osorno suffers, because she is stupid, because she does not open her heart to what God says and she lets herself be carried away by the idiocies that all those people say."

He also said, "The only accusation there was against that bishop was [tossed] by the judicial court." That is not exactly right. In any case, his advice to the faithful was, "Think with your head and do not be led by the nose by all the leftists, who are the ones who put the [scandal] together," i.e. orchestrated the whole business. However much the leftists were using the press to gin things up, it turns out they weren't conjuring from thin air. Also, the way the Holy Father's beats track with those of Santiago's Cardinals Francisco Errázuriz and Ricardo Ezzati suggests that, if some of the faithful of Osorno were being led by the nose, they weren't the only ones.

That the Pope has, after intense and sustained public pressure, finally seen fit to send his point man, Archbishop Charles J. Scicluna of Malta, to look into the matter, changes nothing about his default position, which is one in which the word of high clerics with skin in the game is worth more than that of the laymen his own court believed when it convicted the priest who abused them. Pope Francis may talk a good game sometimes, but when push comes to shove, the very best one can say for him is that he is about the same as all the others, certainly no better, and maybe even worse.

For the Catholic Herald, March 12, 2018

"Five years after his election, this year is make-or-break for Pope Francis"

The election of a Jesuit to the See of Peter thrilled me, even as the resignation of Benedict XVI had crushed my bones. History was happening, and I was not only there, but telling people about it. Sitting at a workstation in the newsroom at Vatican Radio, with my colleague, Christopher Wells, I heard Cardinal Tauran make the announcement—a return to Latin form after the polyglot preface that Cardinal Medina gave in 2005—and had to dig to place the name. When it clicked into place, the first couple of sentences spoken were unprintable. "Goodness gracious, sakes alive!" was the gist of it. That's a sentiment we've all expressed, and heard expressed, more than a few times during the intervening half-decade.

The five-year mark is a good point at which to pause and take stock: to stand still and take a look around, to see where we are, and maybe try to get some idea of our bearing.

There are lots of different ways to take the measure of a leader and his leadership, but none of the standard measures are quite suited to the kind of leadership that Papal leadership is. Everyone knows, for example, that the man who used to be called Jorge Mario Cardinal Bergoglio, SJ, was elected with a reform mandate: there was one thing on which every one of the red hats in the conclave could be reliably supposed to agree, and that one thing was the brokenness of the curial system by means of which the Pope exercises his threefold *munus* of teaching, sanctifying, and governing the Universal Church.

Frankly, the Pope has not seemed terribly interested in reforming the Church's central bureaucracy. Sure, he appointed his Council of Nine "Cardinal Advisers" to study the matter and draw up a reform plan. He also seems to abide by the maxim, "If you want to make sure something never gets done, appoint a committee to study it." He has said so, or said as much, in words. The actual reforms he has announced have been shuffles, in essence, and the principles—such as they are—on which the reform of the Curia is based are ones apt not so much to direct a functional system, as to make it easier for the head man to sidestep the machine and govern directly. In any case, two of the nine members of his kitchen cabinet are dealing with sex abuse scandals (Cardinal George Pell is home in Australia on indefinite leave to face abuse charges, while Cardinal Francisco Javier Errázuriz is trying to respond to the fallout from the Barros Affair, along with Pope Francis himself), and another—Cardinal Óscar Rodríguez Maradiaga of Tegucigalpa—is accused of financial mismanagement (which he denies).

Pope Francis, meanwhile, seems increasingly isolated within the Vatican, even as his "surprises" continue to generate media buzz, though less of it, and less sympathetic. Most recently, his airplane wedding stunt fell flat, and failed to divert attention for more than a few hours from the big story of his trip to Chile and Perú, which was his sufficient, dismissive, frankly insulting and possibly injurious attitude toward victims of clerical sex abuse. In short, the shine has gone off. People in the mainstream secular media are asking questions, and people in the Church—even and especially those, who heretofore have been well disposed to him and to his style of governance—grow tired of waiting and the games that go with it.

At the beginning of 2018, I predicted the year would be make-or-break for Pope Francis: one in which he would have to decide whether to use his gifts to set the project on track, or continue trying to remake Rome into what I described as "Buenos Aires-on-Tiber." The stakes remain at least as high as they were at the turning of the year. It is important to remember that we are still in the first quarter.

"The Vatican's Viganò Problem"

Pope Francis has a problem, and his name is Msgr. Dario Edoardo Viganò. Hand-picked by the Holy Father in 2015 to head the newly created Secretariat for Communication of the Holy See, Viganò's tenure has been rocky from the get-go. After nearly three years on the job, and until last week, the great achievement of Viganò's tenure was an anemic new web portal still in beta testing. That mighty jewel of an accomplishment has now been supplanted by a major scandal, revealing the Prefect's tenuous grasp of personal relationships, professional ethics, moral obligations to the public, and common sense.

What happened? Even the bones of the story are difficult to lay out succinctly, but the nutshell version is that the Prefect of the Secretariat for Communications botched a book launch. That's the sort of thing that can happen to anyone, even to highly competent and well-intentioned publicists. It is also too short by more than half. The controversy—scandal is neither too strong a word, nor inaccurate—began on Monday, and brewed all week.

The details of it are impossible to rehearse succinctly. The broad strokes of it are that Msgr. Viganò tried to score a trifecta: a publicity coup for a series of books published by the

Libreria Editrice Vaticana (which is under the control of the SpC) on *The Theology of Pope Francis*, a tactical media coup to give his principal a boost, and a rhetorical coup in the debates over the nature and scope of Pope Francis's ongoing project of reform in the Church.

Viganò's grand design began to crack when it emerged that he had not only quoted selectively from a letter from the Pope-emeritus, Benedict XVI, responding to a solicitation from Viganò himself for a "brief dense theological page" engaging the theological content of the books—both during the press conference he had called to launch the book and in the press release announcing the launch—but had also altered a publicity photo in a manner that made pertinent portions of Benedict's letter impossible to read and ran afoul of the AP's professional ethical standards.

On Saturday, in the wake of increasingly intense public pressure and media scrutiny, the Vatican Press Office—heretofore not directly involved in the mounting controversy—released the letter from Benedict. At that point, it became apparent that Viganò was not simply using lemons to make lemonade. The full text of the letter from the pope emeritus contains a paragraph that Viganò neither read during the press conference, nor quoted in the press release:

> Just as an aside, I would like to mention my surprise at the fact that among the authors figures Professor [Peter] Hünermann as well, who during my pontificate distinguished himself [It. *si è messo in luce*] for his having headed anti-papal initiatives. He participated in a relevant manner in the release of the *Kölner*

Erklärung [the Cologne Declaration], which, in relation to the encyclical letter *Veritatis splendor* attacked in a virulent manner the magisterial authority of the Pope [i.e. St. John Paul II], especially on questions of moral theology. Also, the *Europäische Theologeng-esellschaft*, which he founded, was initially conceived by him as an organization in opposition to Papal magisterium. Subsequently, the ecclesial sentiment of many theologians impeded this orientation, rendering that organization a normal instrument of encounter among theologians.

I am certain that you will have comprehension for my refusal, and I salute you cordially.

So, it is not only that the Prefect of the Secretariat for Communication of the Holy See was using Benedict to prop up Francis. It is not only that the Prefect of the Secretariat for Communication of the Holy See makes selective use of words of his betters when it suits his purpose. It is not only that his purpose in doing so this time was threefold and underhanded: to hawk books and to score points in a major ecclesial debate and curry favor with his current boss. All that is true, and all that is distasteful.

The upshot of all this is that the Prefect of the Secretariat for Communication of the Holy See, Msgr. Dario Edoardo Viganò, has a communication problem. Specifically, he has a hard time telling the truth. That is indeed a problem for Pope Francis, who put Msgr. Viganò in the job. More importantly, it is a problem for the universal Church. Whether the problem admits of a remedy short of Msgr. Viganò's severance from the department he currently heads is beyond the scope of these considerations, the purpose of which has been merely to say what happened. *Res ipsa loquitur.*

"The Viganò scandal raises serious questions about reform in the Roman Curia"

By now, the news that Pope Francis on Wednesday accepted the resignation of the Prefect of the Vatican's Secretariat for Communication, Msgr. Dario Edoardo Viganò, has made the rounds. The resignation came in the wake of a major scandal and outcry over Viganò's mishandling and misuse of a letter from the Pope-emeritus, Benedict XVI, as part of Viganò's efforts to promote a series of books on *The Theology of Pope Francis*. Several questions remain, however, regarding the project of reform Viganò was tapped to direct, and regarding the broader project of reform in the Roman Curia.

The controversy and scandal that led to Viganò's resignation unfolded all throughout last week, through the weekend, and into the first part of this week, as details emerged, and an already messy story became almost surreal and sordid. Viganò, in his resignation letter, wrote:

> In these recent days, a great deal of polemical discussion has arisen regarding my work, which, quite apart from my intentions, destabilizes the great and complex labor of reform with which you entrusted me in June

of 2015 and that now sees, thanks to the contributions
of a great many persons starting with the personnel,
the completion of the final stage.

Pope Francis responded to Msgr. Viganò's letter with one
of his own, in which he accepted the Prefect's resignation
"not without difficulty" and asked Viganò to stay on with
the Secretariat in a new capacity: "Assessor" to the Dicastery, "so that [he] might give [his] human and professional
contribution to the new Prefect, to the project of reform
desired by the Council of Cardinals, approved by me and
regularly shared." The Holy Father went on to write, "The
reform has now reached the final stage with the imminent
fusion of *L'Osservatore Romano* into the single communica-
tive system of the Holy See and the absorption of the Vatican Typography."

Issues of syntax aside—the sentence was a clunker in the
original Italian—the affirmations it contains raise at least as
many questions as they answer.

To start, why is Viganò being kept around at all? At best,
his presence will be a nuisance to the new Prefect, whoever
he is (though my nickel is on Bishop Paul Tighe, who was
in to see the Holy Father on Thursday of last week, the day
the story now dubbed "Lettergate" really began to go side-
ways for Viganò). At worst, he will "retard, damage, or even
block" the reform—precisely the things Viganò said in his
letter he wishes to avoid by his resignation—just by being
there. In any case, the decision to make him an Assessor—
whatever that is—does not seem to respect Viganò's wish to
"step back" and "step out of the way" so work can proceed,

nor does it seem to accord, therefore, with the Holy Father's acceptance of the resignation. Perhaps the appointment is designed to be temporary, meant to last only as long as absolutely necessary to bring the new head up to speed. That could have been accomplished without an official appointment to an *ad hoc* position.

Another noteworthy and frankly perplexing turn-of-phrase in the Pope's letter is the one that speaks of "the project of reform desired by the Council of Cardinals" and only approved by the Pope. Almost from get-go, the leadership of the Secretariat for Communication has told staffers—of which I was one—that the reform they were enacting was "the Pope's reform" and "the reform desired by the Pope." Is the Pope distancing himself from the reform project, now that the man he chose to head it has resigned?

It does not sound like it, with all the talk of the reform's being in its final stage, but there is no telling, especially since, "The great dedication," and effort Msgr. Viganò has:

> [P]oured out in recent years in the new Dicastery with the style of open and willing exchange of ideas [It. *disponibile confronto*] and docility that [Viganò] was able to demonstrate among collaborators and the organisms of the Roman Curia, has made clear that the reform of the Church is not primarily a problem of organizational charts but rather the acquisition of a spirit of service.

I've been reading *curialese* for nearly two decades now, and this letter might just take the cake. It is not that it says nothing. Saying nothing is easy, and par for the course in Curial discourse. Its great achievement is in that it seems to say—in as literal a translation as comprehension will admit—everything, and also the opposite of everything. In Italian: *Tutto, e il contrario di tutto.*

It seems to say the reform is in its final stage and can't be stopped now, and also the specific shape of the reform doesn't matter. It seems to acknowledge that Viganò's leadership has been ineffective, and then praises Viganò's leadership style (and so in frankly improbable terms, but leave that aside). Taken in its whole complex, the letter from Pope Francis seems to say that Viganò must go, and also stay.

In any case, shortly after the news of Viganò's resignation broke on Wednesday, the go-betweens for the SpC staff and the nocturnal council calling the shots from the SpC head office at *via della conciliazione* #5, called a meeting for 1pm at the building that used to be the headquarters of The Thing That Used To Be Vatican Radio, Palazzo Pio. The nutshell version of their message for staffers was: this changes nothing.

Time will tell, but there are at least two reasons to believe the reform of Vatican communications will continue apace, hence that things will get worse before they ever have a chance to get better. The first is that the real problems with Vatican communications are not located in the communications organs, nor have they ever been. The real problems are in the dicasteries and woven into the fabric of Roman curial culture.

The dicasteries—not just the new one for communication—are stepping stones for the ranking prelates who run them, especially for those who want to trade a purple hat for a red one. Msgr. Viganò's was a particularly garish case-in-point, not only because he wanted a red hat and did not even have a purple one to trade yet, but also—indeed, primarily—because the whole embarrassing fiasco never would have happened had he not been so eager to boost his own stock, that he was willing not only to try and get Benedict to dance for his successor, but when he couldn't, was desperate enough to try and sell a Punch and Judy show for the real thing.

Pope Francis is right when he says that what is needed is a "spirit of service" in the Curia. The thing is, he will not get that spirit, or even create the conditions in which such a spirit (should he or anyone else happen to catch it) will ever be able to become the active principle of curial work, without destroying the bureaucracy as it exists—and that will leave the whole Church without the necessary machinery of governance. I've said it before, and I'll say it again: it is one thing to undertake the reform of bureaucracy, and quite another to undertake the reform of bureaucrats. Confusing the tasks leads to chaos, and so by a very much shorter route than anyone in such a confused state realizes.

To change the communications culture in the Vatican is perhaps feasible. It would, however, require creating communications staffs and budgets within each of the dicasteries. The heads of the communications staffs—ideally lay persons of long experience and significant accomplishment—would have to meet regularly and frequently with each other, and monthly with the dicastery heads all together. More importantly, the communications heads would have to be in the room, both literally and figuratively. They would need to be part of decision-making processes. They would need to have a free hand to work their work, and that would in turn require a commodity more rare and precious than gold in the Vatican: trust. I'm sorry to say I'm not holding my breath.

"Gaudete et exsultate is beautiful for its simplicity, frustrating for its failures"

The project of Pope Francis's Apostolic Exhortation, *Gaudete et exsultate*, is beautiful for its simplicity: Pope Francis wants us to be better Christians. He is using the platform his office affords him to illustrate how we might go about growing in holiness. There's everything right with that. Nevertheless, there are some serious problems with his execution, which tend to make some of the great good in it accessible to many readers only after a great deal of difficulty, if at all. The purpose of this essay is to acknowledge those problems of execution frankly in a general way, and to offer a few concrete examples of both the good and the problematic, in that spirit of parrhesia—that spirit of frankness and forthrightness—for which Pope Francis has called.

The practical advice Francis offers and the insights he shares into our part of the work of becoming holy are in the main very good, and broadly applicable. Some of us will find some things he has to say more helpful than we will find others. Some readers will come to see some things really don't apply to them (though I would not recommend haste in making that determination). That is fine, and that is also how he meant it to be.

Growing in holiness will always involve death to self. It ought not to come as a surprise, therefore, when we find the things we most need to hear are the ones, the hearing of which is most difficult for us. A list of all the things I found challenging and convicting would run to great length. One in particular was Pope Francis's call for an attitude of prompt responsiveness. "Let us ask the Lord for the grace not to hesitate when the Spirit calls us to take a step forward," he says in §139. "Let us ask for the apostolic courage to share the Gospel with others and to stop trying to make our Christian life a museum of memories," Francis continues. We have heard that from Francis before. When I have heard that line before, I have been inclined to receive it as a trope, a slight against anyone drawn to traditional modes of spirituality and orders of worship. This time, however, I hear it as a general warning against sentimental nostalgia and—in my case, at least—the twin pitfalls of complacency and of practicing cowardice and calling it prudence.

Another starkly convicting passage was right in the middle of the Exhortation (§90), and fairly leapt from the page. "Jesus himself warns us that the path he proposes goes against the flow," Pope Francis writes, "even making us challenge society by the way we live and, as a result, becoming a nuisance." Here I thought of the people giving prayerful witness outside the abortion mill in Ealing, or protesting at Alder Hey, where Alfie Evans is on trial for his life on charges of being very small and very ill. I also thought of my Anglican friend, who recently suffered an indignity (happily minor) here in Rome while participating in an ecumenical meal program serving the poor, the homeless, and "clandestine" immigrants as they are called here. I'd told him I was interested in helping, but couldn't get my act together in time to be there the night it happened. My friend is fine. I am not.

"[Jesus] reminds us how many people have been, and still are, persecuted simply because they struggle for justice, because they take seriously their commitment to God and to others," Pope Francis continues. "Unless we wish to sink into an obscure mediocrity, let us not long for an easy life, for 'whoever would save his life will lose it.' (Mt 16:25)" Consciously or not, there Pope Francis was channeling Benedict, who, in one of the most convicting utterances of his pontificate, said (of Our Lady, in 2005 on the Solemnity of her Immaculate Conception), "Looking at Mary, how can we, her children, fail to let the aspiration to beauty, goodness and purity of heart be aroused in us? Her heavenly candor draws us to God, helping us to overcome the temptation to live a mediocre life composed of compromises with evil, and directs us decisively towards the authentic good that is the source of joy." Benedict might have been speaking directly to me. Indeed, he was.

Next, I thought of one of my heroes, Cardinal Nguyên, about whom Pope Francis also writes. "When Cardinal François-Xavier Nguyên van Thuân was imprisoned," Pope Francis says in §17, "he refused to waste time waiting for the day he would be set free. Instead, he chose 'to live the present moment, filling it to the brim with love.' He decided: 'I will seize the occasions that present themselves every day; I will accomplish ordinary actions in an extraordinary way.'" That's when I thought of me, and was ashamed. Pope

Francis is right as well, when he writes about humility, and says humiliation is that quintessential virtue's price in sinful flesh:

> Humility can only take root in the heart through humiliations. Without them, there is no humility or holiness. If you are unable to suffer and offer up a few humiliations, you are not humble and you are not on the path to holiness. The holiness that God bestows on his Church comes through the humiliation of his Son. He is the way. Humiliation makes you resemble Jesus; it is an unavoidable aspect of the imitation of Christ. For "Christ suffered for you, leaving you an example, so that you might follow in his steps" (1 Pet 2:21). In turn, he reveals the humility of the Father, who condescends to journey with his people, enduring their infidelities and complaints (cf. Ex 34:6-9; Wis 11:23-12:2; Lk 6:36). For this reason, the Apostles, after suffering humiliation, rejoiced "that they were counted worthy to suffer dishonor for [Jesus's] name" (Acts 5:41).
>
> Here I am not speaking only about stark situations of martyrdom, but about the daily humiliations of those who keep silent to save their families, who prefer to praise others rather than boast about themselves, or who choose the less welcome tasks, at times even choosing to bear an injustice so as to offer it to the Lord. "If when you do right and suffer for it, you have God's approval" (1 Pet 2:20). This does not mean walking around with eyes lowered, not saying a word

and fleeing the company of others. At times, precisely
because someone is free of selfishness, he or she can
dare to disagree gently, to demand justice or to defend
the weak before the powerful, even if it may harm his
or her reputation. (§118-19)

I am tempted at this point to soften the blow, or assuage
the sting of those lines on my skin and the crush of their
force, which I feel in my bones, perhaps by noting how our
public discourse in the Church and in the worlds of our
societies should be improved if all of us would strive to practice humility in the ways Pope Francis indicates in the lines
above. It is most certainly so. God help me, let it begin with
this sinner.

There is much more of great worth in the Exhortation,
some of which we shall visit at the end of this essay. During
the course of his official encouragement, however, there are
things Pope Francis says, which do little in the way of good,
and make the great good there is in the essay more difficult
than it need be to discover.

One example is in §70, where Pope Francis writes, "Luke
does not speak of poverty 'of spirit' but simply of those who
are 'poor' (cf. Lk 6:20). In this way, he too invites us to live a
plain and austere life. He calls us to share in the life of those
most in need, the life lived by the Apostles, and ultimately to
configure ourselves to Jesus who, though rich, 'made himself
poor' (2 Cor 8:9)." I do not take kindly to clerics lecturing
laity about austerity, who have never had to choose between
fixing the roof or fixing the car, let alone between making
rent or buying shoes and school supplies for their children,

or which utility bill to pay on time, or between a full course of medicine and a full week of groceries.

I think of when Francis decided to forego the usual bonus to employees, in favor of a gift to charity from the Papal purse. The thing was not a wrong, not precisely. It was an indignity, and for the lay persons on the payroll—especially the men and women in the lower pay grades, some of whom might not see much more than €1300 per month, if they see that—the thing was hard. "The hours are going to be long in the coming weeks, darling," a typical conversation might have gone, "but, with the overtime and the bonus (when it comes) we might just be able to [get Maria those braces / replace the boiler / air conditioner / take that vacation / send Mario to Paris for the summer, after all]." I will not speculate on how the conversation went, after news came of the Holy Father's religious economy and exemplary generosity with other people's money.

I very much doubt Pope Francis considered how those conversations might go, either. His appreciation for domesticity generally suggests rather a lack of moral imagination. Listen to him imagine a day in the life of a homemaker (obviously a woman):

> [A] woman goes shopping, she meets a neighbor and they begin to speak, and the gossip starts. But she says in her heart: "No, I will not speak badly of anyone." This is a step forward in holiness. Later, at home, one of her children wants to talk to her about his hopes and dreams, and even though she is tired, she sits down and listens with patience and love. That is

another sacrifice that brings holiness. Later she experiences some anxiety, but recalling the love of the Virgin
Mary, she takes her rosary and prays with faith. Yet
another path of holiness. Later still, she goes out onto
the street, encounters a poor person and stops to say a
kind word to him. One more step.

Leave aside the impression he gives of conviction in the
inveterate proclivity toward and nearly boundless capacity
for gossip that possesses everyone around him, especially
housewives. I do not know of any parent who, faced with
a child desirous of discussing future hopes and dreams,
would not drop everything to listen and participate in their
elaboration. It would certainly be worth a ruined pot. It is
perhaps the only thing as could make this too busy father-
of-a-teenager miss a deadline. Usually, children (including
adolescent children) want to talk about "When is dinner
ready?!?!?" every three minutes for two straight hours before
dinner time, so they can disappear right before you serve the
meal.

He might have run that passage past a parent or two,
before sending it to the printer. He did not have to put it in
at all. He'd made his point already. There are other instances
of superfluous exemplarism and gratuitous cajoling and even
sniping, which, though it were gossip to adduce them, are
already amply cited by partisans on both sides of the ecclesial
divide. I shall not rehearse them here, but only give one particularly egregious example, found in §49, part of the Holy
Father's treatment of "Contemporary Pelagianism":

Those who yield to this Pelagian or semi-Pelagian mindset, even though they speak warmly of God's grace, "ultimately trust only in their own powers and feel superior to others because they observe certain rules or remain intransigently faithful to a particular Catholic style." When some of them tell the weak that all things can be accomplished with God's grace, deep down they tend to give the idea that all things are possible by the human will, as if it were something pure, perfect, all-powerful, to which grace is then added. They fail to realize that "not everyone can do everything", and that in this life human weaknesses are not healed completely and once for all by grace. In every case, as Saint Augustine taught, God commands you to do what you can and to ask for what you cannot, and indeed to pray to him humbly: "Grant what you command, and command what you will."

The sense of superiority Pope Francis impugns is there to be found, and often plain to see, though it is not confined to "Pelagian" or "semi-Pelagian" circles, so-called. To be frank, it strikes me as increasingly transversal and at times systemic. Indeed, it often seems likely the most dangerous heresy plaguing the Body of Christ in these days is Donatism: factions loyal to one disposition or dispensation warring with another over the claim to be the native and rightful heirs of Christ's promise. It makes us weak, silly, incredible. All of us.

In any case, I cannot recall ever meeting anyone, layman or cleric (high or low), who seems to me really to believe that all things—or even anything—is possible by the human will.

Friends I respect and admire, upon whose judgment I have come to rely in forming my own, tell me they have discovered it in themselves. In my experience, there can be found a sort of default belief that people seeking the help of the Church must be made to prove their earnest by "making an effort", sometimes in the form of frankly unreasonable sacrifice, uncharitably required, in order, e.g., to meet parish- (or parish secretary-) imposed "requirements" that really are no such thing, and are often contrary to the letter and the spirit of pertinent Church law. It is hardly a sin exclusively the province of "conservative" or "traditional" Catholics, though both supporters of Pope Francis and his implacable critics often receive it as a sort of dog whistle blown against those of a more conservative or traditional bent. If Pope Francis is aware of the effect his mode of speech has, he shows no sign of it. If he speaks thus for effect, it is ill-chosen and ill-met.

I suspect I would not mind Pope Francis's rather peculiar—not to say, "quirky"—concern with this particular straw man, were it not for the boldness it engenders is certain partisans, who use it as a cudgel. Most galling, however, is the turn-of-phrase, "deep down", which suggests a mind-reading or soul-seeing power that, did he have it, would best be kept tightly under wraps. All of this to say that I understand how hard it is for people who are sore with Francis to hear him. So, too, are persons drawn to the beauty and precision of traditional liturgy, or confused and consternated by his approach to doctrine and discipline, sore with him.

Readers already disappointed with his leadership and discouraged by his governance will find in this and other similar passages confirmation of the Pope's disdain for them.

Perhaps they ought not discover such disdain, but it is easy to understand why they do. Francis does not help when he hectors and cajoles. In *Gaudete et exsultate*, he gives ample evidence of his extraordinary ability to speak hard and needful truths with charity. This makes his failures to do so the more evident, and the more frustrating.

When other readers better disposed to the Holy Father because they see him as the standard bearer of their kind of Christianity take up the call, they appear to their fellows and brethren to be too keen to lay it on thick, or even kick their fellows when they are down. That impression will often be false. It is nevertheless something of which persons well-disposed to Francis and enthused by his style and record of leadership do well to be mindful in both charity and justice when they engage their fellows who see things differently. Persons less enthusiastic with Pope Francis—or even discouraged by him—ought neither be so quick nor so willing to seek confirmation of their worst fears and deepest misgivings in his or his supporters' every utterance.

Sometimes Pope Francis says bad things. Sometimes he says good things badly. If he is not exempt from criticism of his conduct in office—he is not—neither ought we exempt ourselves from criticism, but be willing to hear hard things from any quarter that protests to mean us well. Even if Pope Francis were wicked—he is not—his wickedness would not prove that of his supporters, nor would it be any proof of his opponents' virtue.

"The Christian life is a constant battle," Pope Francis starkly reminds us in the opening lines of Chapter 5. So it is. He also tells us in §114:

> We need to recognize and combat our aggressive and
> selfish inclinations, and not let them take root. "Be
> angry but do not sin; do not let the sun go down on
> your anger (Eph 4:26)." When we feel overwhelmed,
> we can always cling to the anchor of prayer, which puts
> us back in God's hands and the source of our peace."

All of us need to hear that, and pay it heed. Too many suns
have set on our anger with each other.

Pope Francis is a sinner, whose life has been profoundly
touched and moved by God's grace. He desires, as a true son
of Saint Ignatius, to help souls. That he should do so badly
from time to time is inevitable, and may require mention.
When it does, however, the mention of it imposes a duty on
the mentioners in justice to think and to say all the good
they can of him. If justice does not require it, then charity
nevertheless impels the critic to praise as well as criticize.

I have sought to illustrate only a few specific instances in
which I see that the Holy Father has succeeded in his project of encouragement, and where he has not. I began with
praise. Let me conclude as I began.

In §113, Pope Francis tells us, "Saint Paul bade the
Romans not to repay evil for evil (cf. Rom 12:17), not to
seek revenge (v. 19), and not to be overcome by evil, but
instead to 'overcome evil with good.' (v. 21)" It is hard to
hear that when we feel we have been wronged, or slighted,
or slandered—whichever side we are on—but that is when
we need to hear it most, and Francis—whatever his faults—
does us a service in saying it now. "This attitude," Pope Francis goes on to tell us, "is not a sign of weakness but of true

strength, because God himself 'is slow to anger but great in power.' (Nah 1:3) The word of God exhorts us to 'put away all bitterness and wrath and wrangling and slander, together with all malice'." (Eph 4:31) So it does.

Frankly, the Pope could stand to take a bit of his own advice in these regards. He should be more careful, for he tends to overstate matters and to attack weak sisters even when he does not set up straw men. There will be no satisfying his implacable critics, no reaching his detractors, who are determined to take offense. Nevertheless, Francis does give them reason, though he need not. Thus, he loses readers who would be inclined to hear him if his criticism were more kind.

"The saints," Pope Francis tells us in §116, "do not waste energy complaining about the failings of others; they can hold their tongue before the faults of their brothers and sisters, and avoid the verbal violence that demeans and mistreats others. Saints hesitate to treat others harshly; they consider others better than themselves" (cf. Phil 2:3). Pope Francis is right.

CHAPTER 3

CLOUDS GATHER AND SEAS STIR

April – May 2018

For the Catholic Herald, April 11, 2018

"The Pope's apology vindicates Chilean abuse survivors—but why did they have to suffer so long?"

Pope Francis has made a general apology to the victims of sexual abuse and clerical cover-up in Chile and called on the bishops of the country to come and meet him in Rome to discuss the crisis in the Chilean Church. While the Holy Father did not apologize specifically to the victims he accused of calumny while visiting their country—accusations he repeated to journalists several days later on the return trip to Rome—he did say: "I recognize, and so I ask that you faithfully convey, that I have made serious mistakes in the assessment and perception of the situation, owing especially to a lack of truthful and balanced information."

The Archbishop-Emeritus of Santiago de Chile, Cardinal Francisco Errázuriz, who was involved in several mishandled abuse cases, including that of the disgraced former celebrity priest, Fernando Karadima, is a member of the Pope's "C9" Council of Cardinal Advisers. Correspondence between Cardinal Errázuriz and the current Archbishop of Santiago, Cardinal Riccardo Ezzati, strongly suggests the two men were determined to block the nomination of abuse survivor Juan

Carlos Cruz to the Pontifical Commission for the Protection of Minors. Cruz is one of the survivors Pope Francis accused of calumny in connection with the case of Bishop Juan Barros, whom Cruz accuses of having witnessed, enabled and covered up Karadima's abuse of him and many other young people.

The Holy Father went on to say: "Here and now, I apologize to all those I have offended, and I hope to be able to do so personally, in the coming weeks, in the meetings I will have with representatives of the people interviewed."

Pope Francis wrote the letter on the Octave of Easter—Divine Mercy Sunday—after completing his review of the report prepared by his special envoy to Chile, Archbishop Charles Scicluna of Malta, who also stopped in New York to hear evidence from Mr. Cruz as part of his investigation. Archbishop Scicluna spent years as the Vatican's chief sex crimes prosecutor and helped draft the legislation Pope Benedict XVI implemented to combat clerical sex abuse. Scicluna got his special assignment in the wake of worldwide shock, anger and protest at the accusations of calumny Pope Francis levelled against the Chilean abuse survivors who accuse Barros, and after the AP reported that the President of the Commission for the Protection of Minors, Cardinal Sean O'Malley of Boston, had personally delivered a letter from Mr. Cruz detailing Bishop Barros's alleged enormities into the Holy Father's hands several years ago, even though the Pope had claimed he had never heard from any of the victims.

Archbishop Scicluna presented his investigation into abuse and cover-up allegations in Chile, many of which had been public for years, in the form of a 2,300-page report, which Pope Francis says he received on March 20. "With all this in mind," Pope Francis wrote to the bishops of Chile, "I am writing to you, gathered at your 115th plenary assembly, humbly to request your cooperation and assistance in discerning the short-, medium-, and long-term measures to be taken to reestablish ecclesial communion in Chile, with the purpose of repairing the scandal as much as possible and of restoring justice."

Pope Francis went on to write: "I plan to call you to Rome to discuss the conclusions of the aforementioned visit and my own conclusions. I have conceived of this meeting as a fraternal moment, without prejudices or preconceived ideas, with the sole objective of making the truth shine in our lives."

Irish abuse survivor, advocate and founding member of the Pontifical Commission for the Protection of Minors, Marie Collins, who resigned from the Commission in frustration in 2017, told the *Catholic Herald* the vindication of the Chilean survivors is belated, and the prospects for real remedy uncertain. "While it is good to see the survivors in Chile vindicated," she said via email, "it is sad they have had to suffer so long before being believed." She continued: "The representatives of the Catholic Church in Chile who misled the Pope no doubt felt they were protecting the institution and maybe themselves."

"This is a particular case as the Pope is involved," Ms. Collins added, "but it is the same mechanism as has happened in country after country where survivors have come forward and cover up taken place. It will continue to happen until there is real change in the culture of the Church."

"The Pope has said he was 'part of the problem' on abuse. Here's how he can change that"

Pope Francis is master of the grand gesture and of the personal encounter. Again and again we have seen his ability to touch and kindle hearts—not least last weekend, when he met Chilean abuse survivors including Juan Carlos Cruz. "He said he was part of the problem," Cruz told journalists at Wednesday's press conference. Cruz, along with James Hamilton and José Andres Murillo, welcomed Pope Francis's apology and said they had "met the friendly face of the Church, completely different from the one we have seen before." What matters now is action.

The Pope has also shown great willingness to use the power of his office where and when he has seen fit. The question is not whether he can govern, but whether he is willing—and the Chile scandal is a major test. "We hope," the statement prepared by Cruz, Hamilton and Murillo read, "that Pope Francis transforms his loving words of forgiveness into exemplary actions. Otherwise, all this will be in vain."

The three men were sexually abused by Fernando Karadima, Chile's most notorious abuser priest. The survivors have also accused Bishop Juan Barros—one of Karadima's protégés and the current bishop of Osorno, Chile—of turning a blind eye to the abuse they suffered at his mentor's hands. In his January trip to Chile, Pope Francis repeatedly dismissed the survivors' allegations against Bishop Barros as "calumny" and said he had seen no evidence for their claims. Then, the Associated Press revealed that Cruz had written to the Pope in 2014 detailing the allegations—and that Cardinal Seán O'Malley, head of the child protection commission, had promised to hand-deliver it to the Pope. Cue a media storm which led to a Vatican investigation of the Chilean case, and to last weekend's meeting. In short, what began with rumblings about the mishandling of one Chilean case has now brought the Holy Father's entire record of leadership in the fight against clerical sexual abuse under intense scrutiny.

So, this is a personal test for Francis, and the window of opportunity for him to show his bona fides is not getting any wider. There is one radical step he could take: to put Cruz himself on the Vatican's child protection commission. That's what Marie Collins, herself an abuse survivor and a former member of the commission, suggested in response to email inquiries from the *Catholic Herald*. "The Pope should appoint him to his Commission for the Protection of Minors or failing that appoint him a member of the new International Survivor Advisory Panel (ISAP) which is being set up to work with the Commission in advising the Pope," Collins wrote. "Mr. Cruz is in an excellent position to represent those survivors who have seen their cases mishandled and themselves mistreated by the Church. He knows first-hand the ongoing problems and what is needed to bring change."

Collins also hopes the talks with survivors will lead the Pope to take tough action. "He must remove from office the church leaders who tried to destroy these men to protect their colleagues," she said. "He must also take action to ensure a repetition of what happened in Chile does not occur elsewhere." Collins has reason to be skeptical of Vatican reform: a founding member of the child protection commission, she resigned last year in frustration at the lack of action. "So far none of the promises of change have come to pass," she said yesterday. "There is no transparent accountability structure to deal with negligent bishops, mandatory reporting is still not part of church policy, survivors are still looked on by many local churches as at best an inconvenience and at worst, as we saw in Chile, an enemy to be destroyed."

Some of those issues are thornier than others. Mandatory reporting is especially complicated and even fraught, especially in light of some civil jurisdictions' attempts to use mandatory reporting laws to force open the seal of confession. There might have been a threat to the confessional seal anyway. But had bishops responded adequately to the abuse crisis, the Church would be engaging in that fight from a much stronger position.

Transparency is a major outstanding issue for Pope Francis. Cruz told reporters he did not ask Pope Francis whether he had received the letter. So we are still not sure whether Cardinal Seán O'Malley of Boston failed to deliver the now infamous 2014 letter. We still don't know whether the Pope failed to open it, or whether it was read and overlooked. One could even be reasonably uncertain whether the Pope ever really received the letter at all. If the question has been,

"What did Pope Francis know, and when did he know it?" yesterday's press conference did not shed any direct light on the answer.

Meanwhile, Pope Francis is preparing to receive—here in Rome later this month—the bishops of Chile, including Bishop Barros and Cardinals Ezzati and Errázuriz. Those last, respectively the Archbishop and Archbishop-emeritus of Santiago, face intense public scrutiny over whether they did enough to prevent the Chilean crisis. They both strenuously deny wrongdoing. The question now is whether Pope Francis will govern the universal Church as though he really does finally understand how deep the filth and rot run, how truly pernicious are the evils to which a clerical culture of power can give rise.

"Pope Francis has pledged to take action on abuse. Here comes a big test"

When Chile's bishops come to Rome for emergency meetings with Pope Francis next week to discuss the clerical sexual abuse crisis in the Chilean Church, reports are that one senior figure is planning not to be there. Cardinal Francisco Javier Errázuriz, the Archbishop-emeritus of Santiago, member of the "C9" Council of Cardinal Advisers, and a key player in the controversy, has let it be known that he plans not to attend. The reasons Cardinal Errázuriz has apparently given are that he only recently got back from Rome, and has already given a report to the Holy Father on the "Barros Affair"—so called because it revolves around Bishop Juan Barros of Osorno, Chile, a protégé of the country's most notorious abuser priest, Fernando Karadima. The matter is the proximate cause of the scandal and crisis currently playing out. Not to put too fine a point on it, if Cardinal Errázuriz is allowed to skip the gathering, he will be rather conspicuous by his absence.

According to Chile's *La Tercera*, the "long report" is a 14-page document Cardinal Errázuriz gave to the Pope on "the trial of Fr Karadima and the ramifications of the case." He also told the Chilean outlet, "So for that, I've already made my contribution." Though emeritus bishops are not required to attend, the idea that a figure so central to the Church in Chile over the past three decades, as well as to the scandal and crisis facing the Church in the country at present, could simply skip the meetings, has stunned many groups in Chile. *Voces Católicas* and *Laicos de Orsorno* have issued statements expressing disappointment.

Bishop Barros has long faced public accusations, which he rejects, of having played a major role in the coverup of his mentor's crimes. Pope Francis appointed him to the see of Osorno in 2015, over the objections of laity and clergy alike. On a visit to Chile at the start of the year, the Pope accused Barros's accusers of "calumny." After facing widespread criticism, the Pope set up a special investigation, led by Archbishop Charles Scicluna. After reading Archbishop Scicluna's 2,300-page dossier, Pope Francis summoned the bishops of Chile to Rome. In a statement, he asked forgiveness of those he had offended, and said, "I have made serious mistakes in the assessment and perception of the situation, especially because of the lack of truthful and balanced information."

The three victims at the center of the Barros Affair—Juan Carlos Cruz, James Hamilton, and José Andres Murillo—all believe Cardinal Errázuriz is one of the Church leaders who were misleading the Pope. At a press conference in Rome last Wednesday at the Foreign Press Club, following private meetings with the Pope, Hamilton said: "Cardinal Errázuriz covered up for more than five years the crimes of Karadima." Hamilton also said, "According to canon law and for the victims, he's a criminal who covered up for Karadima and his circle."

Cardinal Errázuriz maintains his innocence. So the question now is whether Pope Francis will make sure the cardinal attends the Rome meeting. Presumably Cardinal Errázuriz expects the Pope will let him stay away. But Chileans—and others—will be disappointed if Francis does so. Francis has admitted he was "part of the problem" in Chile's abuse crisis. The meeting of the Chilean bishops is a great test of whether he really is ready to start being part of the solution. The prepared statement of Cruz, Hamilton, and Murillo framed the issue this way:

> We expressed to [Pope Francis] how the Church has a duty to become an ally and a guide in the global fight against abuse, and a refuge for victims, something that unfortunately does not happen today. In our lives, we have met many priests, men and women religious, committed to justice and the dignity of every single human being: honest and courageous people who have made progress in this fight, they are many, and they are essential.

The question facing Pope Francis now is: what sort of leader does he want to be? After spending the weekend hearing hard things from the victims he had accused of calumny, he told them, "There's no turning back now." Regardless of Cardinal Errázuriz's intention, his decision has challenged the Pope to make good on that pledge.

For the Catholic World Report, May 13, 2018

"What did Pope Francis know about Chile, and when did he know it?"

The Chilean bishops are converging on Rome for an emergency meeting this week to which Pope Francis has summoned them in response to the explosion of the clerical sexual abuse crisis and related scandals in their country. Pope Francis is largely responsible for the explosion of the scandal—the crisis is another matter—having garnered international media attention and intense criticism when he accused Chilean sex abuse victims of calumny and then doubled down on his accusation before relenting, ordering an investigation, and eventually recanting. If all that leads to a real address and remedy of the situation in Chile and the worldwide Church, it may prove to have been to the good. Nevertheless, he was, in his own estimation, "part of the problem," according to witnesses who heard him say it.

In the letter he wrote to the bishops of Chile in April, after reading a 2,300-page dossier from his special investigator, Archbishop Charles Scicluna of Malta, Pope Francis wrote, "I believe I can affirm that the collected testimonies speak in a stark way, without additives or sweeteners, of many crucified lives and I confess to you that that causes me pain and shame." He went on in the letter to say, "As for my own responsibility, I acknowledge, and I want you to faith-fully convey it that way, that I have made serious mistakes in the assessment and perception of the situation, especially because of the lack of truthful and balanced information."

There is a great deal about the situation in Chile that we do not know. Based on what we do know, it is diffi-cult to understand precisely what Pope Francis means by, "the lack of truthful and balanced information." There was a letter from Juan Carlos Cruz (one of the victims Francis had accused of calumny) rehearsing in gruesome detail his abuser's predations and the role he alleges bishop Juan Bar-ros played in their coverup. (Barros is at the center of the scandal that is proximate cause of the investigation and the upcoming meeting, after Pope Francis put Barros on the See of Osorno in 2015 despite the objections of clergy and laity in the diocese.)

The President of the Pontifical Commission for the Pro-tection of Minors, Cardinal Seán O'Malley of Boston, is supposed to have delivered the letter to the Holy Father in person. Did he? If he did, it is difficult to understand how Pope Francis can say he "lacked truthful and balanced information." Cardinal O'Malley's spokesman has con-firmed delivering the letter. And Pope Francis has not denied receiving it. If Pope Francis did receive the letter, but did not read it, he needs to explain why he did not. If he received it and read it, but decided not to credit or otherwise heed the contents of it, that simply is not a state of affairs for which "[lack of] truthful and balanced information," is an adequate description. It is one thing not to have informa-tion. It is quite another to have it, and disregard it. What happened to the letter from Cruz is as important an out-standing question as what—if anything—the Pope did with it. Those questions, however, are not crucial to understanding that the Pope's handling of this whole matter has been gravely inadequate.

His failures of leadership, moreover, may not necessarily be attributable to want of information. Pope Francis also apparently knew of the accusations against Barros and of the grounds on which clergy and faithful in Osorno and throughout the country objected to his appointment. The Pope wrote to the bishops of Chile in 2015, in response to a letter from them in which they explained their reasons for believing it best that Barros should not be seated. In his reply, the Holy Father said that he understood the bishops' concerns and was aware—in January 2015—of the difficult situation of the Church in Chile, as well as of "all the trials [the Church] has had to undergo." While he might now protest to the effect that he thought he was well informed at the time, but really was not, the information he did have in January 2015 was enough to raise doubts regarding the opportunity of seating Barros in Osorno or anywhere.

In fact, the Holy Father was convinced it would be best that Barros (and the other bishops in positions of responsibility, who had been protégés of their country's most notorious pedophile cleric) take a year's sabbatical—often church-speak for early and quiet retirement. The letter to the Chilean bishops—obtained by the AP and dated Jan. 31, 2015, reads:

I well remember your visit in February of last year and all the different proposals which I thought were prudent and constructive.

However, a serious problem came up at the end of the year. The Nuncio [Archbishop Ivo Scapolo] asked Bishop Barros to resign and encouraged him to take a sabbatical (for perhaps a year) before assuming any other responsibilities as a [diocesan] bishop. And he told him the same course of action would be taken with the bishops of Talca and Linares, but that nothing should be said to them. Bishop Barros wrote a resignation letter adding [or including—Spanish *añadiendo*] the Nuncio's comment.

As you can comprehend, the Nuncio's comment complicated and blocked any eventual path to offering a year's sabbatical.

Why Barros's mention of the Nuncio's remark should have torpedoed the plan for a quiet sail into the sunset is not at all clear to anyone not in the know, and may not really be any clearer to those who are. In any case, it is more than extremely difficult to see how putting Barros in a diocese should have been any sort of solution. Still, that is what happened, and here we are.

Frank admission of specific failures of governance will be necessary if the Pope wants to have a chance—as he says he does—at being part of the solution to the problem. Transparency will be equally important. Said bluntly, Pope Francis cannot be a credible leader on this issue unless he tells the whole story and tells it straight, even and especially when it will be painful to do so.

For the Catholic Herald, May 14, 2018

"Pope Francis needs to be transparent in his meetings with the Chilean bishops"

The bishops of Chile are in Rome this week for emergency meetings with Pope Francis, who wants to address the crisis of clerical sexual abuse and cover-up in their country. Thirty-one of Chile's sitting bishops will participate, along with a handful of retired prelates—virtually the country's entire episcopate. In a surprise development, Cardinal Francisco Javier Errázuriz, Archbishop-emeritus of Santiago de Chile, decided to board a plane and fly to Rome to participate in the gathering, which opens on Tuesday and is scheduled to run through to Thursday.

Cardinal Errázuriz is very much at the center of the controversy surrounding the crisis. He is accused, by victims a Vatican criminal court has deemed credible in a related matter, of providing cover for Fr. Fernando Karadima, who was once a prominent celebrity priest in Chile, found guilty at trial in the Vatican in 2010. Karadima's conviction came largely on the strength of the testimony of the men who also say Errázuriz covered up Karadima's abuse.

Last week, Cardinal Errázuriz let it be known he would not be joining his brother bishops for the meetings, saying he'd just been to Rome to see the Pope and, "already given my contribution," in the form of a 14-page report on the Barros Affair, which is the proximate cause of the scandal that has led to the upcoming sessions. He also said he couldn't get a room in Santa Marta (the Vatican guest residence where Pope Francis lives and where many bishops stay when they're in town).

Victims' support groups and survivor-advocates in Chile and around the world expressed disappointment in the announcement, while news outlets including the *Catholic Herald* viewed the episode as a test of Francis's resolve and wondered whether Pope Francis would let the prominent cardinal stay away. For whatever reason, Cardinal Errázuriz will be here. He told a reporter for *La Tercera* at Santiago's international airport, "I thought I was not going, but at my age I can change my mind."

Meanwhile, preparations for the three days of sessions here at the Vatican continue. On Saturday, the Press Office of the Holy See released a statement explaining that the meetings would take place in secrecy, and that the Holy Father would be presenting the Chilean bishops with his conclusions on the basis of the 2,300-page dossier his special investigator, Archbishop Charles Scicluna, assembled during the course of his recent mission, but also that the Pope would not be making statements either during or after the sessions. "It is not foreseen that Pope Francis should make any declaration either during or after the meetings, which shall take place in absolute confidentiality," the Saturday statement from the Press Office reads. Whether the bishops of Chile will talk, as happened when representatives of the US bishops had a similar series of meetings in Rome in 2002, remains to be seen.

Survivor-advocates are not sanguine. Marie Collins, an Irish abuse victim who served on the Pontifical Commission for the Protection of Minors as a founding member before resigning in frustration at the commission's toothlessness and the general lack of progress on the issues, said in a Twitter comment, "I hope whatever action the Pope takes against the Cardinals and bishops of Chile for their cover up it will be transparent." She went on to say that letting malefactors quietly resign is insufficient. "Justice," said Collins, "must be seen to be done."

The statement from the Press Office says, "It is fundamental to restore trust in the Church through good pastors who bear witness with their lives to their having known the voice of the Good Shepherd, that they should be able to accompany the suffering of the victims and work in a determined and tireless way in the prevention of abuse." The hierarchical leadership of the Church has a long row to hoe if it would re-establish credibility. For the universal pastor of the universal Church, bringing the faithful into his confidence, so that they may know his thoughts with regard to a major crisis precipitated at least in part by his own failures of leadership, ought to be a no-brainer.

For the Catholic Herald, May 17, 2018

"Abuse crisis: Recent events have revealed a broken culture"

At the start of this week, the eyes of the world were on the Vatican, where Pope Francis was preparing to receive the bishops of Chile in an emergency meeting to discuss the crisis of clerical sexual abuse, the details of which he learned through a special investigation that he ordered after the protracted saga had reached the papers and become a scandal. The three days set aside for those meetings will have come and gone by the time this edition of the *Catholic Herald* is published, so this is an opportunity to step back and take a broader view of the crisis facing the Church at present—a crisis that reaches the highest levels of governance.

Whatever else one may think or say about the present condition of the Church, one thing is certain: the specific culture her clerical and hierarchical leadership inhabits is broken. The brokenness of clerical culture is such that the Church risks mission failure: the Church cannot be a credible witness to the saving Gospel of Jesus Christ if the men who are her leaders care more about protecting their position than they do about protecting children; more about keeping up appearances than they do about keeping child abusers out of the ranks of her clerical leadership.

It has been 16 years since the global scope of the crisis began to be apparent. The damage it has wrought has not been fully surveyed. In his letter to the bishops of Chile summoning them to Rome for the emergency meetings, Pope Francis wrote of "many crucified lives"—lives that certainly number many thousands worldwide. Predator clerics high and low continue to abuse children and get away with it. Half measures will not avail as remedy.

"Justice must be seen to be done," explained abuse survivor and victims' advocate Marie Collins, who was a founding member of Pope Francis's Commission for the Protection of Minors and served three years before resigning in frustration at the commission's ineffectiveness, which she attributed to a lack of support (and even active resistance) within the Vatican. By that standard, one episode in another protracted abuse scandal sets in relief the inadequacy of the prevailing attitude towards the administration of justice in the Vatican: that of the disgraced former Archbishop of Guam, Anthony Apuron, OFM Cap.

The 72-year-old Apuron is a Guam native and member of the Capuchin Franciscans, who served more than 30 years as Archbishop of Agaña, coextensive with Guam's small island territory, where almost everyone is related to almost everyone else. He was a controversial figure at times. In particular, the archdiocese was involved in scandals stemming in part from the acquisition of real estate. Apuron wanted the land in order to block building of the gambling resort, and instead construct and outfit a seminary and theological institute to train men discerning vocations from the Neocatechumenal Way, a lay group founded by Spanish artist Francisco "Kiko"

Argüello as an itinerary of Christian formation for families in the wake of the Second Vatican Council. Apuron has been for decades a strong supporter of the group. He got his way in 2002, though the archdiocese reportedly bid only $2 million for the land (significantly less than the reported bid from Chinese investors, who wanted to build the casino). The *Redemptoris Mater* seminary opened in 2004.

Complaints about the archbishop—including one from a nephew who said he suffered sexual abuse in 1989 or 1990 at a family gathering—are therefore wrapped up and mixed with several intertwined scandals, with allegations and counter-allegations of shady real estate dealing, influence peddling, abuse of office (both civil and ecclesiastical, against Archbishop Apuron and against other major figures in the Church and island society), as well as financial misdoings. The crisis on the island—in which Archbishop Apuron is only one, albeit a central figure—is another protracted one, and the situation still an ugly mess.

A Vatican tribunal investigated and tried Archbishop Apuron in 2017, finding him guilty of two of the six crimes with which he had been charged at the start of the process. What were those six charges? That is a good question. No one not directly involved in the trial officially knows. The Vatican never announced either the charges or the specific counts on which Apuron had been acquitted.

Even Archbishop Michael Byrnes, coadjutor archbishop to Apuron and apostolic administrator of Guam during the trial, did not know what the charges against Apuron were, or what the specific result of the trial was. Byrnes explained to reporters, "I got a phone call saying to go to this site," and read the statement from the Vatican on the matter. The Congregation for the Doctrine of the Faith removed Apuron from office and forbade him from residing within the archdiocese he formerly led, effectively exiling him from the island of Guam.

Since his conviction, Archbishop Apuron has appeared at papal events on different occasions. Earlier this month, he joined several other bishops on the stage with Pope Francis for an event marking the 50th anniversary of the founding of the Neocatechumenal Way. The Holy See press office would not comment on the matter. A source in the Vatican told the *Catholic Herald* that the Vatican probably had no prior knowledge of the persons invited to participate in the celebration, which took place at Rome's Tor Vergata field on May 5, in front of 150,000 people from more than 100 countries.

At a weekly General Audience earlier this year—after the trial was concluded and the verdict reached, though before the Vatican announced it (that took months, adding another Kafkaesque wrinkle to the story)—Pope Francis gave Archbishop Apuron his blessing and exchanged a few words with him in the Paul VI hall.

Archbishop Apuron maintains his innocence and is appealing his conviction. Judicial processes are what they are, and they take time. Nevertheless, confidence in the administration of justice—an indispensable bulwark of credible leadership—cannot be won by means of star chambers and mixed signals.

For the Catholic World Report, May 19, 2018

"Pope Francis's handling of the Viganò scandal doesn't bode well for Chilean crisis"

The unprecedented resignation *en masse* of the Chilean bishops earlier this week sent the entire Catholic world into ferment. Speculation abounds regarding whether Pope Francis will accept any or all of the resignations—and whether he ought to accept them—as well as what it all means and what comes next. Those are questions touching not only the good of the Church in Chile, but also the common weal of the whole Church. They call for sober, informed reflection. Certain recent events may well provide some guidance for those needful considerations, in particular the recent scandal at the highest level of governance within the recently created dicastery for communications.

There and then, Pope Francis appeared to take swift action, though how much really changed is still not clear. The situation within the communications dicastery as well as the Church's central governing apparatus more broadly considered is arguably one not unresembling the driver of *Il gattopardo*, the famous historical novel by Lampedusa: *Se vogliamo che tutto rimanga come è, bisogna che tutto cambi* ("If we desire that everything remain the same, it is necessary that everything change.").

Earlier this year, the Prefect of the Secretariat for Communication, Msgr. Dario Edoardo Viganò, resigned his post as head of the dicastery in the wake of a fake news scandal dubbed "Lettergate". In his resignation letter, Viganò wrote of his desire, "to step aside," though he promised he would be, "available," should the Holy Father decide to make use of him in some other capacity.

The Pope allowed him to resign, but immediately—indeed, in the very same letter by which he accepted Msgr. Viganò's resignation—created a new position for him within the very same Secretariat for Communication from which he was resigning. "Assessor" is what the Pope called his new position: a Vatican catch-all that does as a sort of shadow minister or minister without portfolio (a "Pope's man" in a department) somewhat outside the regular chain of command, but vested with as much or as little effective power as the Pope decides to give—and Pope Francis actually listed him as the #2 man in the dicastery he used to head.

One may be forgiven for having the impression that the moves at the Secretariat for Communication fit something of a pattern: the announcement of the new Commission for the Protection of Minors was greeted with much fanfare, but the Commission itself was born toothless and has proven ineffective. The promise of a special tribunal for trying wayward and negligent bishops, too, eventually got jettisoned, while the much-ballyhooed judicial reforms supposed to make the trial of such prelates easier still has not been tested. Pope Francis often says the right things: he grabs the headlines and starts out well enough, but he does not follow through—and the details of a few significant cases of this lack of follow-through (e.g. Msgr. Viganò's case) might make one wonder whether he ever really meant to follow through at all.

In any case, Msgr. Viganò remains very much the public face of the dicastery and of the Pope's vision for Vatican communications, despite his missteps. That is at any rate a reasonable surmise, if Viganò's public engagements of late are any indication.

The *Catholic News Service* featured Msgr. Viganò in a piece published earlier this week looking at what happens when "Hollywood meets Holy See" in connection with a location shoot at the Vatican for an upcoming Netflix movie, *The Pope*—a fictionalized account of the relationship between Pope emeritus Benedict XVI and his successor, Pope Francis. Several news outlets including *Crux* (where you can find the piece published in full, though it is behind a subscription paywall on the CNS) picked up the story, which was a friendly and informative peek behind the curtain at what happens when movie productions bump into the Vatican gatekeepers:

> The Vatican receives many requests for "images of the Vatican Gardens, the Sistine Chapel, St. Peter's," said Msgr. Dario Vigano, the former prefect of the secretariat, who currently serves as a top counselor to the office. "We are the reference point for these requests from various international production houses."

The CNS story goes on to discuss the recent Wim Wenders documentary on Pope Francis:

Until the Wim Wenders documentary *Pope Francis: A Man of His Word*, which premiered in early May at the Cannes Film Festival, the current pontiff was never directly involved in any motion picture. Francis often "told me that he isn't an actor and doesn't want to be an actor," Vigano explained.

On that basis, he said, the Vatican had always denied requests from production companies to make a day-in-the-life film of Francis, as had been done with Pope Pius XII and St. John XXIII. But the Wenders documentary "was a little different. Why? Because (the pope) was in front of a very poetic director, a Christian director, of great sensibility," Vigano said. "We had a guarantee to be present in the production step by step."

All things being equal, it makes more than a little sense to have Viganò be the go-to guy for this sort of thing: he is a trained cinematographer and film critic. He also caused the worst Vatican media scandal in recent memory—a "fake news" scandal that gravely diminished the reliability of the dicastery he once headed, and gutted his personal credibility. It bears mention as well, that it was Viganò's very peculiar and selective representation of one important aspect of the relationship of the former pontiff to the currently reigning one, that was at the heart of the scandal that led to his resignation.

It was also rather surprising when, late last month—not two full months since his resignation—he appeared on a panel addressing "fake news" and gave a talk on the subject under the panel heading, "Fake News and the Ethical

Responsibilities of Media", during which he discussed the importance of transparency and likened journalists' ethical responsibilities to physicians'. "The journalist, like the doctor, has the ability to poison their readers [but] with one difference, which is that the journalist can poison more readers than a doctor can patients," the *Catholic News Agency* reported Viganò as saying during his talk. We can only suppose the former prefect has taken fully to heart the maxim recorded in Luke 4:23.

All this is perplexing: mixed signals and double standards are things of which the Vatican and Pope Francis personally have arguably less need now than at any other time in recent memory. With the resignation *en masse* of the bishops of Chile at the end of the working week, the world is watching to see what Pope Francis will do. If the "resignation" of Msgr. Viganò is any indication at all of what awaits, then one may reasonably expect acceptance of the resignations—in part or *in toto*—to mean very little one way or the other.

"Pope Francis now faces a terrible dilemma over Chile"

With their resignation *en masse* late last week, the bishops of Chile have put Pope Francis between a rock and a hard place. Basically, he has three options: accept all of them; accept some of them; accept none of them.

If he accepts them all, he leaves the Church in Chile headless, while owning utterly every awful thing that may yet emerge as the crisis unfolds—there is a great deal more in the way of awful things that must come out, if the Church in the country is to recover—and the Chilean crisis is far from over.

If he accepts some, his every decision will be scrutinized—he is bound to make mistakes—and if he takes his time and does it right, as he ought to, the Church will remain paralysed in the meantime and the evil men he has heretofore at least tacitly (though not always tacitly) supported will have time and opportunity to maneuver. A few—like bishops Juan Barros of Osorno, Horacio Valenzuela of Talca, and Tomislav Koljatic of Linares—are no-brainers. These men were protégés of the disgraced celebrity priest, Fernando Karadima: they were just the sort of men abusers seek systematically to insinuate into power structures for their own protection and advancement. Others are not.

If he accepts none of them, he will have to try some of them. Those trials will presumably take place under the procedural rules laid out in the Apostolic Letter *motu proprio*, *As a Loving Mother*, though the dispositions given in that letter remain essentially untried. There will be a learning curve. There will also need to be significant investment in the Vatican court system, which is already overloaded, underfunded, and not exactly bursting at the seams with enthusiasm for the work. Confidence in the ability of the Vatican to administer justice is therefore also very low, indeed.

In short, none of those is a good option—and one gets the impression the Chilean bishops knew exactly what they were doing when they left their letters with the Pope. Even if Pope Francis were to accept some or all the resignations as a quick and dirty stopgap, and immediately move to study the structural reform that everyone agrees is needed, the fact remains that there is virtually no agreement on what that structural reform ought to look like. If it is to have the popular support it will need in order to be even minimally credible from the outset, whatever emerges from the study of the reform question cannot be the result of the top-down approach that Francis has taken to every problem he has really tried to address.

With the Old Guard in place, consultation will be tainted. With the Old Guard removed, there will be no one to direct and moderate the consultation, which must involve the whole People of God in Chile—the Christian faithful of every age and sex and state of life in the Church—if it is to have any hope of success. With the Old Guard replaced, there will likely be too many figures too new to the halls of influence in the Church and unacquainted with the deep grammar of ecclesiastical power to be reliable partners.

One possible workaround could be a sort of ecclesiastical receivership: An Apostolic Visitation with a broad mandate, to work with Apostolic Administrators appointed at the diocesan level. That alternative has its own inherent difficulties and potential pitfalls, most of which must be the subject of another essay. One thing, however, does bear mention here and now. Usually the appointment of new bishops is accomplished through a process that begins with the proposal from the Apostolic Nuncio of three candidates for a given see. In Chile, the Apostolic Nuncio is Archbishop Ivo Scapolo, whose role in the Barros Affair and in the broader Chilean crisis has received much critical attention and deserves much more and much closer scrutiny.

In all this, however, there is one outstanding consideration, one giant red elephant in the room: Cardinal Francisco Javier Errázuriz, whose alleged mishandling of abuse—including alleged active coverup for Karadima—and position of trust and confidence as a member of the Pope's hand-picked inner circle, have placed him at the very center of the ongoing controversy.

The Archbishop emeritus of Santiago de Chile, Cardinal Errázuriz is also a member of Pope Francis's "C9" Council of Cardinal Advisers. Since he already has emeritus status, he did not submit a resignation along with the other bishops, and since the C9 is an extra-juridical "kitchen cabinet" of Pope's men, he technically has no position from which to resign. That does not mean he may not be declared persona non grata. Even if he cannot be juridically removed or punished—and that is a big "if"—there is also no reason he needs to keep his red hat.

That he has faced nothing harsher than a "no vacancy" sign put out for him at the Casa Santa Marta is unsatisfactory to many victims. "In my view," abuse survivor Marie Collins told the *Catholic Herald*, "[Cardinal Errázuriz] should have been removed immediately from this position [on the C9] when the Pope received the details." Collins was a founding member of the Pontifical Commission for the Protection of Minors, and served on the advisory body for three years, before resigning in frustration at the lack of progress (and even active resistance) within the Vatican. "Not clearly sanctioning him in any way would be indefensible," she said, "and send the message that his cover-up and attitude are to be tolerated because of his position as a cardinal."

CHAPTER 4

INTO THE STORM

June – August 2018

For the Catholic World Report, June 7, 2018

"Pope Francis's letter to Chilean faithful is disappointing and insufficient"

At the end of May, Pope Francis delivered a letter he had promised to the faithful of Chile, as part of his response to the burgeoning crisis of clerical sexual abuse and cover-up in their country. There was probably no letter that Pope Francis could have written which would have been adequate under the circumstances. Nevertheless, two failures of the one he did send last week were unnecessary and particularly unhelpful: his insistence on hackneyed language, and his continued evasion of full responsibility.

A letter to the faithful of Chile was a sensible thing to promise and deliver. Pope Francis cannot fix the crisis in Chile or the worldwide Church on his own, and he is very short on trustworthy advisers and capable ministers. He also needs to resist the temptation to rash action taken in order to be seen doing something. Such a letter was never going to accomplish anything in the way of real reform, but it might have given some sign the Pope appreciates the severity and gravity of the crisis.

Instead, the letter to the Chilean faithful reads as a sort of defense—an apologia, rather than an apology. It is as if the author is begging his readers to see what a decent fellow he

is beneath it all, even if he has made some painful missteps
of late, and show how very earnestly he wants to get it right
this time, with their help:

> With you, we can take the necessary steps for a healthy
> and lasting renewal and ecclesial conversion. With you,
> the necessary transformation can be generated, which
> is much needed [sic]. Without you, nothing can be
> done. I urge all the Holy Faithful People of God who
> live in Chile to not be afraid of getting involved, and
> to walk, driven by the Spirit, in search of a Church
> each day more synodal, prophetic and hopeful; less
> abusive, because she knows how to put Jesus at the
> center—in the hungry, in the prisoner, in the migrant,
> in the abused.

The faithful of Chile have been clamoring for action from
the Church's hierarchical leadership for years, even decades.
While Francis has thanked the faithful for their tenacity—
especially the victims he accused of calumny—and renewed
his gratitude to them in this letter, the talk of being in it all
together, and the protestations of helplessness without their
involvement, has a tinny ring to it at best, especially given
his apparent unwillingness to say what really happened and
name his failures of leadership and governance specifically.

The lack of discipline those lines above betray—they are
the closing lines of his missive—is disappointing and frankly
telling. Though he is certainly right to tell us—every time
he does—of our duty to every person who is hungry, every
prisoner, and every migrant, it is nevertheless also true that
"the hungry", "the prisoner", and "the migrant" are among

his most frequent subjects of address, along with "prophetic witness" and especially "synodality". Pope Francis could not apologize for miscarrying in his duty to an entire people, without hitting his favorite talking points. They ought to be the focus of our zeal: here, they are his tropes, with "abuse victims" tossed in at the end.

"*Nunca más!*" Pope Francis had declared earlier in his letter, writing to the pilgrim people of God in Chile:

> The "Never again!" to the culture of abuse, as well as to the system of concealment that allows it to perpetuate itself, requires working together to generate a culture of care that permeates our ways of relating, praying, thinking, living authority; our customs and modes of speaking [orig. *lenguajes*], and our relationship with power and money. Today we know that the best word that we can give to deal with the pain caused is the commitment to personal, community and social conversion, which learns to listen and take care especially of the most vulnerable.

Never again. That is what we heard after the hierarchical leadership of the Church in Ireland imploded under the weight of its own scandalous conduct. That is what we heard after Pope St. John Paul II summoned the US bishops to Rome for a reckoning when it got out they had betrayed the trust of the faithful in their country. One has warrant at this point to doubt whether the bishops—Pope Francis included—really understand what it means, and if they do understand it, whether they really mean it.

More to this: the commitment to personal, community, and social conversion, which Pope Francis proposes as a solution to the crisis, is what the Church calls all of us to seek prayerfully, every day. It is what Christians do. Bishops are Christians, and the Pope is a bishop. What is he doing? What are they going to do? Reminding the faithful that we're all in this together is perhaps necessary, hard as it is, but such a reminder can only come effectively if it is preceded by credible attestations from ecclesiastical leadership—starting with Pope Francis—recognizing their faults, acknowledging their guilt, and committing to repair of the damage they have wrought.

On each of those last three points, the Holy Father's letter to the faithful of Chile is insufficient. "[O]ne of our main faults and omissions," was, according to Pope Francis, "[not] knowing how to listen to the victims. Thus, partial conclusions were drawn that lacked crucial elements for a healthy and clear discernment." He went on to say, "With shame, I must say that I did not know how to listen and react in time." The clerical leadership of the Church in Chile had listened and heard the victims, though. They knew too well what problem they had on their hands.

The statement, "Conclusions were drawn," raises the question: by whom were they drawn? The answer is: by Pope Francis. Pope Francis drew conclusions based on what he'd learned from men who listened to the victims of clerical sexual abuse very carefully, indeed, and heard them loud and clear—the same men, who are credibly alleged to have responded with conduct that was at the very least morally bankrupt. Pope Francis, meanwhile, distrusted the witness of men the Vatican's own criminal court had believed when they gave evidence against Chile's most well-known abuser-priest, the disgraced 87-year-old Fr. Fernando Karadima, found guilty by a Vatican tribunal and sentenced to a life of prayer and penance in 2011.

One of Karadima's victims, Juan Carlos Cruz, wrote a letter to Pope Francis, which the Holy Father's own hand-picked head of the Commission for the Protection of Minors, Cardinal Sean O'Malley of Boston, supposedly delivered to the Pope in person in 2015. That letter detailed the abuse Mr. Cruz suffered, and rehearsed many of the allegations against several of the men Pope Francis trusted over and against Mr. Cruz and his fellows. Pope Francis denied he had evidence of the misdeeds to which Mr. Cruz's letter attested, years after he should have received it. He also stated that no victims had ever come to him, also years after he should have taken delivery of Mr. Cruz's missive.

Cardinal O'Malley has confirmed—albeit through his secretary for communications and public affairs, Terrence Donilon—that he did deliver the letter. Even if the Pope for some reason never got the letter, Mr. Cruz's story and others had nevertheless been before the public for years. Pope Francis's problem was not inadequate information, however incomplete the picture might have been. Pope Francis chose to believe bishops over victims. That is a very different thing.

If Pope Francis's failures contributed to the crisis, his leadership may yet be the thing that begins to stabilize the wounds and repair the damage, even if the necessary real and deep healing of the injuries the Church's clerical over-seers have inflicted on her body and soul will take at least a generation. He needs to get this right: to do that, he needs to trust the people of God with the whole, unvarnished truth; and he needs to get out of his own way. The window of opportunity, however, is closing rapidly.

"Cardinal McCarrick and the crisis of episcopal leadership"

Over the past sixteen years, there has been much praise of the reform efforts the Church's hierarchical leaders in the United States have undertaken in the wake of the clerical sexual abuse scandal that erupted in 2002. Much of that praise has come from the bishops, themselves. From the very start, however, there has been ample reason to take a grim view of the thing, and I confess I have never been too terribly sanguine regarding the prospects for successful reform. When I have heard it said that the US bishops have made the part of the Catholic Church in their charge the safest place in the world for children, I have inwardly—sometimes privately, but never before now publicly—quipped, "Someone needs to tell them that's not a selling point." At best, it's only a little better than saying: The Catholic Church—Now abusing fewer children.

We have heard little about those successes over the past few weeks, especially since several major sees have been caught up in another abuse scandal—this one dating back more than four decades and involving a man, who in the years intervening became a prominent figure in the US

Church: the Archbishop-emeritus of Washington, DC, Cardinal Theodore Edgar McCarrick.

Cardinal McCarrick is accused of abusing a minor this time—hence Church authorities have taken action—though his reputation for license with priests and seminarians, many of whom were his subordinates, has been the stuff of black legend for decades.

Coverage of the story since it broke in the second half of June has made clear the extent to which Cardinal McCarrick's alleged behavior toward young men over whom he exercised spiritual and administrative authority was an open secret. His alleged proclivities were widely known, and where they were not, they were much guessed at, and fairly. Until very recently, however, it seems no witness had ever brought "credible and substantiated" accusations of McCarrick's engagement in the kind of abusive behavior that would put the accused afoul of "the charter"—that's the US bishops' Rome-approved Charter for the Protection of Children and Young People, first adopted in 2002 and revised in 2005, 2011, and 2018—which requires Church leadership to take action in such cases. The statement from Cardinal Timothy Dolan of New York regarding Cardinal McCarrick says, "[This is] the first such report of a violation of the Charter for the Protection of Children and Young People ever made against [McCarrick] of which the archdiocese was aware." Perhaps.

The Diocese of Metuchen and the Archdiocese of Newark, however, knew of Cardinal McCarrick's behavior toward legal adults, for they had settled complaints against him. The shock and sadness expressed over the allegations Cardinal

McCarrick violated the Charter are therefore no more than a red herring.

The bishops' vaunted Charter, which is supposed to be at once a shield for the protection of children and young people and an instrument of reform for the Church in the United States, is instead a tool the bishops use to protect themselves and the cultural status quo: so long as a cleric—high or low—does not fall afoul of it, the bishops can turn a blind eye to his behavior. Anyone on the Church beat will have heard dozens of stories through the years, of clerics high and low behaving badly—on the parish dime in one heartbreaking case.

As Charles Collins wrote in his excellent analysis piece on the McCarrick scandal for *Crux* this week, "If the Church hierarchy continues to turn a blind eye to sexual misconduct involving adults, it will never be able to put an end to the sexual abuse of minors." Meanwhile, the bishops' moral authority is destroyed, and their credibility is in tatters. There is no quick and easy mending of it.

The crisis of clerical sexual abuse is a crisis of clerical culture, and more specifically, a crisis of episcopal leadership: the bishops have lost their way, and they have brought the whole Church with them into a quagmire. The only way out is through, and the only way through the filthy muck and slime of half-truth more devilish than outright mendacity, is veracity. The bishops—all of them and every one of them—must tell the whole, unvarnished truth. In any case, the truth will out.

For the Catholic Herald, July 28, 2018

"Set aside ideology: US bishops are guilty of a collective failure"

Since the allegations against Theodore McCarrick began to emerge over a month ago, one senior US churchman after another has disowned knowledge of his behavior—some more credibly than others. They should have known. They should have made it their business to know. The question we need to be asking, after McCarrick's resignation today, is: why didn't they know?

Bishops must have heard rumors: after all, two New Jersey dioceses had reached settlements over McCarrick's actions, and as more than one writer has noted, stories about the then-cardinal had a wide circulation. The bishops needed to look into those rumors. They didn't. In this, too, they failed: a truly execrable miscarriage of the duty to care.

This failure of the bishops is at once personal, touching each bishop singly, and corporate, touching them all together: they failed as one body—as a college. Some of them knew and did nothing. Those who simply let themselves be fooled are also guilty. This applies to many cases besides McCarrick's. Catholics on every side of every issue in the Church are perfectly aware of the bishops' corporate responsibility for the abuse crisis, and rightly appalled by their haste to plead ignorance and pretend responsibility only lies with the "few" who did the evil.

If some of the bishops have been lions in other fights, they are goats in this one. Nevertheless, many of us are too quick to blame the prelates on the other side of the ideological divide. That temptation will prove fatal to any reform effort. Catholics must resist it. Bishops who have been our allies and standard-bearers—sometimes even our heroes—in other situations may turn out to fail us in this one. In fact, they already have.

Said differently: we can use this crisis as a proxy in our ideological battles, or we can fight this fight together, ruthlessly and without stint, until we have won. We cannot do both. If we choose the first path, we shall make ourselves the evildoers' accomplices. The second path is the only one that offers hope. But it will also require us to smash our own idols.

For the Catholic World Report, August 11, 2018

Interview with Cardinal Wuerl

The Archbishop of Washington, DC, Cardinal Donald W. Wuerl, says the Church is in a moment of grave crisis, and affirms that the laity have a right to participate in roles of responsibility when it comes to the investigation and oversight of bishops' conduct. The statements came in an exclusive interview on Saturday with Christopher R. Altieri, reporting for *Catholic World Report*. Cardinal Wuerl had made remarks to Salt & Light Television earlier in the week, in which he appeared to downplay the significance of the crisis of confidence in the bishops' leadership in the wake of serious misconduct allegations against Cardinal Wuerl's predecessor in Washington, Theodore McCarrick.

McCarrick has resigned from the College of Cardinals and is facing canonical trial on charges he sexually abused at least one minor. Since the "credible and substantiated" accusation first came before the public in June, numerous other persons—many of them clerics or former clerics, or seminarians—have come forward with allegations of grave misconduct dating back years. The information come to light thus far has raised serious questions about the conduct of the US bishops with regard to the policing of their own ranks and their care for the moral culture of the clergy more generally.

Cardinal Wuerl told Salt & Light, "I don't think this is some massive, massive crisis." Speaking specifically of the news about his predecessor, McCarrick, Cardinal Wuerl went on to say, "It was a terrible disappointment." Speaking to the *Catholic World Report* on Saturday morning, Cardinal Wuerl clarified that he does, in fact, believe the crisis to be very serious. Nevertheless, he feels it is not insuperable.

"I think it's important to take a look at, and to listen to the context," he told *CWR*. "The context of that whole discussion [with Salt & Light] was: The Church is facing a very grave situation. There's an erosion of confidence—in fact, there's a breakdown—right now, of credibility." Cardinal Wuerl went on to say, "This is a very grave moment, a situation of very real crisis. That crisis should not overwhelm us. We should be able as lay women, lay men, and bishops, to confront it and to resolve it."

In an interview with the *National Catholic Reporter* published Monday, Cardinal Wuerl had seemed to suggest that the bishops needed to find a way to address the crisis by themselves, and for themselves. "Would we have some sort of a panel, a board, of bishops," he offered, "where we would take it upon ourselves, or a number of bishops would be deputed, to ask about those rumors [of episcopal misconduct]?" He is further quoted as saying, "It seems to me that's one possibility, that there would be some way for the bishops, and that would mean working through our conference … to be able to address the question of sustained rumors."

On Wednesday, Cardinal Wuerl was discussing a sort of partnership between existing structures, which are creatures of the US Bishops' Conference. "What I'm suggesting,"

Cardinal Wuerl told Salt & Light, "is [that] we already have a National Review Board made up of lay people: why don't we take from our Conference a number of Bishops—different committees—to work with and invite the National Review Board to join them. So, now we have a permanent body, and if someone has an accusation they want to bring, they can bring it there."

Cardinal Wuerl on Saturday clarified to *CWR* that he feels there must be a stable and independent oversight body with responsible lay participation. He also feels the body must be established as soon as possible, and that the bishops cannot wait for their Fall meeting to begin discussing the shape it will take, even if a full working-out of the ecclesiological implications of the crisis and its redress will take some time. "[T]he first thing we need is to put into place some sort of mechanism by which we can actually do what's being suggested," he said, "and I have suggested to our conference of Bishops that there should be some sort of an independent board established."

His Eminence also said, "It would have lay women, lay men—but also bishops—on it, and one of its functions would be to receive an allegation, to receive [any] complaint, so there is a place to which that complaint can go, where there is a sense of accountability but also a sense of autonomy." Cardinal Wuerl also said that any such stable and autonomous board must have a broad mandate, not only to deal with future allegations, but also to look into the bishops' past conduct.

He told *CWR* the scope of any investigation and oversight mandate ought to be comprehensive. "Now that board, once it's set up, should also then have as its prerogative to look at what it wants to call into question. Whether it's looking to the past, or whether it's moving into the future, the goal is to establish something that would engage lay women and lay men together with bishops—that is, flock and shepherds—working together to address this very grave crisis of credibility."

An autonomous body with a broad mandate would not only be able to investigate and oversee bishops' behavior toward minors, but also look at their records with regard to clergy, seminarians, and adult lay people. It would also be broad enough to countenance scrutiny of bishops' efforts—past, present, and future—to foster a sane moral culture among the clergy, starting in houses of priestly formation.

CWR asked Cardinal Wuerl whether he believes the laity have a right to roles of responsibility in the necessary investigation and oversight efforts. "[T]he laity do have a place," he responded, "a moral place—a right in that sense—to participate in whatever is going on in the life of the Church."

****

Below is a transcript—slightly edited for clarity—of Cardinal Wuerl's conversation with Christopher R. Altieri for the *Catholic World Report*.

Christopher Altieri for *CWR*: Your Eminence, do you have anything you would like to clarify with regard to the remarks you made in your conversation with Salt & Light?

Donald Cardinal Wuerl: I think it's important to take a look at, and to listen to the context. The context of that whole discussion was: the church is facing a very grave situation. There's an erosion of confidence—in fact there's a breakdown—right now, of credibility, and what I was saying and will say again now is: in the context of clergy and laity, laity and clergy—and I used the example of Shepherd and flock, parishioners and pastors—in that context there should be nothing that is so overwhelming that we can't deal with it. That was the context of those comments I made. This is a very grave moment—a situation of very real crisis. That crisis should not overwhelm us. We should be able as lay women, lay men, and bishops, to confront it and to be able to resolve it.

CWR: You spoke then and seem to be speaking now about going forward: that raises the question about how much looking backward we need to do. There have been calls for an investigation—an independent investigation—one thinks specifically of Bishop Scharfenberger from Albany, who strongly suggested that the laity should have a responsible role in any such investigation. I'm wondering about your thoughts on that: do we need to look back right now?

DCW: I think what we need first of all is to put into place—and this is what I have been saying in all of those interviews and in the material that I have sent out for use—the first thing we need is to put into place some sort of mechanism by which we can actually do what's being suggested, and I have suggested to our conference of Bishops that there be some sort of an independent board established. It would have lay women, lay men, but also bishops on it: and it would have as its—one of its functions—to receive an allegation, to receive some complaint, so there is a place to which that complaint can go, where there is a sense of accountability but also a sense of autonomy. Now that board, once it's set up, should also then have as its prerogative to look at what it wants to call into question: whether it's looking to the past, or whether it's moving into the future, the goal is to establish something that would engage lay women and lay men together with bishops—that is, flock and shepherd—working together to address this very grave crisis of credibility.

CWR: Do the laity then have a right—a moral right, whatever its expression in Canon Law, whether at the universal level or at the level of particular law—whatever that might look like now or in the future: do the laity have a right to responsible participation either in an investigation or in a stable oversight body or mechanism?

DCW: I think one of the things we've already seen—and this is, I believe, a response to the II Vatican Council, and Pope Francis is the strongest voice in this—is the role of the laity in the life of the Church. And I am wondering if we don't have expressions of that now: for example, the National Review Board and our National Advisory Council. But to have the recognition that, as we go forward, in whatever we're doing, lay people should be engaged. I think we're seeing more and more the recognition that that's the best way for the church to move forward.

CWR: Well, I guess I'm asking the question, Your Eminence—if I could just push you a little on this a little bit—because I think there is broad agreement that the laity should be involved as a matter of prudence right now—and you spoke to the question of the credibility deficit that the bishops have: Do the laity have a right—a moral right, independent of the question of the right's expression in Canon Law—to be involved in investigation and oversight in a responsible way?

DCW: How about if we word it this way: because, once you use the word, "right," then—you yourself have already said—are we talking about a canonical right? Are we talking about a constitutional right? Are we talking about a legal right? Are we talking about a moral right? Are we talking about an ecclesial right? How about if we said: It is absolutely clear in the theology of the Church, that the laity have a role in the life of the Church, and that role includes the exercise of their baptismal obligations and their baptismal responsibilities. So, in answer to your question, I think there is a place—a very significant place—for the laity in all the activity of the Church. That's merely confirming what the II Vatican Council affirmed. Now, how that is spelled out is something that—as you said—we're going to need a lot of time to work on that. But, yes, the laity do have a place—they have a moral place—a right in that sense—to participate in whatever is going on in the life of the Church. That has to be seen in the way it is expressed in the II Vatican Council, in the Decree on the Laity, also *Lumen gentium*—the structure and nature of the Church—but in both of those documents, there's a significant role of the laity in the life of the Church, and as Pope Francis keeps telling us, the Church is not just the bishops and clergy.

"The bishops' 'Apalachin moment' has arrived"

The Press Office of the Holy See has issued a statement in response to the Grand Jury Report released in Pennsylvania earlier this week, expressing "shame and sorrow" over the contents of the report, while praising the efforts of Church leaders to implement reforms. "Most of the discussion in the report concerns abuses before the early 2000s," the statement reads. "By finding almost no cases after 2002, the Grand Jury's conclusions are consistent with previous studies showing that Catholic Church reforms in the United States drastically reduced the incidence of clergy child abuse." The statement goes on to say, "The Holy See encourages continued reform and vigilance at all levels of the Catholic Church, to help ensure the protection of minors and vulnerable adults from harm."

The statement from the Press Office also expresses the Holy See's desire "to underscore the need to comply with the civil law, including mandatory child abuse reporting requirements." Pope Francis did not speak to the scandal in his remarks to the faithful at Wednesday's Angelus prayer on the Solemnity of the Assumption, while the Press Office of the Holy See kept silence and declined requests for comment for more than two full days after Pennsylvania authorities released a redacted version of the report, which neverthe-less runs to 1,356 pages. The President of the United States Conference of Catholic Bishops, Cardinal Daniel DiNardo of Galveston-Houston, issued his own statement on Thurs-day, calling for an Apostolic Visitation of the Church in the US.

Prominent voices from across the spectrum of Catholic opinion found the Vatican's two days' silence perplexing and consternating. CNN quoted Massimo Faggioli, Professor of Historical Theology at Villanova University and a colum-nist for *La Croix International*, as saying, "I don't think they understand in Rome that this is not just a continuation of the sexual abuse crisis in the United States." Faggioli went on to say, "This is a whole different chapter. There should be people in Rome telling the Pope this information, but they are not, and that is one of the biggest problems in this pon-tificate—and it's getting worse." *First Things* editor Matthew Schmitz told CNN, "[Francis] needs to act now by authoriz-ing a full investigation of the American hierarchy."

"Victims should know that the Pope is on their side," the Vatican statement says. "Those who have suffered are his pri-ority, and the Church wants to listen to them to root out this tragic horror that destroys the lives of the innocent." Mean-while, news outlets continue to divulge the report's findings, while analysis largely confines itself to sifting details and connecting dots, and commentary ranges in tone and sub-stance from heartbroken plaint to heartbroken rage.

The ball is now in the Holy Father's court, and while his next plays are anyone's guess, one thing is certain: Pope Francis can ill afford to ignore either the Pennsylvania

Grand Jury Report or the enormous groundswell of ire, which threatens the foundations of the Church. His moral authority—already greatly diminished by his handling of the crisis in Chile and his apparent paralysis with regard to the scandal-ridden "C9" Council of Cardinal Advisers he chose to spearhead the curial reform that was supposed to be the hallmark of his springtime pontificate—risks permanent compromise with each passing day. The damage is not only—not even primarily—to this pope or to his pontificate, but to the Office. The papacy has enjoyed greater and lesser esteem through the centuries, though rarely has the efficacy of the institution so much depended upon the high public regard of it, as today.

The question is: does Pope Francis have the stuff to do what circumstances require? He does not seem to be interested in institutional reform, yet it is institutional reform the hierarchy needs. As I put it earlier this year in an analysis piece for the *Catholic World Report*:

> 2017 was a year in which the micro-fissures in the structure began to be visible to the naked eye. 2018 is likely to be the year in which it becomes clear that major structural reform (or engine rebuilding, depending on one's preferred analogy) cannot be postponed.

In an earlier piece, addressing the specific issue of reform of the Roman Curia—or rather the lack of progress in reform, I noted how it struck me that Pope Francis did not seem concerned with it so much as he did with the spiritual renewal of Curial officials:

Spiritual reform, reform of the soul, repentance, conversion, healing, receptiveness to grace, and docility to the promptings of conscience: all these are essential to the life of every Christian, and only more so to the lives of those Christians who are called to assist the Universal Pastor in his governance of the Universal Church. Even so, the Roman Curia is a bureaucracy, and would be a bureaucracy if it were staffed and run by living saints. It is one thing to undertake a reform of a bureaucracy. It is quite another to undertake a reform of bureaucrats.

Fr. Thomas Rosica published an essay a few weeks ago, in which he attempted to say something about what difference having a Jesuit pope has made:

> Pope Francis breaks Catholic traditions whenever he wants because he is "free from disordered attachments." Our Church has indeed entered a new phase: with the advent of this first Jesuit pope, it is openly ruled by an individual rather than by the authority of Scripture alone or even its own dictates of tradition plus Scripture. Pope Francis has brought to the Petrine office a Jesuit intellectualism.

Those remarks are ill considered (and have since been edited), even as an exercise in sycophancy. Their facile parroting of SJ argot does not touch the crux of the matter, which is rather a tension built into the Jesuit character and ethos, for good and for ill. Here is how I placed the matter in another essay for the *Catholic World Report*:

The Society of Jesus has never—not for one single hour of one single day since the promulgation of *Regimini militantis*—had an unproblematic relationship with the hierarchical leadership of the Church. Ignatius wanted his men stalwart "Pope's men" and at one and the same time fearless theological envelope-pushers. The whole Jesuit charism is ordered to the right management—in the Company and in the souls of its members—of the tension that arises instantly and inevitably when those two poles are activated. … The long and the short of it is that, when you put a Jesuit at the head of the hierarchical leadership of the Church, you risk either collapsing that tension, or exploding it. That is one major reason why we never had a Jesuit Pope before now, and it goes a long way toward explaining why we are in the situation, in which we find ourselves, for good and for ill.

Francis, in other words, does not trust institutions—certainly not to reform themselves—and in any case does not seem to know how to run one, except to run it as though it were a Jesuit province and he its superior. At the same time, he trusts the charism of office in a manner ill-befitting a man, whose job is to oversee and discipline the officeholders.

This mismatched mode of trusting was on display in his painfully forthright remarks to pilgrims regarding the sorely tried diocese of Osorno, made on the sidelines of a weekly General Audience in May, 2015, after several months of agitation over the nomination of a bishop to the see, widely believed to have been complicit in the systematic abuse of minors and the coverup of that abuse. "The Osorno community is suffering because it's dumb," he told the group. Francis generally has been too willing to take the word of bishops over that of the lay faithful. Unfortunate under any circumstance, such willingness is disastrous when it comes to clerical impropriety.

"[The Church in Osorno] has lost her freedom," he told those pilgrims at the Audience in May of 2015, "by letting her head be filled with [words of] politicians, blaming a bishop without any proof, after 20 years of being a bishop." It turns out there was proof—evidence, at any rate—and Pope Francis had it, too, against Bishop Juan Barros of Osorno, who allegedly turned a blind eye to the predatory behavior of his mentor, the disgraced former Chilean celebrity priest, Fernando Karadima.

After accusing Barros's accusers of calumny and facing major blowback, Francis ordered an investigation that led to the resignation of the entire Chilean bishops' conference, though he has yet to accept the lion's share of the resignations, including that of Cardinal Ricardo Ezzati, accused of covering up Karadima's predations. Meanwhile, the civil authorities in Chile are investigating the Church, and have conducted multiple raids on bishops' offices, including—this week—on those of the bishops' conference.

Pope Francis has taken some steps, such as demanding that the disgraced former archbishop of Washington, DC, Theodore McCarrick, turn in his red hat. He has also removed bishops for impropriety—Juan José Pineda, the former auxiliary bishop of Tegucigalpa, for instance—though he has supported Pineda's principal, Cardinal Óscar Rodriguez

Maradiaga, a papal friend and confidante who is embroiled in a money scandal of his own and widely suspected of having given the allegedly perverse and lecherous Pineda the run of his archdiocese.

Pope Francis commuted the sentences of two priests convicted of molestation and punished with laicization—an act he later described as a mistake. He also rehabilitated Cardinal Godfried Danneels, inviting him to participate in the 2014 Extraordinary Assembly of the Synod of Bishops on the Family, some four years after Cardinal Danneels was caught on tape pleading with a victim of sex abuse by a bishop—Roger Vangheluwe, the victim's uncle—to keep silent. Danneels went into retirement with his reputation in tatters.

In short, Pope Francis's approach to abuse seems very much ad hoc and more precisely *ad personam*. It is also rather susceptible of influences other than the evidence at hand and the sense of duty to the faithful, which is proper to the office he holds in the Church. Whether he shall discover the resolve necessary to face the crisis—now indisputably global in scope and growing daily—remains to be seen. His record thus far has been, with rare notable exception, frankly dismal.

Meanwhile, there can be no doubt of the US bishops' moral standing either in the Church or in society more broadly: it is squandered; utterly trifled away. Committees, review boards, commissions of inquiry: none of it will suffice—not even the measures Cardinal DiNardo—who trained and served in Pittsburgh and was an officer of the chancery there before going to staff the Congregation for Bishops in Rome—outlined on Thursday:

> The Executive Committee has established three goals: (1) an investigation into the questions surrounding Archbishop McCarrick; (2) an opening of new and confidential channels for reporting complaints against bishops; and (3) advocacy for more effective resolution of future complaints.

While the United States Conference of Catholic Bishops issue statements firmly resolving "with the help of God's grace, never to repeat it," (rinse, repeat); invite the Holy See to investigate (in language that sounds fair but smells foul); and call for "advocacy for more effective resolution of future complaints," (advocacy within their own ranks, as though their solution is to call themselves to lobby one another—or advocacy at the Vatican, because "only the Pope has authority to discipline or remove bishops," so that this hellish debacle should be his problem, not theirs?); the faithful read news articles containing the gruesome details of the Pennsylvania Grand Jury Report released on Tuesday and reach the conclusion of the Grand Jurors: "While each church district had its idiosyncrasies, the pattern was pretty much the same. The main thing was not to help children, but to avoid 'scandal'."

Even the very first criterion is an exercise in blame shifting and obfuscation: "The first goal is a full investigation of questions surrounding Archbishop McCarrick," DiNardo wrote. That's too easy by half. Even an Apostolic Visitation of the Church in the US, which DiNardo's statement invites, is destined to fail if its scope is limited to McCarrick, even if it illuminates every dark corner in which McCarrick's baleful influence is hiding. Still, once the Vatican is involved, it will be the Vatican to determine both the real scope of inquiry and the vigor with which to conduct the inquest. Even so, if the faithful permit the scapegoating of McCarrick, they will be guilty of moral failure not less grave than that of the bishops themselves. McCarrick came from somewhere. McCarrick did not act alone.

Nor will it do, then, for bishops of other places in the US to say that they do not deserve the weight of judgment, which the bishops of Pennsylvania bear. The Grand Jury Report shows how priests were sent to and from the Commonwealth with great ease, and details the facile communication and serene discourse among bishops and their chanceries when it came to "problem cases"—some of them predators, others committed perverts, still others inveterate lechers of the Old School—amounting to a system of cover-up that not only permitted the abuse of minors to continue, but allowed and even fostered a corrupt and morally insane culture throughout the whole body of the clergy, high and low.

The first head of the US Bishops National Review Board, former Oklahoma governor Frank Keating, was not wrong to say of the bishops, in 2003, "To resist grand-jury subpoenas, to suppress the names of offending clerics, to deny, to obfuscate, to explain away; that is the model of a criminal organization." Cardinal Roger Mahony condemned Keating's remarks, and several lay members of the board joined the then-Archbishop of Los Angeles in decrying them. Asked to apologize, Keating refused and resigned.

"I was curious," Keating told me in a recent interview, "that the cardinals were the ones that were seemingly most offended by what was coming," i.e. "an anticipated reversal of what went before—a complete change of the clerical culture, in what was permitted and what wasn't." In many ways, the Pennsylvania report's release is—or deserves to be at any rate—a sort of "Apalachin moment" for the Church in the United States.

Apalachin, New York, was home to Joseph "Joe the Barber" Barbara, a mafia don who hosted a meeting of organized crime families from all over the country in 1957, at his house in the "sleepy hamlet" on the southern bank of the Susquehanna River. Local law enforcement noted the influx of fancy cars with out-of-state plates and took a closer look. Eventually, authorities intervened. They broke up the meeting and made dozens of arrests. Not many indictments came from those arrests—it isn't a crime to host a house party, after all—and those there were proved hard to make stick. Nevertheless, the readiness of those policemen once and for all gave the lie to the notion—long-espoused by FBI director J. Edgar Hoover—that there was no nationwide organization of underworld outfits in the United States.

Once facts came to light and rendered that fiction no longer viable, law enforcement at every level from the federal government to the states to every major city set about building dedicated organized crime task forces, which are still in place today. In this case, it may be that bishops with questionable or troubling records are sincere in their protestations of good faith: if they are sincere, then it is difficult to understand how they can be morally fit for office. If they are not moral imbeciles, then it is all but impossible to avoid the conclusion that they are wicked. *Tertium non datur.*

For the Catholic Herald, August 17, 2018

"The bishops will have to sacrifice power and privilege to resolve the abuse crisis"

The US bishops are panicking over the burgeoning crisis in the United States following the release of a Pennsylvania Grand Jury Report that portrays in gruesome detail how bishops built and maintained for seven decades a system designed to cover up abuse and protect predator priests. The Vatican has noticed and has caught the panic as well. That is the short version of the story as of Friday morning.

The longer version begins with two statements that appeared late in the day on Thursday, one from the President of the US Conference of Catholic Bishops, Cardinal Daniel DiNardo, the other from the Press Office of the Holy See. Both statements regarded the report out of Pennsylvania, the release of which came on the back of revelations concerning the abominable behavior of a very senior churchman, Theodore McCarrick. Neither statement was adequate, or even close to it.

Couched in the language of "sadness, anger, and shame" and promising bold, decisive action "to avoid repeating the sins and failures of the past," Cardinal DiNardo's statement nevertheless deserves to be judged as an exercise in blame-shifting and obfuscation. The statement from

Cardinal DiNardo—who grew up in Pennsylvania and went through priestly formation with the now-Bishop of Pittsburgh David Zubik—outlines three "goals" the US bishops have established for themselves:

> (1) an investigation into the questions surrounding Archbishop McCarrick; (2) an opening of new and confidential channels for reporting complaints against bishops; and (3) advocacy for more effective resolution of future complaints. These goals will be pursued according to three criteria: proper independence, sufficient authority, and substantial leadership by laity.

There are questions regarding McCarrick, the 88-year-old former Archbishop of Washington, who last month resigned from the College of Cardinals in disgrace after news of a "credible and substantiated" accusation he sexually abused a minor unleashed a torrent of other misconduct allegations involving priests and seminarians as well as at least one other minor.

Most of those questions focus on who knew what and when they knew it; why they kept silent; who had reasonable suspicion and what they did with it; why the Vatican apparatus—including the last three popes—did nothing to stop him. Those questions deserve answers. Even if we got answers to all of them, we would still be no closer to beginning to address the overriding question: why did the bishops not know, not see, not act against McCarrick?

In short, the bishops of the United States want attention to focus on McCarrick, because they want to escape scrutiny—real scrutiny—of themselves. As I argued at length in a piece that appeared Thursday in the *Catholic World Report*, "Even an Apostolic Visitation of the Church in the US, which DiNardo's statement invites, is destined to fail if its scope is limited to McCarrick, even if it illuminates every dark corner in which McCarrick's baleful influence is hiding."

Working to establish "an opening of new and confidential channels for reporting complaints against bishops" sounds good, but keeps the focus on the future, rather than on the bishops' disastrous record of leadership. Cardinal DiNardo tells us the bishops "firmly resolve, with the help of God's grace, never to repeat" the "moral catastrophe" that is "failure of episcopal leadership" as a result of which "scores of beloved children of God were abandoned to face an abuse of power alone."

Calls for "new policy against evil", as one biting headline in the *National Review* put it, are useless so long as the bishops who "came up" through this system and saw nothing wrong with it until their names started appearing in the wrong sort of articles are in charge. The US bishops know it, and they are scared—terrified—of losing their power, their privilege, their place. They are unable to countenance the fact that they have squandered and wantonly trifled away the trust of the faithful and cannot earn it again. They are grasping at straws.

It took the Vatican two days to respond to the 1,300-plus page dossier out of Pennsylvania, which contains evidence of a possible criminal conspiracy not confined to the six dioceses of the Commonwealth that were the subject of the two-year investigation that led to the report. "While each church district had its idiosyncrasies," the report's introduction states, "the pattern was pretty much the same. The main thing was not to help children, but to avoid 'scandal'."

Though the scandal is in full ferment, the Vatican statement offered bromide: "Regarding the report made public in Pennsylvania this week," the statement began, "there are two words that can express the feelings faced with these horrible crimes: shame and sorrow." The statement goes on to assure us, "The Holy See treats with great seriousness the work of the Investigating Grand Jury of Pennsylvania and the lengthy Interim Report it has produced. The Holy See condemns unequivocally the sexual abuse of minors." Of course, it does.

As the revelations regarding Cardinal McCarrick amply attest—though they are hardly the only witness to the corrupt moral culture of the clergy worldwide—the sexual abuse of minors is not the only form of wickedness that has been tolerated within the clerical ranks for generations. "The Church must learn hard lessons from its past, and there should be accountability for both abusers and those who permitted abuse to occur." To hear the Vatican tell it—echoing one of the US bishops' favourite talking points—the problems are largely in the past:

> Most of the discussion in the report concerns abuses before the early 2000s. By finding almost no cases after 2002, the Grand Jury's conclusions are consistent with previous studies showing that Catholic Church reforms in the United States drastically reduced the incidence of clergy child abuse. The Holy See

encourages continued reform and vigilance at all levels
of the Catholic Church, to help ensure the protection
of minors and vulnerable adults from harm. The Holy
See also wants to underscore the need to comply with
the civil law, including mandatory child abuse reporting requirements.

Here is the rub: what is unfolding now is unfolding now,
in the present. The same rotten culture that gave rise to the
awful abuses detailed in the Pennsylvania report, and also
served for decades as a perverted playground for McCarrick
and his ilk, persists in the present day. Frankly, the myo-
pia, deafness, and olfactory dullness of the Vatican in these
regards is such that one is almost tempted to admire their
restraint in waiting until the fourth paragraph to begin the
self-congratulation.

The Archbishop of Boston and President of the Pontifical
Commission for the Protection of Minors, Cardinal Sean
O'Malley, OFM Cap.—who recently opened an investigation into allegations of moral turpitude at the flagship seminary of his archdiocese—issued his own statement Thursday.
"The clock is ticking for all of us in Church leadership,"
O'Malley said. "Catholics have lost patience with us and
civil society has lost confidence in us. But I am not without
hope and do not succumb to despondent acceptance that
our failures cannot be corrected."

The question is not whether the failures can be corrected.
The question is whether the men who have heretofore per-
petuated the crisis, may now be trusted with any part of
fixing it. Of that, there is ample reason to doubt.

"Pope Francis's letter on abuse was not enough. We need action"

Pope Francis has written another letter in the wake of the revelations regarding clerical sex abuse in Pennsylvania. From start to finish, his latest "Letter to the People of God" is full of language we have seen before, or minor variations on themes that have become clichés—little more than what folks in the trade call "boilerplate." It is devoid of practical considerations regarding the reform of clerical leadership worldwide, which many within and without the Church now universally recognize as necessary and urgent. The letter is, in a word, inadequate: like the statement from USCCB president Daniel Cardinal DiNardo, an exercise in misdirection, blame-shifting, and obfuscation.

The letter is riddled with cliché

Its incipit takes a quote from the First Letter of St. Paul to the Corinthians (12:12-26) and misapplies it—for though the Church is indeed one Body, her sickness is in the head. His next sentence is self-serving, as it attempts, with all the subtlety of a mallet strike, to remind the reader of all the times the Popes and other Church leaders have given us high-sounding words of execration for the evils that were the run of the mill on their watch. "These words of Saint Paul forcefully echo in my heart as I acknowledge once more the suffering endured by many minors due to sexual abuse, the abuse of power and the abuse of conscience perpetrated by a significant number of clerics and consecrated persons," Pope Francis writes.

A "significant number," indeed, and telling that he does not say, "bishops,"—an omission to which the Director of the Press Office of the Holy See, Greg Burke, called attention when he attempted to rectify it. Burke offered, "Pope Francis says that greater accountability is needed, not only for those who committed these crimes but those who covered them up, which in many cases means bishops." That is what Burke said. Pope Francis says that he 'makes his own' the words of then-Cardinal Ratzinger:

> How much filth there is in the Church, and even among those who, in the priesthood, ought to belong entirely to [Christ]! How much pride, how much self-complacency! Christ's betrayal by his disciples, their unworthy reception of his body and blood, is certainly the greatest suffering endured by the Redeemer; it pierces his heart. We can only call to him from the depths of our hearts: Kyrie eleison – Lord, save us! (cf. Mt 8:25)

That was 2005, this is now. Thirteen years have passed since we first heard that cri de coeur, and still the People of God await the cleansing of the house. Meanwhile, we are fed on what may charitably be called euphemism: "We have delayed in applying these actions and sanctions that are so necessary," Pope Francis writes, "yet I am confident that they will help to guarantee a greater culture of care in the present and future." Such words as these, given in this moment, are a grotesque parody of John the Seer:

> [The angel] said to me, 'Take the book, and eat it up: and it shall make thy belly bitter, but in thy mouth it shall be sweet as honey.' And I took the book from the hand of the angel, and ate it up: and it was in my mouth, sweet as honey: and when I had eaten it, my belly was bitter.'

The hierarchical leadership of the Church have "delayed" taking actions that the faithful have demanded, and which they themselves have promised. The hierarchical leaders have delayed so long—and without any reasonable justification—that the faithful now want to know the reason for the bishops' delay. The bishops seem unwilling to act against their own interests—interests many and varied, but all converging on an insane culture of clerical power, privilege, and insulation from consequence.

"With shame and repentance," writes Pope Francis, "we acknowledge as an ecclesial community that we were not where we should have been, that we did not act in a timely manner, realizing the magnitude and the gravity of the damage done to so many lives." If Pope Francis is reticent to share the power of governance necessary to address the crisis and repair the Church—as he appears to be, given his unwillingness thus far even to disclose his mind in these regards beyond platitudinous generalities—he is nevertheless quite willing to share the blame with the whole body of the faithful. "The heart-wrenching pain of these victims, which cries out to heaven, was long ignored, kept quiet or silenced," Pope Francis writes. "But their outcry was more powerful than all the measures meant to silence it, or sought even to resolve it by decisions that increased its gravity by falling into complicity."

The first sentence of that passage is bromide: mere rehearsal of fact, without even an attempt to warm over the stale descriptors. The second is an exercise in linguistic gymnastics that would make the Ministry of Truth blush. The clerics, who counselled and made the decisions that "tried to resolve it" by means of cover-up were not trying to resolve the abuse crisis at all. They were trying to eliminate a threat to their position—hence to their power, their prestige, and their place. Such clerics did not "fall" into complicity: they dived in, head first. To keep the evil under wraps, they employed means as despicable as the acts they meant to cover up: bribery, intimidation, threats, and character assassination. Others acquiesced to the program.

The letter is devoid of practical considerations regarding reform

Pope Francis has had ample opportunity to acknowledge the bishops' role in the perpetuation of a system, which to this day not only permits but fosters the insane moral culture of the whole body of the clergy, high and low. So far, he has not so much as named it. While we hope only a very few bishops are guilty of the worst crimes and sins, they remain as a body committed to the maintenance of the culture that has allowed the wicked to flourish. The Pope's general condemnations of "clericalism" and calls for "repentance" are, therefore, likewise unsatisfactory:

> It is essential that we, as a Church, be able to acknowledge and condemn, with sorrow and shame, the atrocities perpetrated by consecrated persons, clerics, and all those entrusted with the mission of watching over and caring for those most vulnerable. Let us beg forgiveness for our own sins and the sins of others. An awareness of sin helps us to acknowledge the errors, the crimes and the wounds caused in the past and allows us, in the present, to be more open and committed along a journey of renewed conversion.

All the faithful have a duty to do penance for their own sins and for the sins of the world, as they have a duty in charity to solicitude for the salvation of the souls of their bishops. More public penance is necessary. It is not sufficient. There is a cancer in the head, which we must remove. This means we must be willing to risk the operation, even if the body is sick and weak. We need the advice of an expert surgeon. Pope Francis's prescriptions are indistinguishable from any spinster aunt's homespun cure for the common cold.

The letter is inadequate

As was the case when he decided to write to the faithful of Chile, there was likely no letter the Pope could have written which would have been adequate to address the crisis. It is certain that no letter on the same broad subject addressed to the whole people of God could have any hope of doing any real good on its own. The best any such letter could have done—what it needed to do—was name the crisis plainly, frankly recognize the specific kind of failure in leadership that plagues the Church, and offer at least some broad view of the practical steps he is considering in the way of reform. The letter we have from Pope Francis does not do a single one of those things.

"The only way that we have to respond to this evil that has darkened so many lives," Pope Francis writes, "is to experience it as a task regarding all of us as the People of God." He needs to start acting as though he believes it. If he does have even the rudiments of a plan, he has not brought the People of God—especially the laity—so far into his confidence as to share it, or any part of it. If he is at a loss for practical remedies, he has given no sign of interest in hearing suggestions.

The Holy Father's latest letter is an even more egregious failure than his letter to the faithful of Chile. If Pope Francis has not squandered this latest chance to treat the faithful as though they are a responsible part of the Church, instead of saying that they are and acting as though they are not, he must be close to squandering it.

The faithful have every reason to doubt that the bishops are on their side in this. In late April of this year, the Pope apparently told victims he had repeatedly accused of calumny only a few months earlier, "I was part of the problem." This letter suggests he still is. If Pope Francis would have us believe that he—a bishop—is on our side, then he must prove it. This letter rather tends to confirm the status quo. That is unacceptable.

For the Catholic World Report, August 26, 2018

"If Viganò's 'Testimony' is true, Pope Francis has failed his own test"

The former Apostolic Nuncio to the United States, Archbishop Carlo Maria Viganò, has written a letter alleging systematic coverup of the disordered and abusive behavior of the former Archbishop of Washington, Theodore McCarrick, who has resigned from the College of Cardinals and awaits canonical trial on charges he molested at least one minor. Since that charge became public on June 20th, other accusers have come forward, some of them alleging they suffered abuse in seminary or as priests, while at least one other accuser—the first person McCarrick baptized as a priest—alleges his abuse began when he was aged 11 years.

McCarrick's behavior appears to have been an open secret, though high-ranking prelates close to McCarrick claim they were unaware of any hint of impropriety. They include McCarrick's successor, Cardinal Donald Wuerl, and Cardinal Kevin Farrell of the Dicastery for Laity, Family and Life. The records of both men deserve the most careful and relentless scrutiny, but not here.

Here, the concern is the set of assertions Archbishop Viganò has made in his letter, in which he details a nearly two decades' coverup of McCarrick's misconduct. It involves three popes and three Secretaries of State, as well as at least a half-dozen other high-ranking Vatican officials.

Archbishop Viganò, who was Nuncio from 2011 to 2016, asserts that Cardinal Angelo Sodano, when he was Secretary of State under Pope St. John Paul II, knew of the allegations against McCarrick. Viganò strongly suggests Sodano was nevertheless instrumental in securing McCarrick's appointment to the See of Washington, DC. Viganò speculates that Sodano would have been able to pass McCarrick's nomination across the desk of the weak and sickly Pope St. John Paul II, from whom he would have kept information regarding McCarrick's habits.

Some knowledge of McCarrick's proclivities would have come to Cardinal Sodano and other Vatican officials—and should have gone to the Pope—by way of a letter written by Fr. Boniface Ramsey, OP, some time before November of the year 2000, when then-Nuncio to the US Gabriel Montalvo should have forwarded it to Sodano.

In his letter of the year 2000, however, Fr. Ramsey apparently only noted his concern regarding what he had heard from students about McCarrick's bizarre sleeping arrangements during his frequent excursions to his beach house: that McCarrick would always bring one more guest—generally seminarians or young priests—than there were beds in the house, and then "solve" the logistical difficulty by sharing a bed with one of the visitors. None of that was, strictly speaking, criminal, though it ought to have been enough to kibosh a nomination to any See. It was not.

Viganò asserts that, sometime between 2006 and 2008, Benedict XVI became aware of further, more gruesome allegations against then-Cardinal McCarrick, no later than when news reached him of a memorandum of indictment written by a laicized priest who was himself an abuser. That document detailed sexual aggressions McCarrick and other priests and seminarians of the Newark archdiocese (which McCarrick led from 1986 to 2000), as well as other allegations detailed in a letter by the former cleric, Richard Sipe, whose career focused on the psychological study of clerics' aberrant and abusive behavior. Viganò says that sometime thereafter, the then-Prefect of the Congregation for Bishops, Cardinal Giovanni Battista Re, told him Benedict had imposed disciplinary measures on McCarrick.

"I learned with certainty, through Cardinal Giovanni Battista Re, then-Prefect of the Congregation for Bishops, that Richard Sipe's courageous and meritorious Statement had had the desired result," Viganò writes in his testimony. "Pope Benedict had imposed on Cardinal McCarrick sanctions similar to those now imposed on him by Pope Francis: the Cardinal was to leave the seminary where he was living, he was forbidden to celebrate [Mass] in public, to participate in public meetings, to give lectures, to travel, with the obligation of dedicating himself to a life of prayer and penance."

If this rehearsal of the facts is accurate, it raises the question why Benedict should have kept the matter secret, not to mention why McCarrick was allowed to keep his red hat. There are other questions the former Nuncio's letter raises, as well. It was not accompanied by a dossier containing the many memoranda and other correspondence on which he draws in his construction of events, even though it appears he kept copies of at least some of the documents to which he averts in his letter. At one point, Viganò says:

> [A]round April 21-23, 2008, the Statement for Pope Benedict XVI about the pattern of sexual abuse crisis in the United States, by Richard Sipe, was published on the internet, at richardsipe.com. On April 24, it was passed on by the Prefect of the Congregation for the Doctrine of the Faith, Cardinal William Levada, to the Cardinal Secretary of State Tarcisio Bertone. It was delivered to me one month later, on May 24, 2008.
>
> The following day, I delivered a new memo to the new Substitute, Fernando Filoni, which included my previous one of December 6, 2006. In it, I summarized Richard Sipe's document, which ended with this respectful and heartfelt appeal to Pope Benedict XVI: "I approach Your Holiness with due reverence, but with the same intensity that motivated Peter Damian to lay out before your predecessor, Pope Leo IX, a description of the condition of the clergy during his time. The problems he spoke of are similar and as great now in the United States as they were then in Rome. If Your Holiness requests, I will personally submit to you documentation of that about which I have spoken."

One wonders where the documentation to which Archbishop Viganò refers, both in the passage above and elsewhere throughout his testimony, might be. If he has it, he should share it—indeed, should have included it in his "testimony". If he is no longer in possession of the documents, he ought to say so, and say why and how he came to be dispossessed of them. It could be simply that they remain on file with the Nunciature and/or the Secretariat of State. If that is the case, there is a strong case to be made for their immediate release to the public.

In any case, the former Nuncio's narrative continues to detail further misdeeds, the most damning of which he attributes to the Holy Father. In essence, Archbishop Viganò claims that Pope Francis knowing of the allegations against McCarrick and aware of the sanctions Benedict had imposed on him, did not act on the allegations and lifted the sanctions, allowing McCarrick to travel freely and function as a priest and a bishop. Reading Viganò's recollection of his conversations with the Holy Father regarding McCarrick—in June of 2013, only a few months after Francis's election—one notes that Viganò never says he explicitly mentioned any specific allegation against McCarrick. He also does a good deal of reading between the lines, and attributes motive:

> I began the conversation, asking the Pope what he intended to say to me with the words he had addressed to me when I greeted him the previous Friday. And the Pope, in a very different, friendly, almost affectionate tone, said to me: "Yes, the Bishops in the United States must not be ideologized, they must not be right-wing like the Archbishop of Philadelphia, (the Pope did not give me the name of the Archbishop) they must be shepherds; and they must not be left-wing—and he added, raising both arms—and when I say left-wing I mean homosexual." Of course, the logic of the

correlation between being left-wing and being homo-sexual escaped me, but I added nothing else.

Immediately after, the Pope asked me in a deceitful way: "What is Cardinal McCarrick like?" I answered him with complete frankness and, if you want, with great naiveté: "Holy Father, I don't know if you know Cardinal McCarrick, but if you ask the Congregation for Bishops there is a dossier this thick about him. He corrupted generations of seminarians and priests and Pope Benedict ordered him to withdraw to a life of prayer and penance." The Pope did not make the slightest comment about those very grave words of mine and did not show any expression of surprise on his face, as if he had already known the matter for some time, and he immediately changed the subject. But then, what was the Pope's purpose in asking me that question: "What is Cardinal McCarrick like?" He clearly wanted to find out if I was an ally of McCarrick or not.

Without regard for the question of motive—and granted that he assumes, rather than demonstrates, Francis's knowl-edge of the specific kinds of enormities McCarrick is alleged to have committed—a candid reader must nevertheless admit that, unless Archbishop Viganò is cutting the story from whole cloth, it is impossible for Pope Francis to claim he had no knowledge of McCarrick's behavior prior to this past June, when the Review Board of the Archdiocese of New York deemed an accusation McCarrick committed numerous acts of sexual assault on an altar boy over a period of years—including one in the sacristy of St. Patrick's Cathedral during preparations for Christmas Mass, 1971, "credible and substantiated."

The testimony Archbishop Viganò offers is neither perfectly crafted, nor immune to criticism. In addition to its presumption of motive, it also speculates—not wildly, but—without foundation as firm as one would want with matters of such gravity. Archbishop Viganò's letter is also intemperate at times. In it, Viganò names several men, at whose roles in the affair he can only guess. Among the men named are Cardinal Francesco Coccopalmerio and Archbishop Vincenzo Paglia, who, says Viganò, "belong to the homosexual current in favor of subverting Catholic doctrine on homosexuality," along with Cardinal Edwin O'Brien and Cardinal Renato Martino. Those claims—without respect to their merit or basis in fact—in the absence of explicit and detailed discussion of their specific pertinence to the narrative, approach slander.

Nevertheless, if the allegations contained in Archbishop Viganò's letter are correct, then it is difficult to escape the conclusion the former nuncio reaches in his testimony: "In this extremely dramatic moment for the universal Church, he must acknowledge his mistakes and, in keeping with the proclaimed principle of zero tolerance, Pope Francis must be the first to set a good example for cardinals and bishops who covered up McCarrick's abuses and resign along with all of them."

If there is even a little truth to the allegations, then Francis has failed his own test: he has not practiced what he has preached—transparency and zero tolerance—nor has he

tried adequately to become part of the solution, as he supposedly promised to Juan Carlos Cruz, James Hamilton, and
José Andrés Murillo, whom he accused of calumny before
praising their courage and resolve when his former position
became untenable.

"The root of the abuse crisis"

Surveying the ravaged landscape of the Church today, one question presses itself upon the viewer of the scene with palpable urgency: how did we get here? There have been many answers to that question, none of them completely satisfactory. Some people say that the problem is the infiltration of homosexual predators into the ranks of the clergy. That is certainly a significant element of the crisis, but we need to ask far-reaching questions about how and why abusers were able to operate within the Church.

Certainly, the naiveté of some pastors contributed to the exacerbation of the problem. On the advice of expert psychologists, bishops treated sex offenders in the clergy as though they were sick and capable of being cured. That, however, was no excuse for returning the men to positions of trust, where they went on to abuse other victims. The failure to see the sexual abuse of minors as anything other than a crime cannot find explanation, nor the guilt of the failure mitigation, in a protestation of bad information from doctors. That is a moral failure so basic as to disqualify anyone guilty of it.

The American bishops and the Vatican were appraised as early as the 1940s of the futility of any attempt to cure them.

Fr. Gerald Fitzgerald, the founder of the Congregation of the Servants of the Paraclete—a religious order dedicated to caring for and rehabilitating struggling and wayward priests, principally those suffering alcoholism and other addictions—also treated pedophiles at the beginning of his Congregation's ministry.

Fr. Fitzgerald quickly became convinced that cure was impossible and spent more than 20 years explaining to Church leaders the nature of the predilection and the impossibility of treating men who had it. In 1957, he wrote to Archbishop Edwin Byrne of Santa Fe, New Mexico—the archdiocese in which the Paracletes had their flagship facility—to say, "Experience has taught us these men are too dangerous to the children of the parish and neighborhood for us to be justified in receiving them here."

In 1962, Fr. Fitzgerald wrote to the Holy Office, which had solicited his opinion on the matter. "We [of the Congregation] feel strongly that such unfortunate priests should be given the alternative of a retired life within the protection of monastery walls or complete laicization," he said. Fr. Fitzgerald also met Pope Paul VI, shortly after the latter's election in 1963, to discuss the same matter, telling him in a summary letter after their meeting: "I am not sanguine of the return of priests to active duty who have been addicted to abnormal practices, especially sins with the young."

Even Fr. Fitzgerald, however, had a blind spot: "The needs of the Church must be taken into consideration and an activation of priests who have seemingly recovered in this field may be considered, but is only recommended where careful guidance and supervision is possible." Fitzgerald went on to write: "Where there is indication of incorrigibility, because of the tremendous scandal given, I would most earnestly recommend total laicization." The needs of the Church. Christ established His Church as a hierarchy, with bishops and priests sharing the governance of her, but bishops and priests are not the Church. Here, we are closer to the problem.

Zooming in for a moment on the present, Pope Francis is right to attribute the evils that beset the Church to "clericalism." Blaming the current crisis in the Church on clericalism, however, is like blaming plane crashes on gravity. The hard truth is that, with respect to clerical abuse and misconduct, as well as the necessary reform of the warped clerical culture bent to the preservation of corrupt power, of which the perverse lifestyles of too many clerics are only a major symptom and not the true root cause of the disease, the failure of the Church's hierarchical leadership—including papal leadership—is protracted and endemic.

We could move all the predators out of the priesthood and into jail cells, and there would still be a crisis of moral culture in the clergy, high and low, almost as bad as it was the day before the purge. That is because the motor of the clerical culture we have right now—and this is true across the board, top to bottom, without respect to ideological leanings or theological inclination—is the intrinsically perverse *libido dominandi* (will to power), rather than a perversion of the *libido coeundi* (sex drive). The former makes use of the latter, and the latter is often a consequence of the former. But the only way men given over to the latter gain any power or place in any society is by addiction to and direction of the former. Therefore the underlying problem is power.

Some of the US bishops are clearly terrified of losing theirs, along with their position and status. One has the impression that they are at a loss over what to do to fix things, precisely because their lust for power makes them blind to the truth.

Nor have the last four popes—excluding John Paul I, who reigned only a little more than a month—exercised their power well to discipline the Church's hierarchical leadership in these regards. Pope Francis did not create Theodore McCarrick and he did not cause the crisis. Neither did Pope Benedict XVI nor Pope St. John Paul II, nor Paul VI cause it. That we are only now—perhaps—beginning to understand the scope of the crisis, tells us that none of them dealt effectively with it.

We have seen that Paul VI had the benefit of Fr. Fitzgerald's experience and cannot be excused on grounds of perfect ignorance. Too often, John Paul II would neither see nor hear evil in these regards: a fact illustrated by his appointment and elevation of McCarrick and epitomized by his constant support of the wicked and vicious founder of the Legion of Christ, Fr. Marcial Maciel, who preyed on women, seminarians and minors (including at least one of his own illegitimate children). Benedict XVI dealt strongly with Maciel, ordering him without trial into a life of prayer and penance. Nevertheless, he let the Legion of Christ—the organization of clerics Maciel founded as a front in support of his twisted double life—to continue to operate. Benedict's failure to suppress the Legion was almost certainly his greatest mistake.

Benedict XVI began to overhaul the Church's legal system, but the rough and dirty work of reform proved too much for him. He gave it up unfinished when he renounced the See of Rome. Put simply, Benedict was a weak governor when he needed to be strong. His record needs examination, and his apparent failures—including those with respect to McCarrick—must be reckoned with.

If Benedict XVI's record is spotty, Francis's record thus far has been mostly dismal—and Francis is Pope now. It is said that he has recognized that he has been part of the problem. He has promised to be part of the solution. We need to hold him to that promise. Doing so will require stern resolve. It will also demand rigorous thoughtfulness and the most careful mindfulness of human frailty: his, and our own.

It is hard to confront horrible things and seek out the truth, while not being fully convicted of the worst until one has all the evidence necessary to support the conviction. Nevertheless, that is precisely what the bishops failed to do, with disastrous consequences. The full truth might be harder still, but it must out.

CHAPTER 5

WINDS HOWL AND WATERS RISE

September – November 2018

For the Catholic World Report, September 12, 2018

"Is Pope Francis serious about addressing the abuse crisis and its causes?"

Anyone who is praising the announcement on Wednesday of Pope Francis's convocation of the presidents of the world's bishops' conferences for a meeting in February on clerical sex abuse has not been paying attention.

For one thing, the sexual abuse of minors by clerics is only the peculiarly gruesome tip of an ocean-tipping iceberg; the systematic coverup of abuse is the level just beginning to be brought to the surface—the depth and extent of rot in clerical culture, high and low, is what we have yet to fathom—and although the Press Office statement that accompanied the announcement—from the "Council of Nine" cardinals—of the February meeting did make mention of "vulnerable adults", the whole thing reads as pre-packaged and contrived.

For another, the wording of the announcement strongly suggests that the C9 cardinals had to persuade Pope Francis of the need to do something—anything—to address the issue. "The Holy Father, Francis, having heard the Council of Cardinals, has decided to convoke a reunion with the Presidents of the Episcopal Conferences of the Catholic Church, on the theme of 'protection of minors,'" the statement reads.

That's the way—in *curialese*—to tell people you had to twist the boss's arm to get what you got.

Whatever else it might be, another meeting of episcopal minds to think through and talk about the issue cannot be any real part of a serious address of this very urgently pressing crisis. Pope Francis, meanwhile, appears to have a very different view of the Church's circumstances and their cause. He claimed on Tuesday that the bishops are the victims of a diabolical plot, to which the faithful are at best unwitting accomplices. "In these times, it seems like the 'Great Accuser' has been unchained and is attacking bishops," he said on Tuesday morning at Mass in the Casa Santa Marta.

"True, we are all sinners, we bishops," Francis went on to say. "[The Great Accuser] tries to uncover [our] sins, so they are visible, in order to scandalize the people." One would think that, after all we've been through in the past eight months—not to mention the last 16 years and more—the proposition that people have a right to know the character and conduct of bishops would not be too controversial. Again, Pope Francis apparently has a different idea.

In one sense, he's quite right. The devil prowls the earth like a roaring lion, 1 Peter 5:8 tells us, seeking souls to devour. We also know the devil likes the taste of bishop. The problem is that the bishops who have winked at moral turpitude and covered for the wickedness of too many clerics over too many decades have betrayed the trust of the people—including priests—the souls of whom God has entrusted to their care.

Pope Francis appears genuinely to believe that airing bishops' dirty laundry is not the right thing to do, because God chose them, and doing so will compromise their mission-effectiveness. That is a large part of the attitude that got us to this point in the first place. "I was part of the problem," the abuse survivor and victim-advocate, Juan Carlos Cruz, has quoted Francis as having said after the Chilean theatre of the global crisis exploded in his face. If that was a moment of clarity for Pope Francis, it is now apparent that he has recovered from it. The tendency toward trolling and gaslighting the faithful, who are fed up with the corruption, incompetence, tone-deafness, and plain old blindness and deafness of the bishops, is certainly "part of the problem." If this assessment is inaccurate, Francis needs to prove it so in deed.

Does the Church have enemies? Yes. Have those enemies used the abuse crisis as a club with which to beat the Church? Yes. They shall continue to do so. The ineluctable fact of the matter is that the hierarchical leaders of the Church are largely responsible for fashioning the weapon and putting it into her enemies' hands. The ultimate goal in all this must be moral recrudescence in the whole Church, especially in the ranks of clerical and hierarchical leadership. The cultural crisis in the Church is complicated, however, by the admixture—inevitable, this side of the celestial Jerusalem—of the general ills of the age.

In our age, enlightened and democratic as it is, we do not often hear talk of the sin of *prosopolempsia*—literally, "face-taking"—which is usually rendered "respect of persons." "What," one might ask, "is wrong with respecting persons?" To be a "respecter of persons" in the possibly sinful sense means, in essence, to deal with people according to their social rank, prestige, or perceived standing in a community, rather than according to the quality of their character. It might help to think of it as being a respecter of someone's persona—and it is dangerous, even when the persona to which one is at risk of standing in thrall is that of a bishop, especially the Bishop of Rome.

The great cautionary tale in this regard is Hans Christian Andersen's short story, *The Emperor's New Clothes*. In that story, everyone sees what there is—and is not—to see, but only a child without the worldly wit to know the stakes is capable of saying what there is to say. "Be like the child," is the facile takeaway. It is not wrong, as far as it goes, but it misses the point of what is, again, a cautionary tale. Do not be like everyone else in the story, from the emperor on down: unable to say, because one is unwilling to admit—because of what the admission would say about oneself—that the emperor is naked as the day he was born.

"USCCB admits 'great harm' caused by 'some bishops', outlines steps to address crisis"

The US Conference of Catholic Bishops released a statement today, which for the first time gives Catholics some small reason to hope that maybe—just maybe—the episcopal leadership of the Church in the United States, at least, is beginning to understand the nature and gravity of the crisis their protracted failure has precipitated. Issued by the Administrative Committee of the USCCB—the principal governing body of the Conference outside plenary session—the statement outlined four steps the Administrative Committee has taken on its own authority to address the crisis. Those steps are, in full:

- Approval of the establishment of a third-party reporting system that will receive confidentially, by phone and online, complaints of sexual abuse of minors by a bishop and sexual harassment of or sexual misconduct with adults by a bishop and will direct those complaints to the appropriate ecclesiastical authority and, as required by applicable law, to civil authorities;

- Instructions to the USCCB Committee on Canonical

Affairs and Church Governance to develop proposals for policies addressing restrictions on bishops who were removed or resigned because of allegations of sexual abuse of minors or sexual harassment of or misconduct with adults, including seminarians and priests;

- Initiation of the process of developing a Code of Conduct for bishops regarding the sexual abuse of a minor; sexual harassment of or sexual misconduct with an adult; or negligence in the exercise of his office related to such cases;

- Support for a full investigation into the situation surrounding Archbishop McCarrick, including his alleged assaults on minors, priests, and seminarians, as well any responses made to those allegations. Such an investigation should rely upon lay experts in relevant fields, such as law enforcement and social services.

The Administrative Committee acknowledges that these steps are not adequate to address the full scope of the crisis. "This is only a beginning," they write. They go on to call for broad consultation with concerned Catholics, including lay experts as well as clergy and religious, in order to develop and implement further measures. "We humbly welcome and are grateful for the assistance of the whole people of God in holding us accountable," the Administrative Committee writes.

"Broad consultation" will likely not be enough to satisfy either the faithful or civil authorities with respect to the bishops' bona fides in these regards. Responsible involvement of laity has become a sine qua non of any response to the crisis that wishes to have a hope of being credible. Nevertheless, for the first time, the bishops frankly acknowledge that there is a general corrosion of moral culture within the ranks of the Church's clerical and hierarchical leadership, which has destroyed the trust on which the bishops' ability to lead must be based.

"Some bishops, by their actions or their failures to act, have caused great harm to both individuals and the Church as a whole," the Administrative Committee writes at the top of their statement. "They have used their authority and power to manipulate and sexually abuse others," they continue. "They have allowed the fear of scandal to replace genuine concern and care for those who have been victimized by abusers." So forthright an admission of widespread failure and miscarriage of duty has been a long time coming. It is welcome, even though it does not satisfy.

One of the criticisms commentators and analysts—including this writer—have made of the bishops' response, is that they have focused too exclusively on the case of Theodore McCarrick, giving the impression that they would have the faithful believe he was the problem, and not merely a grotesque and awful symptom of a systemic disease. If such an acknowledgment was too long in coming and still not enough, it is a small step in the right direction. "For this, we again ask forgiveness from both the Lord and those who have been harmed," the Administrative Committee says. "Turning to the Lord for strength," they promise, "we must and will do better."

The Administrative Committee concludes its statement with protestations of filial love for and loyalty to Pope Francis. "Acting in communion with the Holy Father, with whom we once again renew our love, obedience, and loyalty," they write, "we make our own the prayer of Pope Francis in his August 20 letter to the people of God: 'May the Holy Spirit grant us the grace of conversion and the interior anointing needed to express before these crimes of abuse our compunction and our resolve courageously to combat them'."

The Executive Committee of the US Conference of Catholic Bishops met with Pope Francis last Thursday to discuss the crisis. There were high hopes for that meeting heading into it, as the USCCB's president, Cardinal Daniel DiNardo of Galveston-Houston had announced his intention to ask the Holy Father to sanction an Apostolic Visitation into the McCarrick affair and related issues. The result of that meeting was an expression of desire, "[of] continuing our discernment together identifying the most effective next steps."

Now, it falls to the US bishops to make good on their commitments. It belongs to the faithful to hold them to the promises they have made, and to demand a responsible part in even stronger measures—ones really apt, as the Administrative Committee says, "to repair the scandal and restore justice." Whether this is a real beginning of that long and arduous work, or merely more empty words, remains to be seen.

"Pope Francis and the current crisis of leadership"

The crisis of leadership in the Catholic Church is protracted, persistent, and global. It is already almost unbearably awful in its details, and has barely begun to be reported. What follows is neither reportage—except incidentally—nor analysis, strictly speaking—but commentary, and it is personal.

In January, I predicted that 2018 would be a make-or-break year for Pope Francis—a year in which he would have to decide whether to use his gifts to set his project of curial reform and Church renewal on track, or whether to continue his efforts to remake Rome into "Buenos Aires-on-Tiber."

In March, on the fifth anniversary of Francis's election, I considered that the year had got off to a rough start, but noted that we were still in the first quarter. Now the third quarter is rapidly approaching its end, and things have not improved for Francis, who, whatever the external pressures on him, just can't seem to get out of his own way.

The election of Francis thrilled me, as it did many others, despite my concerns at having a Jesuit pope—concerns perhaps paradoxically rooted in my love for the Ignatian charism and my many personal spiritual debts to great Jesuits, living and dead—and I must say his early forays into pot-stirring and mess-making did not dissuade me from my hope that he was most, at any rate, of what he was cracked up to be.

Read in context, his remark about gay priests—"Who am I to judge?"—was unexceptionable, and had enough of the wily Jesuit in it to make me think that his play was inspired. He brought faithful Catholics of every age and state of life in the Church out of the woodwork and into the public conversation to say what the Church really teaches—and people who otherwise wouldn't have, perked up and listened.

It was more gambit than gamble—there was a downside—but I was game for it, even after I had read reports regarding the case of the specific figure, which gave rise to the question that elicited the now famous answer—Msgr. Battista Ricca—whom Francis apparently trusted, based on limited personal acquaintance and the absence of any official condemnation in Ricca's jacket, even though the Apostolic Nuncio under whom Ricca had worked in Uruguay did not, owing to serial ambiguities in Ricca's personal moral conduct. It is worth revisiting Pope Francis's full response to the question from Brazilian journalist Ilze Scamparini:

> About Monsignor Ricca: I did what canon law calls for, that is a preliminary investigation. And from this investigation, there was nothing of what had been alleged. We did not find anything of that. This is the response. But I wish to add something else: I see that many times in the Church, over and above this case, but including this case, people search for "sins from youth", for example, and then publish them. They are

not crimes, right? Crimes are something different: the abuse of minors is a crime. No, sins. But if a person, whether it be a lay person, a priest or a religious sister, commits a sin and then converts, the Lord forgives, and when the Lord forgives, the Lord forgets and this is very important for our lives. When we confess our sins and we truly say, "I have sinned in this", the Lord forgets, and so we have no right not to forget, because otherwise we would run the risk of the Lord not forgetting our sins. That is a danger. This is important: a theology of sin. Many times I think of Saint Peter. He committed one of the worst sins, that is he denied Christ, and even with this sin they made him Pope. We have to think a great deal about that. But, returning to your question more concretely. In this case, I conducted the preliminary investigation and we didn't find anything. This is the first question. Then, you spoke about the gay lobby. So much is written about the gay lobby. I still haven't found anyone with an identity card in the Vatican with "gay" on it. They say there are some there. I believe that when you are dealing with such a person, you must distinguish between the fact of a person being gay and the fact of someone forming a lobby, because not all lobbies are good. This one is not good. If someone is gay and is searching for the Lord and has good will, then who am I to judge him? The Catechism of the Catholic Church explains this in a beautiful way, saying … wait a moment, how does it say it … it says: "no one should marginalize these people for this, they must be integrated into society". The problem is not having this tendency, no, we must be brothers and sisters to one another, and there is this one and there is that one. The problem is in making a lobby of this tendency: a lobby of misers, a lobby of politicians, a lobby of masons, so many lobbies. For me, this is the greater problem. Thank you so much for asking this question. Many thanks.

That was then. This is now. The pope's basic instinct may well be sound—he's not wrong to say, "If someone is gay and is searching for the Lord and has good will, then who am I to judge him?" There are many men in priestly ministry who experience same-sex attraction and struggle to live chastely. Sometimes they fail. They are not to be lumped in automatically with the evil men who sought Holy Orders for the target-rich environment and protection a collar affords, while never intending even to attempt a life of chastity.

The real lavender *Mafiosi* groom boys for membership in their ranks, but that is not all they do—they work their work across the board, and may exploit a straight priest's dalliance just as easily as they might a gay one's. Exploiting the confusion and naiveté of an adolescent struggling to understand his identity is worse, on the whole, but exploiting the foibles of a grown man is still very bad. The more disorderly men there are in the clergy, the more powerful the lavender mafia will be, regardless of their marks' status as members or affiliates of the syndicate.

We need to know the extent of the rot, which may—as I have noted elsewhere—go all the way up, and all the way through.

Nearly a month has passed now, since the former papal nuncio to the United States, Archbishop Carlo Maria Viganò, published his 11-page "testimony", and while pundits and professional Catholics continue debate whether the Francis pontificate will survive the scandal, the pope himself keeps silence. Sort of. Two weeks ago, Pope Francis devoted his morning reflections—billed as homilies, though they aren't really homilies, but brief moral exhortations based loosely on the Readings of the Day—or fervorini to use the Italian word for the genre, to the Great Accuser, saying he attacks bishops especially, trying to expose their sins and scandalize the faithful, whose default disposition is to love their bishops.

Last week, he returned to the theme and enlarged upon it, saying that it was the people who cried out for Jesus's crucifixion, and it was Jesus, who kept compassionate silence because "the people were deceived by the powerful." Francis went on to say the true shepherd chooses silence when the Great Accuser attacks him "through so many people." On Thursday, Pope Francis offered:

> [T]he Church, when she journeys through history, is persecuted by hypocrites: hypocrites, within and without. The devil has nothing to do with repentant sinners, because they look upon God and say, "Lord, I am a sinner, help me!" and the Devil is impotent; but he is strong with hypocrites. He is strong, and he uses them to destroy, to destroy the people, to destroy society, to destroy the Church. Hypocrisy is the Devil's workhorse, for he is a liar. He makes himself out to be

> a prince, powerful and beautiful, though from behind
> he is an assassin.

On a good day, comparison of the bishop—who stands among his flock in Christ's stead, as their pastor—to Our Lord, ought to be aspirational. In the midst of worldwide outcry for accountability from bishops, who have sinfully miscarried in their duty of care and used their power to coverup terrible wrongdoing—their own, and that of others in their charge—and coupled with juxtaposition of the faithful thus alarmed with the people who sought Christ's blood, such comparison is so far beyond the bounds of reasonable discourse, that one is embarrassed for all those who saw the remarks published on their watch.

If Pope Francis did not have the current crisis of leadership in mind when he uttered those words, then it is fair to say he ought to have been more careful in his choice of them. That he did not, frankly beggars credulity. In any case, he cannot have it both ways: silence is silence, and talk is talk.

The US bishops seem to have begun to grasp the nature of the crisis, and its gravity. They announced new oversight measures this week. However well intentioned, those measures will likely prove toothless without precisely that support from Rome, in the absence of which they announced them.

Last Friday, Pope Francis did accept the resignations of two more bishops in Chile—where he faces a terrible dilemma—but his piecemeal response to that theater of the global crisis has done little to convince the faithful—there or elsewhere—that he even understands how bad things are, let alone that he is serious about addressing the crisis. The bishops he removed on Friday are both credibly accused of abusing minors, yet it took him four months to accept their resignations, even though both had been accused of abuse years ago.

The removals have done little to reassure Catholics in the United States of Francis's commitment, especially in light of his apparent refusal to support the US bishops in their efforts. Even Cardinal Timothy Dolan of New York—who last week announced the appointment of an independent investigator in his archdiocese—has voiced his impatience with the Pope.

Cardinal Dolan's impatience is eminently understandable: Theodore Edgar "Uncle Ted" McCarrick was a priest of the archdiocese of which Dolan now has charge. McCarrick—who did not rise in the ranks alone—ordained hundreds of priests, and oversaw the formation of hundreds more. For every one that has come forward with allegations of untoward behavior suffered at McCarrick's hands, there could be dozens who have not. Whether their silence is due to complicity, or to fear of repercussion, the situation is appalling and untenable. Francis did not cause the crisis, but he is pope now. If his recent predecessors' records of leadership must be given the most careful scrutiny, that the People of God may judge them candidly—and there must be such a reckoning—Francis sits on Peter's throne, and is the only one with power to dispose of our circumstances.

In an open letter I wrote to Bishop Thomas Tobin of Providence in July, I said, "I believe I speak for many of our brothers and sisters in Christ, when I say that we will not fail to support any shepherd who proves his willingness to toil and to suffer in this cause for our sake and Our Lord's." I said to a friend recently that I still believe the sentiments I expressed to Bishop Tobin to be true, and pray God that Francis of Rome, His vicar on earth, will be that shepherd. If Francis will not be that shepherd, I pray God send us another. What follows is the rest of my response, with minor cosmetic editions:

> God will act in His time, not ours, and by means inscrutable to us. In the mean, I am the Pope's man, God help me, to the last gasp and—*quod Deus avertat*—the last drop. Finally, there is no other stance for any Catholic to take.
>
> If Francis or anyone else thinks that I or any other member of Christ's Body as such owes him anything other than this promise and the *parrhesia*—the manly frankness—for which he himself has called, then he is mistaken. It is because Francis is the Pope, that we must speak our minds to him. It is because Christ is Lord, that we must speak our minds to one another.
>
> There will be hard words in the days and weeks and months to come.
>
> Let us remember that this too, shall pass: that we share one Faith and one Baptism; that nothing we say or do should jeopardize the place of any one of us at the heavenly feast, which is our common hope.

To this, I would add something else I've been saying lately—to myself and to others—in essence that, as all this continues to unfold, we must remember that God is good. His mercy—the response of self-subsistent Charity to sinful creatures—is severe: stern as death, and not less terrible than His wrath. His Church is true: She is His bride, and she must be spotless; He will not have her any other way. There is one Lord, one Faith, one Baptism: one Church founded by Christ on St. Peter for the forgiveness of sin, the redemption of flesh, and the salvation of the world.

For the Catholic Herald, September 29, 2018

"Dismissing Karadima from the clerical state will do little to help the crisis"

Pope Francis has "laicized" Chile's most notorious abuser-priest, Fernando Karadima. He took the step on Thursday, September 27, effective immediately. A statement in Spanish from the Press Office of the Holy See released on Friday afternoon in Rome, announced the measure. Karadima was convicted and sentenced—in 2011—to a life of prayer and penance. He is 88 years old, and reported to be in failing health. He is a symptom of the disease plaguing the Church, but he is hardly a lynchpin of the corrupt power structure, either in Chile or in other places. Press Office director Greg Burke told reporters: "There are two keys to understanding this decree: the first, that the Pope does [this] in conscience. The second key, the motivation: for the good of the Church." Burke went on to say:

> Pope Francis is acting as a pastor, as a father, for the good of the entire People of God. The dismissal from the clerical state of Fernando Karadima is another step in the iron line of Pope Francis on abuse. We were facing a very serious case of rot and it had to be rooted out.

Anyone intrigued by the use of the past tense will be reassured to know that Burke clarified the point for the *Catholic Herald*: he was referring specifically and exclusively to Karadima's case, not to the whole Chilean theatre of the crisis. "This is an exceptional measure," Burke recognized in his remarks to reporters, "but the serious crimes of Karadima have done exceptional damage in Chile." The measure is indeed exceptional: it comes to punishment by fiat.

Considering the decision in light of the global crisis, it appears arguably typical of a leader who perceives the need to be seen doing something—anything—but either knows not what to do, or dares not do it. The Chilean crisis has been simmering for decades. It exploded in January, when Pope Francis repeatedly accused three of Karadima's victims of calumny, prompting sustained popular outcry around the world and garnering intense media scrutiny that shows no signs of abating.

The laicization of Fernando Karadima is not likely to be a major part of any solution to the grave crisis engulfing the Church in Chile. For one thing, the octogenarian is no longer a danger, and is punished for his crimes. If anything, removing him from the clerical state lessens the practical control Church authorities have over him. It may well be that the sentence Karadima received in 2011—a life of prayer and penance—was too light. Nevertheless, it was the sentence the trial court imposed—seven years, eight months and 11 days before Pope Francis's extraordinary measure.

Karadima's laicization also sets in relief the things Pope Francis has not done in Chile, where prosecutors have raided several diocesan chanceries, other offices, and even the offices of the Chilean bishops' conference. The written release from the Press Office stated: "The Holy Father has exercised his 'ordinary power, which is supreme, full, immediate and universal in the Church' (Code of Canon Law, canon 331), conscious of his service to the people of God as successor of St. Peter." That same ordinary power allows him to do many other things: to depose bishops, for example, though he has thus far limited himself to accepting a handful of resignations from Chilean prelates—seven of them, all told—and he has taken eight months to get to that point.

Meanwhile, Cardinal Francisco Javier Errázuriz, emeritus of Santiago de Chile, remains a cleric in good standing, even though he is accused of covering up for Karadima— charges he vigorously denies—as well as a member of the "C9" Council of Cardinal Advisers, the Pope's "kitchen cabinet" of trusted counsellors to whom he has given the task of drafting the blueprint for the reform of the Church's central governing and administrative apparatus, the Roman Curia.

Cardinal Ricardo Ezzati—Errázuriz's successor in Santiago—is still in his see, though he likewise faces serious charges—which he also denies—including covering up of abuse. Archbishop Ivo Scapolo, the Apostolic Nuncio to Chile, also retains his post, even though he has been criticized for his role in the appointment of Bishop Juan Barros, a close associate of Karadima, to the Diocese of Osorno. The Barros affair led to the extraordinary summons of the entire Chilean episcopate, and the submission of their resignations *en masse*, earlier this year.

Before the ecclesiastical politics, however, there is a prior consideration to make: Pope Francis has said repeatedly that he believes "clericalism" to be at the root of the crisis. Right or wrong, it cannot escape the consideration of any candid observer, that the worst possible measure Church law as currently written envisions and places at the disposal of the Supreme Pastor and Governor of the Church on earth for the punishment of any cleric guilty of grave wrongdoing, is to make that cleric a layman.

"Analysis: Pope's 'thorough study' of McCarrick files unlikely to satisfy"

The Press Office of the Holy See released a communiqué on Saturday afternoon, offering the first direct response to the 11-page letter of "testimony" published in late August by the former Apostolic Nuncio to the United States, Archbishop Carlo Maria Viganò. The Vatican communiqué promises "to ascertain all the relevant facts, to place them in their historical context and to evaluate them objectively." The subject of the effort to ascertain "all the relevant facts" is to be "the entire documentation present in the Archives of the Dicasteries and Offices of the Holy See regarding the former Cardinal McCarrick." In other words: we are in essence looking at a promise to review documents on file.

The Holy See promises the review will be "thorough," though it says nothing about who will be conducting the "thorough study" or with what precise mandate, let alone what powers of discovery—if any—those tasked with the "thorough study" are to have. The paperwork review will be "combined" with the information gathered during the Archdiocese of New York's preliminary investigation, which the Archdiocese forwarded to the Congregation for the Doctrine of the Faith.

It is hard to say what the "thorough study" promised by the Vatican will be. For one thing, "The entire documentation present in the Archives of the Dicasteries and Offices of the Holy See regarding the former Cardinal McCarrick," could be very vast, or relatively thin, depending on what construction one puts on the word "regarding." It is easy to say what the "thorough study" will not be: An independent, transparent, and credibly complete investigation, apt to discover the extent of the rot in the Roman Curia (let alone the reach of McCarrick's corruption in the United States).

In his letter, Viganò alleged a cover-up of the conduct of the disgraced former Archbishop of Washington, DC, going back nearly twenty years and involving three popes—including Francis—as well as three Cardinal Secretaries of State—including the current one, Cardinal Pietro Parolin—and dozens of other very senior Churchmen.

McCarrick fell spectacularly over the summer, but he did not rise alone, or unaided—and while he was ascendant, he brought men with him. The state of affairs leaves the entire US hierarchy under a cloud of suspicion. The US bishops' credibility is in tatters, and they are by their own admission unable to police themselves. Their requests for assistance from Rome to investigate their own conduct have not been granted.

The announcement of a credible accusation and the referral of McCarrick's case to the Congregation for the Doctrine of the Faith came in June of this year. More than a month later, Pope Francis accepted McCarrick's resignation from the College of Cardinals. A statement from the Press Office of the Holy See announcing the acceptance of McCarrick's resignation from the College reported that Pope Francis had also, "ordered [McCarrick's] suspension from the exercise of any public ministry, together with the obligation to remain in a house yet to be indicated to him, for a life of prayer and penance until the accusations made against him are examined in a regular canonical trial."

The Communiqué from the Holy See on Saturday reiterates the measures in place against McCarrick—suspension from ministry and a life of secluded prayer and penance—but made no mention of a trial. The Communiqué also promises, "The Holy See will, in due course, make known the conclusions of the matter regarding Archbishop McCarrick," though it is not clear from the Communiqué what "the matter" is.

There is language in the Communiqué to suggest we might expect some unflattering reports regarding Pope St. John Paul II and Pope-emeritus Benedict XVI. "The Holy See," the Communiqué says, "is conscious that, from the examination of the facts and of the circumstances, it may emerge that choices were taken that would not be consonant with a contemporary approach to such issues." It is also unlikely that either Cardinal Angelo Sodano or Cardinal Tarcisio Bertone—former Secretaries of State under Francis's two most recent predecessors—will escape with their reputations intact. Both were implicated in Archbishop Viganò's August letter. Both by rights ought to have known about McCarrick.

Sodano would have received the letter solicited by the Apostolic Nuncio to the US at the time, Archbishop Gabriel Montalvo. Written in late 2000 by Fr. Boniface Ramsey,

OP, after the announcement of McCarrick's appointment to Washington, the letter detailed reports Ramsey had heard from seminary students regarding McCarrick's penchant for inviting himself into bed with seminarians. Cardinal Bertone allegedly received evidence from Archbishop Viganò's immediate predecessor, the late Archbishop Pietro Sambi, stemming from an Indictment Memorandum prepared by a priest punished with laicization for abuse of minors, Gregory Littleton of Charlotte, and summarized by Viganò in his capacity as Delegate for Pontifical Representations.

"As Pope Francis has said," the Communiqué continues, quoting the Holy Father's own remarks of September 27, 2015, in Philadelphia, Pennsylvania, to a group of victims of sexual abuse, "'We will follow the path of truth wherever it may lead.' Both abuse and its cover-up can no longer be tolerated and a different treatment for Bishops who have committed or covered up abuse, in fact represents a form of clericalism that is no longer acceptable." Right now, the path the Holy See is following seems to lead away from Pope Francis.

The concluding paragraph of the Communiqué commences with a renewal of Pope Francis's "pressing invitation to unite forces to fight against the grave scourge of abuse within and beyond the Church, and to prevent such crimes from being committed in the future to the harm of the most innocent and most vulnerable in society." It goes on to remind us of the meeting of the Presidents of the world's bishops' conferences, scheduled for February of the coming year. The Communiqué then quotes the Holy Father's August 20 Letter to the People of God. "The only way that we have to respond to this evil that has darkened so many lives," the quoted portion says, "is to experience it as a task regarding all of us as the People of God. This awareness of being part of a people and a shared history will enable us to acknowledge our past sins and mistakes with a penitential openness that can allow us to be renewed from within."

This "thorough study" could be a very little step in the right direction—certainly too little and arguably too late, given the legitimate impatience of the faithful and the manifest readiness of Caesar to clean the Church's house. There is little reason to credit it as anything other than a time-buying measure: in essence, a delaying tactic. In any case, it is something for Pope Francis to talk of sharing responsibility for fixing this unholy mess, when he is the only one with any power to do anything about it.

"Cardinal Ouellet's letter forceful, but does not provide substantial refutation"

To cut to the chase: Cardinal Ouellet's open letter has confirmed there were restrictions on then-Cardinal McCarrick. This has been a major point of contention in the press, but it is really a secondary or an ancillary consideration. I've been saying from the start—I called it on August 27, in the *Catholic Herald*—that the "sanctions" of which Archbishop Viganò wrote in his original *J'Accuse!* were in essence a sort of ecclesiastical double-secret probation. Nevertheless, there, you have it.

Cardinal Ouellet has expressed incredulity regarding Viganò's recollection of the conversation, that constitutes the core of his accusation against Pope Francis: that Viganò informed Pope Francis of McCarrick's character, behavior, and proclivities, in a private exchange on June 23, 2013, on the sidelines of an audience with Apostolic Nuncios.

Archbishop Viganò's direct report of his own speech has always been rather incredible on its face. He protested too clear a recollection of his precise words, given—as that report was—at more than five years' remove. Viganò was also irresponsible in his more fanciful interpolations and colorful surmises of Pope Francis's motives and state of mind. A rehearsal of the substance and the facts would have sufficed, and been more effective.

Nevertheless, Cardinal Ouellet offers nothing in the way of substantial refutation. Insofar as its probative value is concerned, Ouellet's opinion of the matter is irrelevant. An expression of incredulity is simply insufficient, especially when coupled with so anemic a qualification as that, which Ouellet's defense of the Pope in this regard does offer. "I very much doubt that McCarrick interested [Pope Francis] to the point that you would have us believe," Ouellet writes—and here it does bear mention that Viganò claims it was Pope Francis, who raised the issue of McCarrick with him during the course of their colloquy. "[McCarrick] was an 82-year-old Archbishop emeritus, who had been seven years without an assignment," Ouellet went on to offer.

"It seems unjust to me," writes Cardinal Ouellet in his open letter, "to conclude that the persons once responsible for discernment are corrupt—even if, in this specific case, some evidence provided by testimonies should have been examined further." Ouellet, in other words, concedes that there were failures of oversight. It comes to an admission in the weak-kneed middle voice of bureaucratic functionaries: mistakes were made. "The prelate in question," i.e. McCarrick, "was able to defend himself with great skill from the doubts raised about him," Ouellet goes on to say.

"On the other hand, the fact that there may be people in the Vatican who practice and support behavior contrary to the values of the Gospel in matters of sexuality, does not authorize us to generalize and declare this or that and even the Holy Father himself unworthy and complicit," writes

Cardinal Ouellet. "Must not the ministers of the truth guard themselves in the first from slander and defamation?"

Every reader not already poisoned by partisanship will concede the point, whether made in reference to the perpetrators of such crimes, or to the victims of them. Nevertheless, the idea that the moral turpitude of clerics high or low is no concern of high Curial officials, unless there is significant evidence of crime, is frankly disturbing. The specific language Cardinal Ouellet entertains also constitutes admission that the presence of a so-called "lavender mafia" might not be so far-fetched, after all.

The fact remains, however, that Archbishop Viganò named lots of men in his letter, and leveled many allegations of many different kinds. Too many allegations, in fact, and with an intemperance and evident animus that could expose Viganò to a charge of slander. Rather than let this sordid epistolary soap opera play out any further, a pastor who was also a statesman and a leader would summon Archbishop Viganò to answer for his crimes, on pain of sanction—very real, and very public—should he fail to appear. The time for star chambers is past.

My suggestion: let Archbishop Viganò be tried for his crimes, publicly. Then, he would have counsel and recourse to witnesses. He would have rights of discovery and access to compulsory process. Let the work of justice be done in the light of day, before a candid world. The longer the Holy See delays such a measure, the more readily credible will be the surmise that the Holy See is afraid of doing so, precisely because it would allow Archbishop Viganò to make his case.

Nor will appeals avail to discretion and care for the reputations of men at any rate protected. For one thing, that ship has sailed. The allegations are published. For another, they are misplaced. The current, secret system can only do further harm to good men falsely accused, even as they further the cause of wicked men intent on concealing their crimes.

Instead, we are promised more secret commissions to study the matter. The Holy See on Saturday promised a "thorough study" of its McCarrick files. The promise is not worth much. Carefully parsed, it is not even clear that the results of the "thorough study" will be fully disclosed. That promise—of full disclosure in due course—appears immediately after a discussion of the abuse charge, and before any mention is made of the documentary review.

The Holy See is implicated in this devilish business: whatever they release will be about as credible as the Nixon administration's redacted transcripts of the Oval Office conversations about the Watergate cover-up. It is true: *Apostolica Sedes a nemine iudicatur*—the Apostolic See is judged by no man. Here, however, another maxim equally applies: *Nemo iudex in causa propria*—No man is to be judge in his own case. Make no mistake: they're trolling us now.

Cover story: "Shadow over the synod"

Hilaire Belloc once remarked that the Catholic Church must have a divine origin, because "no merely human institution conducted with such knavish imbecility would have lasted a fortnight." Belloc's gallows humor applies rather well in the current circumstances. The crisis of clerical sexual abuse and cover-up has demonstrated just how much incompetence and wickedness have disfigured the Church. As bishops from around the world meet in Rome this month for the Synod on Youth, that crisis is inescapable—and, at the outset, some bishops see the problem more clearly than others.

On Thursday, October 4, the first day of real working sessions, several bishops spoke with commendable forthrightness. One was Bishop Frank Caggiano of Bridgeport, Connecticut, who told the synod hall: "We must continue to face courageously and honestly the betrayal of young people by clerics to whom they were entrusted. This sin must never again be found in our midst. Only in this way can the youth of the world believe our synodal call to offer them reassurance, comfort, hope, and belonging."

One might quibble with Bishop Caggiano's apparent belief that the Church has begun to face her leaders' culture of betrayal courageously and honestly. The bishop also spoke generally of "clerics," but it is bishops who have often neglected to police the general moral culture of the clergy, high and low, or to foster a candid spirit among the men who are the Church's leaders and among the seminarians who will succeed them. Nevertheless, Bishop Caggiano put the issue front and center.

The Vatican's media men tried to give a different emphasis at the start of the synod: what this month is really about, they said, is a process of collective discernment. At one of the daily briefings last week, Fr. Antonio Spadaro, SJ, a close advisor to Pope Francis and a senior communications figure at the synod, spoke about a new rule, introduced by Pope Francis: after every five speeches, there will be three minutes' silence.

Fr. Spadaro says that the practice is rooted in the Ignatian charism, and put in place in order to facilitate serene reflection on what speakers are saying. That's reasonable, but Fr. Spadaro discussed one further element. It is, he said, a mistake to get caught up in worrying about the rules. Not to put too fine a point on it: if the rules aren't all that important, then why did Pope Francis just change them? As for the three minutes' silence, it is only perhaps a little too cynical to note that one might as well call a bathroom break by its name.

To be fair, the rules of procedure inside the hall appear not to have changed all that much. That's what Bishop Godfrey Onah of Nsukka, Nigeria, told me at an off-campus event at Rome's LUMSA university on Thursday evening. Bishop Onah, who spent several years as a consultor to the

General Secretariat, said there were some minor tweaks, but nothing too complicated in the way of procedural change.

The basic sub-division of the three weeks' work follows the outline of the *Instrumentum laboris*, which has three main sections: recognizing, interpreting, choosing—slight variations on the threefold process of discernment dear to Pope Francis: see, judge, act. Each section will be discussed in general congregation, followed by small group sessions. There are 14 small groups, organized according to language, each of which will make a report to the whole body at the end of each "unit of work". At the conclusion of the three units, the Commission for the Elaboration of the Final Document will meet to prepare a draft that is supposed to integrate the fruits of the Fathers' labors with the *Instrumentum laboris*. The synod has just one afternoon, on Wednesday, October 24, to debate the draft.

Whatever the Synod Fathers produce, their work is likely to be judged by how it addresses the ongoing crisis. There is one way the Fathers might do this, while keeping to the packed agenda: Recognize—in words—that the crisis is really one of episcopal leadership, the remedy for which cannot be found without real institutional house-cleaning and permanent commitment to the moral reform of clerical culture. Without such recognition, it is unlikely that the Synod Fathers will be able to speak effectively to any other major issue. For example, there is the question of how to teach in a way that is accessible to young people steeped in a culture that won't countenance talk of order or disorder. This is an issue affecting not only the developed societies that incubate this stunted moral and spiritual state, but also reaches those societies threatened by what Pope Francis has called "ideological colonization."

Archbishop Charles Chaput of Philadelphia spoke to this in both his interventions during the first half-week. "The wealthy societies of today's world that style themselves as 'developed'—including most notably my own—are in fact underdeveloped in their humanity," he said in his second intervention. "They're frozen in a kind of moral adolescence; an adolescence which they've chosen for themselves and now seek to impose upon others." In his opening salvo, Archbishop Chaput said the Synod's working document is strong on sociological analysis, but does not offer a spiritual diagnosis, much less a cure. "If we lack the confidence to preach Jesus Christ without hesitation or excuses to every generation, especially to the young, then the Church is just another purveyor of ethical pieties the world doesn't need."

There is anxiety among some bishops that the synod may go soft on the Church's hard teaching in an effort to reach young people. They say that's exactly the wrong way around: the Church's doctrines, including (though not limited to) those about disordered sexuality, are often where they find Jesus Christ at work in their lives.

Cardinal Wilfrid Napier of Durban shared a letter from a young woman illustrating this point. His correspondent, 22-year-old Courage member Avera Maria Santos, experiences (in her words) same-sex attraction. She wrote that she has found the faith preached to her whole and undiluted to be a heady draught and effective medicine. "Telling me that my cross of same-sex attraction is too heavy for me to love as Christ calls me to is not just degrading, it is also a lie. God did not abandon me when man first sinned in the beginning. He will not abandon me now."

The letter spoke more directly than almost any bishop has managed so far at the synod. "Like Christ remembered me from the cross," Santos writes, "I pray that you would remember me, and my brothers and sisters like me, dear bishops, as you pray about and discuss how to help young people ... especially in regard to the topic of homosexuality." Cardinal Napier, by the way, has been elected to the liaison group for communicating with the press, styled the Commission for Information. We were reminded early on that this has often been a controversial area.

At the briefing on October 4, the under-secretary of the General Secretariat, Archbishop Fabio Fabene, confirmed that Cardinal Robert Sarah had been elected to the position first. But Cardinal Sarah refused to serve, citing "personal reasons". Pressed by journalists, Archbishop Fabene did not elaborate.

Cardinal Sarah, however, has been frankly critical of the methods adopted in the last two synod assemblies—in 2014 and 2015—on the family. Cardinal Napier, who took the place when Cardinal Sarah refused, has also been critical of process in the past. At the 2014 synod, an interim report was published, claiming that the synod was taking a looser approach to the questions of divorce and homosexuality. Cardinal Napier expressed the alarm of his fellow bishops: "The message has gone out and it's not a true message," he told the press ruefully.

The test the Synod Fathers need to pass is threefold. It corresponds to the divisions in the working document.

Can they recognize the nature and scale of the crisis beset-
ting the Church because of their failures? Can they address
the challenges facing them? Can they choose wisely and
courageously?

For the Catholic Herald, October 12, 2018

"Cardinal Wuerl is gone—or is he?"

In Pope Francis's acceptance of Cardinal Donald W. Wuerl's resignation from the See of Washington, DC, we see an unmistakable pattern emerging. By accepting Wuerl's resignation, but also keeping him on as Apostolic Administrator, the Pope shows he is working to a particular *modus operandi*. There seem to be three basic steps: (1) ignore criticism and impugn critics' motives; (2) when that becomes impracticable, make a big show of doing something, without actually doing much of anything; (3) if necessary, remove a high-profile figure, but not really.

With Cardinal Wuerl, Pope Francis has done exactly this: he is officially out, and also officially in. The Pope's letter expresses support for Cardinal Wuerl and confidence in his record of leadership. It also indicates reluctance to accept the resignation. "You have sufficient elements to 'justify' your actions and what it means to cover up crimes or not to deal with problems, and to commit some mistakes," Pope Francis writes. "However, your nobility has led you not to choose this way of defense," he continues. "Of this, I am proud, and thank you."

The New York Times reports Wuerl as saying he expects to keep his roles in various powerful dicasteries, including the Congregation for Bishops. The Pope did something very similar in his management of the dust-up at his Dicastery for Communication and in his handling of the crisis in Chile. In March of this year, Pope Francis's hand-picked prefect of the Secretariat for Communication, Msgr. Dario Edoardo Viganò (not to be confused with whistleblower Carlo), landed himself in hot water over doctored photographs and manipulative claims about a letter from Benedict XVI. Msgr. Viganò resigned after several days of increasingly intense media scrutiny. In the same letter announcing acceptance of Viganò's resignation, Pope Francis also praised him and announced he had created a special position for him within the Secretariat.

In Chile, Pope Francis first accused the now-disgraced and retired Bishop Juan Barros's principal accusers of calumny, then said he'd seen no actual evidence against Barros even though he's had a letter from one of Barros's accusers since 2015. Then Francis ordered an investigation into the whole hierarchy, then he summoned the bishops of Chile for a pow-wow at the Vatican, obtained their resignations, and began to sit on all but seven of them while the Chilean government continues to raid chanceries and offices of the national bishops' conference.

Meanwhile, three central figures remain in place, despite serious misconduct allegations pending against them (allegations all three strenuously deny): Cardinal Ricardo Ezzati continues in peaceful possession of his see—the capital Archdiocese of Santiago de Chile—while Ezzati's predecessor, Cardinal Francisco Errázuriz, remains a member of the Pope's C9 "kitchen cabinet" of cardinal-advisers, and

Archbishop Ivo Scapolo remains in place as Apostolic Nuncio. There have been varying degrees of emphasis on different parts at different times, but the basic pattern is fairly straightforward.

For the Catholic World Report, October 12, 2018

"Analysis: Pope's acceptance of Wuerl resignation puts governance front and center"

Pope Francis accepted the resignation of Cardinal Donald W. Wuerl from the See of Washington, DC, on Friday, though Francis made Wuerl apostolic administrator of the capital archdiocese until the Pope names a successor—an unusual move given the circumstances of controversy, scandal, and crisis of confidence in Wuerl's leadership and of the whole US hierarchy.

Cardinal Wuerl's leadership of the Archdiocese has been under intense scrutiny since news broke on June 20 regarding his immediate predecessor, Theodore McCarrick, who is credibly alleged to be an inveterate pervert and serial abuser of children. Wuerl denies any prior knowledge of his disgraced predecessor's proclivities, and claims to have been utterly deceived with respect to his predecessor's character.

Wuerl continued to face increasingly severe criticism throughout the summer, especially in the wake of the Pennsylvania Grand Jury Report, which offered some qualified praise of Wuerl:

> On June 30, 1989, Bishop Donald Wuerl sent a letter
> to the Vatican with respect to several diocesan priests

who had recently been accused of sexually abusing children and whose cases had generated significant publicity. In the letter, Wuerl documented his diocesan policies for sexual abuse and stated his responsibility as Bishop was to determine the course of action in these cases. Wuerl wrote that Catholic parishioners had a right to know whether a priest accused of such crimes had been reassigned to their parish.

Further, Wuerl advised that due to the scandal caused by these priests, he initiated a review of any previous cases of diocesan priests who had been accused of "pedophilic activities" with minors. Wuerl warned the Vatican that Catholic bishops and dioceses could become liable once they are made aware of sexual abuse complaints and that priests who deny the "crime" of pedophilic activity with minors is "common in pedophiles" and that pedophilia is "incurable."

The short version of the last few months is that Cardinal Wuerl was either telling the truth about his ignorance or was not—and either way lost the confidence of the faithful and his clergy. The revelations regarding Cardinal Wuerl's record of leadership in Pittsburgh, however, were arguably what sounded the knell for him.

The report also recounts numerous of Wuerl's failures of leadership as bishop of Pittsburgh, including Wuerl's handling of the case of Fr. George Zirwas, repeatedly accused of abusing teenaged boys. The Pennsylvania report details that Zirwas was first sent to St. Joseph Hospital for evaluation in March 1988, after a February allegation. Wuerl was named bishop of Pittsburgh in February, and was installed on March 25, 1988. In November, Wuerl sent Zirwas for further evaluation at St. Luke's Institute following other complaints, and again returned him to ministry after Zirwas threatened to sue the diocese. The Grand Jury Report further details how then-Bishop Wuerl convinced Zirwas to recant a claim he knew of other sexual predators among the clergy in the diocese, ostensibly in exchange for an increase in the monthly cheque Zirwas received for living expenses.

In fairness to Cardinal Wuerl, those failures were in part conditioned by circumstance. Nor ought Francis be faulted for Pope St. John Paul II's failure to police episcopal culture thirty years ago, or for Benedict XVI's decision to raise a man capable of such failure. Painful as it must be, the whole history of failure from top to bottom must out, and soon. Francis is pope now, and the one man with power of right to bring what lurks in darkness into the light of day.

Cardinal Wuerl's leadership does deserve criticism and rigorous scrutiny, both of which will likely confirm and flesh out what we already know: that Wuerl is a complex and complicated man of considerable talent and ability, who has been weak when he needed to be strong, and has too often been his own worst enemy. At bottom, however, this is not about Cardinal Wuerl, or even his dastardly predecessor, "Uncle Ted" McCarrick. This is about Pope Francis's governance of the Church in a time of crisis.

As a governor of the Church, Pope Francis seems to want it both ways. He praises Cardinal Wuerl as a Christ-like shepherd for his request that Francis accept his resignation, even comparing Wuerl's professed concern over the unity of the Church to Christ's own high priestly prayer at the Last Supper. Francis even praises Wuerl's "nobility" in giving his *nunc dimittis*:

> You have sufficient elements to "justify" your actions and distinguish between what it means to cover up crimes or not to deal with problems, and to commit some mistakes. However, your nobility has led you not to choose this way of defense. Of this, I am proud and thank you.

The issue here is not the sincerity of Wuerl's or Francis's desire to act for the good of the Church. Fr. David Poecking of the Diocese of Pittsburgh told the *Catholic World Report*, "With Pope Francis, I can believe that the Cardinal truly resigned for the good of the Church." Fr. Poecking also told *CWR*, "In his former role as Bishop of Pittsburgh, Cardinal Wuerl in my experience persistently held the clergy accountable to the standards of civil law." Fr. Poecking went on to say, "Pope Francis, in a letter perhaps intended as much for Cardinal Wuerl as for the general public, alludes to 'mistakes' in a manner that might seem dismissive to those affected by the sexual abuse of minors, but otherwise correctly distinguishes mistakes from 'what it means to cover up crimes or not deal with problems'." In any case, neither Pope Francis nor Cardinal Wuerl may reasonably expect the faithful to be satisfied that, with Wuerl out, the Church in the capital archdiocese—or the United States or anywhere else—can return to business as usual. Nevertheless, that is the thing for which both seem to hope.

"The Holy Father's decision to provide new leadership to the Archdiocese can allow all of the faithful, clergy, religious and lay, to focus on healing and the future," said Cardinal Wuerl in a prepared statement. Cardinal Wuerl's desire to let the healing begin appears to dovetail with some expressions found in the closing lines of Pope Francis's own letter. "In this way," Pope Francis writes, "You make clear the intent to put God's Project first, before any kind of personal project, including what could be considered as good for the Church."

One wonders why Pope Francis should have seen fit to offer such mellifluous—if not improbable—praise. There are also the outstanding questions regarding the Papal Foundation and the $25 million loan Cardinal Wuerl secured as the Foundation's chairman, an act of loyalty to the Holy Father that has already done significant damage to reputations both personal and institutional, and could do worse, yet.

Pope Francis has accepted resignations from high-profile Churchmen in the past, including from high-profile figures who have got themselves in hot water. One thinks of the man, who was his personal choice to lead what is now styled the Dicastery for Communication, Msgr. Dario Edoardo Viganò, whose spectacular botch of a book launch in March led to his ouster—sort of.

Whether Pope Francis's apparent reluctance to remove figures of proven loyalty is due to a belief in the policy of standing by one's allies, or propensity for resistance to pressure—especially when it comes in the form of bad press—or from a desire to keep trusted advisers close by, rigorous adherence to the policy is not without a significant downside. Regardless, whether Wuerl is in or out, the McCarrick scandal is not going away. It sits as a cloud over the whole US hierarchy, even as it reaches the highest echelons of governance of the universal Church.

"Analysis: Justice by papal fiat points to serious lack of trust within the Church"

The Vatican announced on Saturday that Pope Francis has reduced two Chilean bishops to the lay state. One of the defrocked is an 85-year-old man reported now to be suffering senile dementia, Francisco José Cox Huneeus, who was bishop of La Serena from 1990 to 1997. The other is 53-year-old Marco Antonio Órdenes Fernández, who served as bishop of Iquique from 2006 to 2012.

Allegations against Mr. Cox go back at least to 1974, the documentation of which contains gruesome details. Mr. Órdenes had what can only be described as a meteoric rise, becoming in 2006 the youngest bishop in Chile's history, at age 42. He would retire a half-dozen years later, citing ill health. Órdenes has apparently lived a quiet and secluded life since handing in his letter, while Cox bounced around for a while—with the help of another high-ranking Chilean prelate (and Cox's confrère in the Schönstatt fraternity), Cardinal Francisco Javier Errázuriz—before settling at the Schönstatt General House in Germany sometime in 2002.

While no one can reasonably deny that the men thus reduced deserved at least what they got from Pope Francis, the manner in which the Holy Father has done the thing brings questions of his ability to govern the Church into tight focus. The statement announcing the moves came on Saturday. *CWR's* translation from the Spanish follows:

> The Holy Father has dismissed from the clerical state Francisco José Cox Huneeus, Archbishop emeritus of La Serena (Chile), member of the Institute of the Schönstatt Fathers, and Marco Antonio Órdenes Fernández, Bishop emeritus of Iquique (Chile).
>
> In both cases, Article 21 § 2.2 of the motu proprio *Sacramentorum sanctitatis tutela* has been applied, as a consequence of manifest acts of abuse of minors. The decision adopted by the Pope last Thursday, October 11, 2018, admits no recourse.
>
> The Congregation for the Doctrine of the Faith has already notified the interested parties, through their respective superiors, in their respective residences. Francisco José Cox Huneeus will continue to be part of the Institute of Schönstatt Fathers.

Sacramentorum sanctitatis tutela is the piece of special legislation governing the gravest delicts—the most serious crimes—in canon law. Article 21 § 2.2 states that the Congregation for the Doctrine of the Faith, which has ordinary jurisdiction over such crimes, may present the gravest of the most grave cases to the Pope for his decision with regard to dismissal from the clerical state or deposition, together with dispensation from the law of celibacy, when it is manifestly evident that the delict was committed and after having given the guilty party the possibility of defending himself.

The Vatican, in other words, was at pains to make it clear that this was Pope Francis's decision. It was also a decision taken outside the Church's normal system of judicial procedure: in short, Cox and Órdenes were laicized with no judicial process—no trial—to speak of. Even in normal circumstances, canonical trials are paperwork affairs—conducted in secret, to boot—and that is a problem. Said simply: (at risk of sounding like a broken record) justice must be seen to be done. There must be independent investigations conducted in the light of day, and reasonably transparent processes for the adjudication of criminal charges against clerics high and low.

Vatican City has the rudiments of such investigative and judicial mechanisms, and has used them recently in connection with crimes both financial and moral. For reasons both juridical-political and practical, the Vatican City system could not possibly be used to process canonical cases. Nevertheless, the existence of the system shows that the Church at the highest levels of governance is not unfamiliar with either the process or the reasons for it.

In any case, Cox and Fernandez received summary justice by papal fiat—and that is a bigger problem. If the Church's continued use of secret trials is a hindrance to the recovery of trust, insofar as it renders reasonable persons incapable of confidence in her capacity to administer justice, so much more will naked exercises of raw power serve to undermine and indeed destroy the very ground on which any such confidence must be based: the reasonable belief in the Church's own bona fide commitment to doing justice at all.

With specific regard to the Chilean theater of the global crisis, there can be no doubt, but that Pope Francis faces a terrible dilemma. When the bishops of Chile resigned *en masse* in May of this year, they created a serious conundrum for Pope Francis. Basically, they left him with a set of three alternatives: accept all the resignations and start from scratch; accept some of the resignations and sit on others; accept none of the resignations and proceed piecemeal.

Each of the three options poses its own set of peculiar dangers, and none of them is without a downside. Francis seems to have opted for an out-of-the-box hybrid solution in Chile, somewhere between door number two and door number three. Seems, one says, because Pope Francis has not shared his plan with the faithful—not even in broad strokes—even as he has constantly insisted we are all in this together.

While the breakdown in trust among bishops and bodies of the faithful in virtually every ecclesiastical jurisdiction is heartbreaking and truly scandalous, there appears to be an even more grievous breakdown in trust within the bishops' own ranks. The dilemma facing Pope Francis with regard to the world's bishops is even more terrible than the one facing him in Chile: he can't trust any of them.

Pope Francis also appears to be wary of the faithful. In his recent letter to Cardinal Donald W. Wuerl accepting his resignation and congratulating him on a job well done after the Cardinal's defensiveness and lack of candor lost him the confidence of the clergy and the faithful in his archdiocese, Pope Francis wrote:

I recognize in your request the heart of the shepherd
who, by widening his vision to recognize a greater good
that can benefit the whole body (cf. Apostolic Exhortation *Evangelii gaudium*, 235), prioritizes actions that
support, stimulate and make the unity and mission
of the Church grow above every kind of sterile division sown by the father of lies who, trying to hurt the
shepherd, wants nothing more than that the sheep be
dispersed (cf. Matthew 26:31).

Whatever else these lines do, they certainly tend to confirm
the worst suspicions of those, who read his series of September fervorini as showing that he believes the faithful to be a
ginned-up mob, and at best the tools and playthings of the
Devil.

From his dismissal of the faithful in the small Chilean
diocese on which he foisted the hapless and unready Bishop
Juan Barros—"Osorno is suffering because it is dumb,"—to
his juxtaposition—if not comparison—of the faithful desirous of transparency and accountability from the Church's
leaders to the bloodthirsty crowds calling for Christ's crucifixion, Francis has shown astounding insensitivity to the
concerns of the faithful. If his eyes were ever opened to the
callousness of his disregard for the real hurt of the people he
professes to love, it appears he has repented of his discovery.

Perhaps it is the case that Pope Francis himself believes—
as the Catholic News Agency's level-headed and judicious
JD Flynn, in an excellent piece of news analysis, recently
speculated Vatican officials may believe—that the crisis in

the Church is somehow playing out as a referendum on his leadership?

It is certain that elements in the Church are using the crisis to make political hay. This weekend, during a press conference to mark the anniversary of the final apparition of Our Lady of Fatima, the bishop of Leiria-Fátima, Cardinal Antonio Marto called l'Affaire Viganò an "ignoble attack" on Pope Francis. "[The whole business] is nothing more than a political montage, with no real foundation," he said. At best, he's half right.

Even without Viganò's extraordinary "testimonies"—the original 11-page letter and the follow-up, to both of which Cardinal Marc Ouellet responded last weekend—we have more than enough to know there is rot in the Church that reaches the Curia. We need to discover the extent of its spread and the vectors of its spreading. The Archbishop of Munich and Friesing and C9 member, Cardinal Reinhard Marx, admitted as much at a press event October 5 to launch a training initiative on safeguarding efforts at Rome's Pontifical Gregorian University. "[The crisis with its fallout] has not been caused by the press doing their job properly," he said. "It's caused by the Church leadership." Said simply, the faithful have a right to know.

In order to begin to address the crisis at its root, Pope Francis needs to earn back some small measure of trust. He simply cannot do that by displays of raw power given piecemeal against old men who used to be someone, or secluded perverts that nobody likes and few even realized were still breathing. Instead, he needs to come up with a plan for reform apt to produce the necessary transparency in governance—especially insofar as the administration of justice is concerned—and he needs to be transparent about that. If he has such a plan, he needs to submit it to the faithful, who have rights in the Church both moral and legal.

Even the Archbishop-emeritus of Washington, DC, Cardinal Donald W. Wuerl—a close adviser and papal favorite—admitted as much when pressed. "[Y]es," he told *CWR* this past August, "the laity do have a place: they have a moral place—a right in that sense—to participate in whatever is going on in the life of the Church." So do victims of wicked clerics. So do the men accused of wicked deeds, though it does not gratify our thirst for vengeance to say so. Even if the laity did not, they are a resource Pope Francis simply cannot afford not to tap.

"Give him time," said Archbishop Charles Scicluna of Malta, at a recent press briefing on the doings of the Synod Assembly underway in Rome, in response to a question regarding what the attitude of the faithful should be with respect to Pope Francis's leadership. With due respect to Archbishop Scicluna—who may be the closest thing to a good guy one is like to find in this whole sordid business—Pope Francis has had plenty of that.

For the Catholic World Report, October 19, 2018

"Archbishop Viganò's third testimony indicates a way through the current morass"

While the Church in the United States faces the prospect of an autumn to make Chile's seem tame and even idyllic by comparison, the grotesque spectacle of "he said / he said" continues at the highest levels of ecclesiastical governance. To call it enervating would be terrible understatement. Wretched as the business is, three things nonetheless emerge from Archbishop Viganò's latest "testimony" that are worthy of note, not least because they offer some inkling of a way through this lamentable morass:

- Viganò's claims are subject to verification (or falsification) of a documentary nature;
- Viganò concedes the semantic point regarding "sanctions" even as he reaffirms the substance of his allegation with regard to them, noting rightly that Cardinal Ouellet in his own letter confirms that specific allegation's substantial correctness;
- Viganò abandons his call for Pope Francis to renounce the See of Rome.

It may well be that the best we dare hope in the way of a resolution is the "documentary review" Pope Francis has promised. Viganò's affirmations in these regards tell us what we know ought to be there, on file. If the documents he has indicated are there, they will either bear him out, or not. If they should not be forthcoming, a full investigation will be inevitable. This provides a frame for the issues, which does not rely on personality, character, or motive for their resolution.

The semantic concession likewise strikes an acceptable compromise and allows discussion to move past what is in any case a secondary, if not an ancillary point. It comes to an admission of poorly chosen language. An outright apology for such a poor choice of words would perhaps have been preferable, but the perfect ought never to be the enemy of the good. After all, the former nuncio did receive substantial vindication on this and several other matters of substance.

As far as resolution of the impasse is concerned, the third point is the most important, for it speaks directly to the principal cause of the Pope's recalcitrance and entrenched refusal to investigate Archbishop Viganò's claims: the plausible charge of rebellion.

In his original letter, Archbishop Viganò concluded with a call for Pope Francis to resign—his word—for the good of the Church. That appeal was premature and deeply misguided. It framed the controversy in starkly political terms, and put Francis on the defensive, precisely when Francis needed to be persuaded of the practical political advantages in full disclosure.

In short, Archbishop Viganò exposed himself to being cast, rightly or wrongly, as the Pope's enemy—a mitred Catiline—when he needed to be a Cicero (if he could not be a Damian).

If Viganò's allegations are correct, it is difficult to avoid his conclusion. We must avoid it, nonetheless. Another renunciation would cripple the Papacy in a manner far more severe and lasting than would a few more years with a morally crippled Pope on the throne. Francis must reign when he breathes his last. Archbishop Viganò now professes something like loyal opposition. "I am charged with disloyalty to the Holy Father and with fomenting an open and scandalous rebellion," he writes. "Yet rebellion would entail urging others to topple the papacy. I am urging no such thing." Viganò goes on to say:

> I pray every day for Pope Francis—more than I have ever done for the other popes. I am asking, indeed earnestly begging, the Holy Father to face up to the commitments he himself made in assuming his office as successor of Peter. He took upon himself the mission of confirming his brothers and guiding all souls in following Christ, in the spiritual combat, along the way of the cross. Let him admit his errors, repent, show his willingness to follow the mandate given to Peter and, once converted let him confirm his brothers (Lk 22:32).

That is still a hard thing for Pope Francis to hear, and might not strike him as perfectly fair. Nevertheless, it is a very different tune, and one that ought not be disagreeable to a leader graced with a moment's magnanimity.

Archbishop Viganò's closing paragraphs, however, represent a return to provocative—if not rebellious—form. In essence, he tells his brother bishops they have a choice between keeping silence or saying what they know. That is true, though Viganò places the matter in a way that equates silence with more-or-less willing complicity in wicked conspiracy. Said simply, that is unjust to men, who have sworn an oath to keep the secrets of their offices.

Archbishop Viganò believes his violation of his own oath justified by circumstance. He may well be right. Nevertheless, to hear him describe as cowards men who keep their oaths, without considering that they might do so honorably, or for reasons blameless if not praiseworthy, cannot fail to distress the candid observer.

Pope Francis could put an end to this whole debacle, by ordering an investigation worthy of the name. Archbishop Viganò has taken steps—small steps, but determined and measurable—toward the very reconciliation to which Cardinal Ouellet called him. The longer the good of the whole Church is held hostage to a clash of personality, the more, and more lasting damage will she suffer. Today, as yesterday, Pope Francis holds all the power to right the ship.

For the Catholic World Report, October 28, 2018

"Opinion: Francis's remarks about the Great Accuser distract from lack of resolve, leadership"

The burgeoning crisis of leadership in the Catholic Church that is the result of organized coverup and winking at rot in the moral culture of the clergy, high and low, was largely absent from the reports of the Fathers' consultations at the XV Ordinary General Assembly of the Synod of Bishops over the past weeks. Nevertheless, Pope Francis's remarks to the prelates on Saturday, at the close of their work, show unmistakably that the crisis continues to occupy his mind.

In extemporaneous remarks to the Synod Fathers gathered in the Synod Hall shortly after they voted to approve the final document, Pope Francis first made his perfunctory thanks to the organizers. Then he said, "Because of our sins, the Great Accuser seizes the advantage, and—as the first chapter of the Book of Job tells us—goes about the earth looking for whom to accuse." It is a theme that has become familiar over the past several weeks.

"In this moment, he is accusing us strongly," the Pope went on to say, "and this accusation becomes persecution." Francis noted the persecution of Christians in Iraq and other parts of the Middle East, as well as in various other parts of the world. Pope Francis said the persecution of which he speaks also takes the form of "continuous accusations," the purpose of which is "to sully the Church." Then, he offered this:

> The Church is not to be sullied: her children, yes, we are all dirty, but the mother is not—and this is the moment to defend our Mother—and we defend our Mother from the Great Accuser by prayer and penance. This is why I asked, in this month that ends in a few days, for people to pray the Rosary, to pray to St. Michael Archangel, to pray to Our Lady, that she might always cover Mother Church. Let us continue to do so. This is a difficult moment, because the Accuser, through us, attacks our Mother—and no one is to lay a finger on our Mother [the Church]. This, I had it in my heart to say at the end of the Synod.

On the one hand, he acknowledges that the bishops are to blame: "[T]he Accuser, through us, attacks our Mother." On the other, the bishops seem to get a pass, because they are simply sinners just like everyone else. It is as if he will not see that the bishops have already harmed the Church by their winking and coverup, while the people within the Church, who are clamoring for transparency and accountability from the bishops, are motivated by the very filial love he praises.

The final document of the Synod does contain some reference to the crisis. In Paragraph 30 we read, "It has become clear that our work is cut out for us, when it comes to eradicating the forms of exercise of authority on which the various forms of abuse are grafted, and of countering the lack of accountability and transparency with which many cases have been managed." Paragraph 30 of the final document goes on to say, "Desire for domination, the lack of dialogue and transparency, the forms of double life, spiritual emptiness, as well as psychological fragilities: these are the terrain on which corruption flourishes."

Francis is not wrong to call for prayer and penance—no Christian can fail to confess that we need much more of both—but the Church must be governed, and Peter's office is for the governance of the Church. Governing means putting aside personal interests—not ignoring the noise of division and agitation, but rising above it—and acting for the true good. In any case and inescapably now, the presence of serious rot reaching the highest echelons of Church governance is laid bare. We must fathom the full extent of it. We must discover its origin, as well as the proximate and more remote causes of it. We must have it out.

Pope Francis alone in the Church holds power by indisputable right to make the source and reach of the rot known, and to begin at any rate to rid us of it. That is the one thing needful, and that is the thing Francis refuses to give. The documentary review he has promised is at best a half measure. At worst, it is a scrap thrown to dogs about the table.

Pope Francis did not create this crisis. He is not to blame for the rise of evil men before he assumed the supreme governance of the universal Church, nor is he to be saddled with the guilt of his predecessors' unhappy decisions and unready responses. Francis is Pope now, however, and that means he is chiefly responsible for her earthly welfare.

Whatever one thinks of Archbishop Carlo Maria Viganò, it is largely owing to his testimony that the rot is exposed. Some in the Church are of the opinion that the former nuncio to the United States is a hero of the faith. Others believe he is a scheming Machiavel, ambitious and cunning, and thirsty for the ruin of men by whom he feels himself wronged. It is evident that his motives—like those of all men—are alloyed: he used his original letter to impugn the reputations of men with no discernible tie to his core allegation, or to sully the names of certain others in ways not strictly necessary to the making of his case.

There is another fact, bright-shining, adamant and ineluctable: Archbishop Viganò's motives are largely irrelevant. If his aim was to topple the pontificate of Francis, then it was a fool's errand from the start: *Apostolica Sedes a nemine iudicatur*—the Apostolic See is judged by no man—and if part of his purpose was to destroy his enemies in the Curia, let him be tried for it in open court and pay the price of his folly. Such a trial would also give him ample room to make his case before a candid world, and expose the miscarriages not only of the reigning Pontiff, but of the last two and their underlings, as well. If Francis would right the Church and see Archbishop Viganò held to account for his intemperances, then there is arguably no better way to achieve both in one.

I think that Archbishop Viganò drew too facile an equation of silence with complicity in his third testimony, when he addressed himself to his brother bishops. Many of them—especially those in the Roman Curia—are legitimately pained in conscience, racked between love of the

Church and fear for their souls' safety, should they abjure an oath sworn in good faith. Nevertheless, Viganò was right on the fundamental point. Those two goods can never be the poles of a dilemma for any true son of the sinless Mother, nor can they ever face a true spouse of the spotless bride as genuine alternatives in a devil's choice. *Salus animarum suprema lex.*

Pope Francis still has a chance—perhaps his only one left—to right the ship. There is no wicked power in the universe that can reach him, and no faithful son or daughter of Holy Church, who would not support him to the last in any sincere and whole-hearted effort to set her aright. If he does not make that effort, and soon, then it will become impossible to avoid the conclusion that the interests he is pursuing do not constitute the true good of the Church. That effort must begin with transparency: justice must be seen to be done.

"The Vatican's carelessness is on display as new US scandals break"

Si cela vous plaît, très Saint Père, pouvons-nous avoir notre Visite Apostolique maintenant?

The US and Roman theaters of the crisis in the Catholic Church have entered a new phase of carelessness—of the reputations of men who may or may not have done grave wrong; of the rights of Christians of every age and sex and state of life to know the truth; of the good of the Church.

That we are entered upon such a phase is amply attested by the removal of Bishop Martin D. Holley from the See of Memphis, the allegations that Bishop Richard Malone of Buffalo covered up for priests accused of abuse, and the revelation that the Vatican was informed as early as 1994 about the strange proclivities of the disgraced former archbishop of Washington, DC, "Uncle Ted" McCarrick.

Now, we learn that another bishop—New York's 74-year-old auxiliary John Jenik—has a "credible and substantiated" allegation against him. The allegation reportedly concerns incidents that date back many years, and involves a victim who was a minor at the time. The Archdiocese of New York has offered no further details, though the *New York Times* on Wednesday reported that the victim is 52-year-old Michael

Meenan, who was 13 at the time the alleged abusive relationship began.

Meenan has also complained of abuse committed in 1984 by his religion teacher at Fordham Prep; he received compensation for the incident in 2016. Meenan told the *Times* he brought his allegation against Bishop Jenik to the archdiocese in January; he says the archdiocesan review board interviewed him last week.

Bishop Jenik wrote a letter to the parishioners of Our Lady of Refuge parish, where he has been pastor for more than 30 years. He denied the allegations, of course. In fairness, "credible and substantiated" is a low standard: it basically comes to mean the allegation is not manifestly false, and is capable in principle of being investigated. Jenik also managed in his letter to mention his recent hip surgery, and his upcoming operation on the other hip.

In a letter of his own addressed to the parishioners of Our Lady of Refuge, the archbishop of New York, Cardinal Timothy Dolan, wrote, "Although Bishop Jenik continues to deny the accusation, loyal priest that he is, he has stepped aside from public ministry, and, as we await Rome's review, may not function or present himself as a bishop or priest."

Why did it take the archdiocese 10 months to interview Meenan after he made his allegation against Bishop Jenik? Was the archdiocesan review board investigating the allegation, and if so, what was Bishop Jenik doing while the investigation was underway? Was he under any sort of restrictions? If so, of what sort? When did the Archdiocese of New York inform Rome of the allegation against Bishop Jenik? Those are just a few of the questions a minimally candid statement on the matter would answer. For that matter, the statement might have mentioned that Cardinal Dolan ordained Jenik a bishop in 2014. Did he ask Pope Francis specifically for Jenik as an auxiliary?

Any family in which the head of the household failed to disclose such pertinent information in similar circumstances would be fairly judged dysfunctional. Cardinal Dolan has said he is "impatient" with the Holy Father's handling of the crisis. Now, it appears he has taken a page from the Vatican's book.

The Vatican's carelessness is on display in the matter of Bishop Holley. A summary of all the claims and counter-claims in the Holley case would run to significant length. Suffice it to say that we know the Vatican cited a "manage-ment issue" in justification of Holley's removal. The apostolic administrator appointed by Pope Francis to lead Memphis in the interim, Archbishop Joseph Kurtz of Louisville, Ken-tucky, gave an interview to *CWR* in which he did not deny knowing more about the reason for Holley's ouster, but only said, "I have to rely on statements of the Vatican about this; I can't speak beyond that."

Archbishop Kurtz demurred when *CWR* asked him whether Bishop Holley's removal is unusual, and took care to explain that he is not in Memphis as an investigator or a fixer. "I can't comment on how unusual it is, other than to say that sometimes there are changes," he said. "As I told the people in Memphis, my task is not to deal with what went on before this change, but what is happening presently."

One reason for the Vatican's caginess regarding Holley's removal may be a general reluctance to be seen as managing too closely the affairs of ordinary ecclesiastical jurisdictions. Such behavior does not appear to comport well with the Vatican's claims—behind which it has successfully shielded itself from civil liability in abuse cases—that bishops are not agents or employees of the Holy See in any legally pertinent sense.

The real reason behind Holley's ouster may be so grave that the bishop of Memphis could not be allowed to stay one more day in his See, and the danger to the Church so sinister that disclosure of even a part of the reason would further imperil her. If it is not, then the refusal to disclose the reasons for Holley's removal is, at the very least, inexcusably careless of Holley's reputation, not to mention the rights of the faithful to know the truth about the state of the Church and the conduct of their pastors.

Suppose for a moment that the "management issue" is no more than run-of-the-mill poor job performance. Why is that enough to earn this bishop a pink slip, while elsewhere all manner of moral negligence and even malfeasance seem to be tolerated for long periods of time? For example, Pope Francis let Bishop Michael Bransfield retire—not altogether peacefully—at 75, though Bransfield was under a cloud of suspicion for years and is now under investigation along with the diocese he used to lead. There are plausible reasons for handling Bransfield as the Vatican did, but the long-suffering faithful (and many of the clergy) in Wheeling-Charleston are impatient with half-truths and assurances that all is well in hand.

If mismanagement is a reason for removal, then it is worth asking how much longer Bishop Richard Malone will remain in the See of Buffalo. Earlier this week "60 Minutes" aired an interview with Bishop Malone's whistle-blowing former executive assistant:

> The hundreds of pages Siobhan O'Connor uncovered included personnel files and memos. They revealed that for years Bishop Malone allowed priests accused of sexual assault such as statutory rape and groping to stay on the job.

The August exposé by local ABC affiliate WKBW that led to the "60 Minutes" report is more detailed, and more damning. Here is the case of Father Art Smith, suspended in 2011 after school officials complained of grooming behavior. Malone rehabilitated Smith when he took over the diocese in 2012:

> [D]ocuments show the principal reported to the diocese that Father Smith refused to stay away from the school, showing up outside a classroom in April 2012. The principal fired off a letter to the diocese saying, "This man is a predator and a groomer of young children. Something needs to be done... As school principal, I feel the students in grade 8 have been injured and troubled by the actions of this man more than originally thought."

The WKBW report then details how Malone returned Father Smith to active ministry, giving him a post at a nursing home. Smith also heard confessions at an event for young people that included hundreds of teenagers. When she heard of it, Principal Hider wrote to Malone:

> If a teacher would have been grooming children and
> had inappropriate relations with a minor, they would
> have been fired and lost their license to teach... Yet a
> priest that has a history of inappropriate contact with
> the youth was among the youth ministering the sacra-
> ment of Reconciliation.

WKBW reports that Bishop Malone replied to Hider to the
effect that Father Smith's behavior was not technically in
violation of the Charter for the Protection of Young People.
Let that sink in.

Bishop Malone issued a statement ahead of the "60 Minutes" report, explaining his reasons for declining an interview with the program:

> First, the Church is in the eye of a storm largely as a
> result of wrong decisions made decades ago and even
> some made recently, as I have acknowledged. But, our
> efforts and our focus have always remained steadfast:
> protect the children and reconcile with the victims.
>
> Second, while "60 Minutes" is free to interview
> whomever they wish for this story, it is clear to me and
> my staff that your roster of interviews did not include
> those who are aware of the full extent of the efforts
> of our Diocese to combat child abuse. Nor does it
> include those who urge me every day to stay the course
> and restore the confidence of our faithful.

The first reason is at best self-serving. That second one,
though—boy, howdy. Had he accepted the interview, Bishop
Malone would have been on the roster. Is there perhaps

someone in his diocese better informed on the matters he listed who might have gone in his stead?

On Wednesday, Bishop Malone's communications office released a statement calling Siobhan O'Connor's testimony "plainly and embarrassingly contradictory," and published several emails the diocese claims "demonstrate [O'Connor's] complete admiration for [Bishop Malone] and his efforts to lead the Diocese." The diocese does not address the allegations, but attacks the woman who brought them—with proof—before the public.

Was Bishop Holley's mismanagement worse than that of which Bishop Malone was first accused in August? At the very least, a power responsible for oversight of bishops' conduct should open an investigation into Malone and his management of the Buffalo diocese. If Pope Francis believes he can stonewall, or go to ground and wait for the anger to subside, he is sorely mistaken.

The sweltering summer of 2018, which saw the simmering discontent of the long-suffering Catholic faithful in the United States boil over and set fire to the kitchen, will spread rapidly to other rooms in the house. Indeed, the anger has already spread beyond the confines of the visible Church: more than a dozen states in the US have opened or are considering criminal investigations; the District of Columbia—which has no authority to conduct criminal investigations—has opened a civil investigation; US attorneys are conducting a broadening federal probe.

If Church leaders' concerns are for scandal, then their silence—from the Vatican on down—is terribly miscalculated. The true scandal is the carelessness at every level of

Church governance toward the broad public who have a right, as I put it in an open letter to Bishop Thomas J. Tobin of Rhode Island at the start of the summer, "to the Gospel and therefore a right to the Church as Christ intends her to be, rather than as you have made her." In any case, the Catholic Church's house will be clean. The only questions are whether it shall be God's Vicar on Earth who cleans it, or Caesar, and whether the cleansing shall come before or after the fire sale.

"February's meeting of bishops will not succeed without a radical change of culture"

February is still a good way off, but it is not as far off as it might seem. Presumably, the Vatican is already busily preparing for the meeting of the heads of the world's bishops' conferences, scheduled for February 21-24. There's a lot riding on the meeting. To say that public perception of the Pope's handling of the burgeoning global crisis is not good would put one in the running for understatement of the year.

From Chile—where the latest chapter exploded in January—to Germany, the Netherlands, several countries in Africa (where women religious especially are reported to have been subjected to horrendous abuse), and India (where one bishop has been arrested on rape charges and another has had his diocese essentially placed in ecclesiastical receivership over shady real estate deals)—not to mention Ireland and the United States—Pope Francis has demonstrated a range of attitudes running from reluctance to near-total paralysis. The February gathering could therefore represent the Pope's last chance to convince people he is serious about addressing the crisis. There is, however, good reason to believe the meeting is doomed from the start. That bodes ill not only or even primarily for the Vatican's PR cache, but for the whole Church, which cannot afford to be without effective leadership.

Pope Francis's troubled C9 "kitchen cabinet" of Cardinal Advisers announced the meeting on September 12, saying the theme of it would be "protection of minors." A summary specified that the meeting would also concern itself with the safeguarding of "vulnerable adults."

Though the Vatican has not clarified what "vulnerable adults" means, it is generally understood to refer to persons who struggle with self-sufficiency because of physical or intellectual handicaps. So, not seminarians, for example, though their vulnerability to evil superiors has been amply attested over the past several months. The problem is two-fold: the bishops have not been merely ineffective in addressing the abuse crisis, they have been complicit in sexual abuse and cover-up; although abuse and cover-up are the swollen and festering boil on the Church's body, the crisis facing the Church is one of episcopal leadership generally: the bishops' protracted failure to police the moral culture of the clergy, high and low.

Keeping minors and vulnerable adults beyond the reach of lascivious men of the cloth is certainly necessary, but even the most fool-proof and iron-clad system of defense could never be a real solution. To fix the problem at its core, to root it out really, there must be a thorough reform of clerical culture and of power structures within the Church. If the old Jesuit maxim, *repetita iuvant*, is to be credited, the thing bears repeating: this crisis is global, protracted, and persistent. The genesis and trajectory of this meeting suggest

Pope Francis still does not get it. In any case, relying on the heads of the bishops' conferences to put their heads together and find solutions on their own must be a long shot: the bishops—and Francis is one of them—are the problem.

It could be that Francis believes he needs to soften up the Church's hierarchical leadership and ease them into the idea that they must relinquish—or at least loosen—their titanic grip on the reins of power. If so, it's an awfully long play.

For the Catholic World Report, November 6, 2018

"Buffalo and the silence of the bishops"

US Attorneys contacted the diocese of Buffalo, NY, in late May, to inform officials of their interest in documents related to abuse reports after 1990 and therefore susceptible of prosecution under federal criminal statutes. Terrence M. Connors, attorney for the Diocese of Buffalo, clarified the chronological point in remarks to reporters during a press conference at Infant of Prague parish, Cheektowaga, on Monday evening.

Charlie Specht, the chief investigative reporter for Buffalo's ABC affiliate, WKBW, first reported the May date in mid-October, but this is the first time any agent or official of the Buffalo diocese has publicly confirmed the report. The point of chronology is significant, since it means the news regarding federal criminal probes that has been coming in cascade since October is not, in fact, merely a response to the Pennsylvania Grand Jury Report. It gives the lie to narrative presumptions of reaction on the part of opportunistic prosecutors eager to strike while the iron is hot. US attorneys wrote to the US Conference of Catholic Bishops in early October to instruct the Conference to advise chanceries throughout the country to keep their files, and not to destroy them. Nevertheless, this reckoning is a long time coming.

We should have known it would come to this. The writing was on the wall in 2002, when the bishops gave themselves a pass. The vote to change the language of the Dallas Charter for the Protection of Children and Young People so it exempted bishops was a sign in flaming letters: *Mene, Mene, Tekel, Upharsin*. If the judgment was meant for the bishops, the message was written for us, the laity, as well. We did not see the words written. We did not want to. We wanted normal.

We wanted to go back to the good old days, the happy time, when ignorance was bliss and Father could be trusted and the Bishop was a smiling cipher who confirmed our children and otherwise did neither good nor harm in any way we could discern, or cared to. We wanted what we knew, which was little, and we wanted all of it.

What we have is Bishop Richard J. Malone, standing at a makeshift podium in a tricked-out parish gym and saying—with a straight face—"I don't think I lack empathy [for victims of clerical sexual abuse]," and then, "I don't avoid meeting victims at all. I want them to call—I don't want to be ambushed, either by you people [i.e. journalists] or a victim."

That was right before Bishop Malone called his auxiliary, Edward Grosz, to the podium to offer, "Perhaps the person [who claims never to have heard from the bishop or his office after complaining of abuse] didn't go through the proper channels." Bishop Grosz handles much of the paperwork and bureaucracy for his principal in abuse cases.

This is not normal. This is not even close to normal, though the silence of bishops in the face of manifest evil is commonplace these days. They will not denounce Malone— though they tried to scapegoat Uncle Ted McCarrick and they failed—nor will they defend him. As a body, the bishops too often behave as men devoid of sense, and destitute of shame.

Not a single one of Bishop Malone's confreres has publicly corrected him, let alone called for his resignation. We continue to hear from some quarters the pious platitudes about the "good bishops" who love their people. If one of them were good, he would denounce his brethren for their cravenness. He would rend his vestments. He would don sackcloth and ashes and do penance. He would say what he knows, or reasonably suspects. Who is that man?

The evidence suggests their mitred highnesses are all terrified: of losing their place? No. Of being found out? No, again. Nor is their fear for what may befall them, should they keep silence. It is for what might befall them, should they speak. They are afraid of being expelled from the club— or worse—having spoken, of becoming a pariah within it.

May we reasonably hope for any good from their Fall Meeting? Their silence bespeaks a general pusillanimity, unbecoming men ordained to be shepherds for God's holy flock and high priests blameless in His sight, ministering to Him night and day. The worst are quite possibly criminal. To continue to place any sort of trust in this Quisling brotherhood is folly. It is maudlin. It is morally criminal.

Let one of them—one—stand up and say he shall no longer be a part of this fiasco. Let one of them own the crisis without stint, for all the brethren, come what may. Let one of them raise his voice and cry out, *Ecce adsum!*

For the Catholic World Report, November 12, 2018

"Why has Pope Francis hamstrung the U.S. bishops?"

Pope Francis has ordered the Catholic Bishops of the United States to refrain from voting on a code of conduct and a lay-led oversight body to investigate bishops accused of misconduct. The President of the USCCB, Cardinal Daniel DiNardo of Galveston-Houston, told prelates of the Pope's instruction as they were gathered for the opening session of their highly anticipated Fall Meeting in Baltimore.

The reason given for the delay is that the Holy See desires the US bishops' action be informed by the discussions scheduled to take place among the heads of the world's bishops' conferences in February at the Vatican. Upon hearing the announcement, Cardinal Blase Cupich of Chicago immediately took the floor to suggest the bishops stick to their agenda, and take a resolution ballot in lieu of a binding vote. "As you [Cardinal DiNardo] are our representative going to that meeting, we need to be very clear with you where we stand," Cupich said, "and we need to tell our people where we stand." Cardinal Cupich also said, "It is clear that the Holy See is taking seriously the abuse crisis in the Church, seeing it as a watershed moment, not just for the Church in this country, but around the world, in putting so much emphasis on the February meeting."

The Vatican announced the February meeting in September, at the end of a three-day gathering of the paralyzed and scandal-ridden C9 Council of Cardinal Advisers—the Pope's hand-picked "kitchen cabinet" tasked with drawing up the blueprint for reform of the Roman Curia—in the wake of Archbishop Carlo Maria Viganò's dossier alleging systemic corruption and rot in the Curia, including a cover-up of the disgraced former Archbishop of Washington, DC, Theodore Edgar "Uncle Ted" McCarrick, that stretches back at least twenty years and involves three popes and three secretaries of state, as well as a host of other more-or-less senior Curial officials.

The Holy See has not published a list of those officially invited to the meeting—though it is supposed to involve all the heads of the world's bishops' conferences—nor has the Holy See said which dicastery is principally responsible for organizing the meeting. There is no agenda, nor is there any specific mandate. When the C9 Cardinals announced the February meeting, this Vatican watcher had the distinct impression they had to twist the Holy Father's arm to get him to agree to do anything at all with regard to the burgeoning crisis.

The Holy See apparently did not have similar scruples when it came to action on the part of French bishops, who last week voted to establish an independent commission to investigate their hierarchy's response to abuse since 1950, and make reform recommendations. In a message to the French bishops sent through his Secretary of State, Pietro

Parolin, Pope Francis called on the French hierarchical leadership to continue their efforts at reform. News.va reported last week:

> [T]he Pope encourages the [French] Bishops to persevere in the fight against pedophilia, urging them to continue in their implementation of a "zero tolerance" stance against sexual abuse committed by certain members of the Church, without ever forgetting, he says, "to recognize and support the humble fidelity lived in daily life, with the grace of God, by so many priests, men and women religious, consecrated and lay faithful." He also stresses the importance of listening to the victims whose wounds, he adds, will never be healed by a prescription.

It remains to be seen whether the Holy See will intrude on the Italian bishops, who are slated to consider similar proposals at their own extraordinary assembly, which also opened Monday in the Vatican.

Addressing the US bishops on Monday morning in Baltimore, shortly after they had received news of the Vatican order, the apostolic nuncio to the United States, Archbishop Christophe Pierre, said, "There may be a temptation on the part of some to relinquish responsibility for reform to others than ourselves, as if we were no longer capable of reforming or trusting ourselves, as if the deposit of trust should be transferred to other institutions entirely."

Archbishop Pierre went on to say, "Assistance is both welcome and necessary, and surely collaboration with the laity is essential. However, the responsibility as bishops of this

Catholic Church is ours—to live with, to suffer with, and to exercise properly." The laity, in other words, are welcome to pray, and will foot the bill for the bishops' incompetence, negligence, and wickedness, but have no say otherwise. Whether the US Department of Justice will see it quite that way, or any of the more than a dozen states currently conducting or considering whether to open their own criminal probes into the conduct of senior US Church leadership, remains to be seen.

After the nuncio's remarks, Cardinal DiNardo announced his intention to lead the US bishops in discussion of their proposals. "We remain committed to the specific program of greater episcopal accountability," he said near the top of his presidential address. "Consultations will take place," he continued. "Votes will not be [cast] this week, but we will prepare ourselves to move forward for action." Cardinal DiNardo went on to say, "Whether we will be regarded as guardians of the abused or the abuser, will be determined by our actions."

When the Executive Committee leadership of the USCCB met with Pope Francis in September, and asked him to authorize a special investigation—an Apostolic Visitation—into the rise of McCarrick, Pope Francis refused. Though the Holy See never gave a reason for the refusal—never actually said the Pope had refused—the general picture that emerged in the wake of the meeting was one in which the blunderbuss procedure of USCCB leadership in announcing their intention in mid-August to request the Apostolic Visitation before talking things over with the Holy See, coupled with Archbishop Viganò's highly publicized *J'accuse!* toward the end of that month, led to Pope Francis feeling unduly pressured, not to say painted into a corner.

McCarrick is credibly accused of abusing at least one minor in St. Patrick's Cathedral and alleged to have subjected the boy who was the first child he baptized as a priest to a decade and more of sexual violence. McCarrick, now known also for his serial abuse and harassment of seminarians, nevertheless advanced to the rank of Cardinal before Francis was forced by circumstance to have his hat. Francis also suggested the bishops forego their Fall gathering entirely, in favor of a spiritual retreat.

Just to be clear: expectations from the US bishops' Fall meeting were generally low already. The proposals on the table amounted to things the bishops admit they should have been doing all along—indeed, things that no morally competent individual or group could fail to do as a matter of course. The measures were a code of conduct that CNA's editor-in-chief, JD Flynn, described as "a seven-page document in which bishops promise to do things they're mostly obliged already to do," and a reporting mechanism that had no real teeth and no real funding mechanism.

It also would have involved the apostolic nuncio as *de facto* referee. The reporting mechanism would have to report to the nuncio. If the Pope's defenders will urge that it does not appear entirely unreasonable to demand the US bishops not foist the arrangement upon the Holy See, it is at least equally reasonable to urge in response that the nuncio is already responsible for knowing what the bishops are doing in the country to which he is appointed.

If the Holy See wants to contend that the responsibility for making sure the bishops the Pope appoints do not rape, assault, abuse, harass, or otherwise mistreat any member of their flock, or condone, allow, wink at, or otherwise tolerate any mistreatment or malfeasance of any kind, should somehow be placed under terms or subject to negotiation, let the Holy See say so in words.

In any case, the nuts and bolts of the arrangement—which the US bishops' administrative committee approved on September 19—are the sort of thing the USCCB leadership and the competent curial officials could have worked out together, either in the run-up to the Baltimore gathering, or during the three days of sessions, themselves, or even subsequent to the vote. The measures would at any rate have been likely to offer precious little in the way of direct address of the core problem: not so much the bishops' failure to police their own ranks with respect to the abuse of minors and the cover-up of said abuse—appalling and egregious as that failure is—as the bishops' dereliction of their duty to foster a sane moral culture among the clergy, high and low.

Here's the point on which the whole thing hangs: neither Cardinal DiNardo, who in his presidential allocution said of himself and his fellows, "In our weakness, we fell asleep," nor Pope Francis, who has called the February meeting around the theme of "safeguarding minors" or "minors and vulnerable adults," comes close to acknowledging either the nature or the scope of the crisis. The bishops were not merely negligent: many of them were complicit. As a body, they are widely viewed as untrustworthy. Francis appears more concerned with making sure everyone understands that he's in charge, than he is with actually governing.

For the Catholic World Report, November 18, 2018

"Making sense of the USCCB fall assembly and its aftermath"

In the wake of reports that the intrusion of the Holy See on the proceedings of the USCCB fall meeting in Baltimore was even more extensive than previously understood, and that the Holy See's intrusion involved high-ranking members of the Conference in its organization and execution, frustration and outrage has increased across broad quarters of the Catholic body. Some of that frustration and outrage will inevitably result in railing and denunciation, but this moment in the life of the Church and in the US theater of the global crisis calls for cold analysis.

"Wuerl's plan"

The Archbishop-emeritus of Washington, DC (who is the current apostolic administrator of the same), Cardinal Donald W. Wuerl, and the current Archbishop of Chicago, Cardinal Blase Cupich, are the two US members of the Congregation for Bishops. That Congregation was directly responsible for conveying the "request" to USCCB leadership, that the bishops refrain from voting on reform measures at their Fall Meeting.

On Friday, Catholic News Agency reported that Cardinal Wuerl and Cardinal Cupich collaborated extensively on a proposal presented to the bishops as an alternative to the proposals on which the Holy See instructed them not to vote. "Wuerl's plan," as CNA reports it was known in the Congregation for Bishops, would have seen allegations of episcopal misconduct sent to the metropolitan archbishop, and eventually to archdiocesan review boards, with accusations against metropolitans being investigated by the senior bishops of the metropolitan's own ecclesiastical province. Basically, bishops would investigate bishops under the Wuerl-Cupich plan, with underlings investigating their bosses in case of accusation against metropolitan archbishops. And two men who are known to be the Pope's men, each with ties to Uncle Ted McCarrick, are architects of the proposal.

The US bishops gathered for their Fall Meeting did not take even a straw vote on either their original proposals, or the Wuerl-Cupich alternative, though Cardinal DiNardo did agree to appoint a task force comprised of former USCCB presidents—Cardinal Timothy Dolan, Archbishop Joseph Kurtz, and Archbishop Wilton Gregory—to develop both sets of options and give them to DiNardo to present at the meeting of the leadership of the world's bishops' conferences scheduled for February 21-24 in the Vatican.

The optics are very bad. Viewed from any vantage point, the collapse of the US Conference of Catholic Bishops beneath the weight of its members' corruption, cowardice, and incompetence is an awful thing. That circumstances, at least, make it appear quite possibly to have been aided by two men already tainted by the crisis, who also are known to be "in" with Pope Francis, does nothing to improve appearances.

The Pope's messengers

It will take a good deal of feeling around to get it, but we start well by skipping debate over optics: Pope Francis did this thing. When it comes to the leadership of the USCCB, and their ability to guide the ship through the troubled waters in which she finds herself, Pope Francis has given what is in essence an unequivocal vote of no confidence:

- He made the Conference leadership wait nearly a month for a meeting in which to make their formal request for an investigation into the rise of the disgraced former Archbishop of Washington, DC, Theodore Edgar "Uncle Ted" McCarrick;
- He rejected their request for an investigation;
- He suggested they skip their Fall Meeting entirely and hold a spiritual retreat in lieu of it;
- He "requested" they not vote on their reform proposals, even as he allowed two other major national conferences—France and Italy—to adopt their own measures.

As if in order to remove any doubt, the Apostolic Nuncio to the US, Archbishop Christophe Pierre, said in his remarks to the bishops, "If we are together, in real hierarchical communion—hierarchical communion that permeates our hearts and are not merely words—we become the visible sign of peace, unity, and love, a sign of true synodality." We all know who is at the head of that hierarchical communion. At this point, it should be clear that "true synodality" is whatever that chief hierarch says it is.

Archbishop Pierre also said, "As said from the time of diplomacy in the Greek City-States, 'Don't shoot the messenger.' (And, as a Nuncio, I can assure you it is a phrase very dear to me!)" Archbishop Pierre was in the quoted passage from his address speaking specifically to the role of the media in highlighting the failures of the bishops. Nevertheless, the message was clear: everyone in that room knew whose messenger Pierre is.

Cardinal DiNardo's attempt to place responsibility for the thing at the door to the Congregation for Bishops is not likely to convince anyone. "We are Roman Catholic bishops, in communion with our Holy Father in Rome," DiNardo told reporters on Monday afternoon. "He has people around him who are what we call congregations or offices, and we're responsible to them, in that communion of faith," he added.

Legal ramifications

In any case, the intrusion of the Holy See on the proceedings in Baltimore may have created more trouble than Francis wanted. Plaintiffs on Tuesday of last week filed a lawsuit in the United States District Court for the District of Columbia, naming both the USCCB and the Holy See as defendants in the civil RICO complaint. The Holy See has shielded itself—thus far successfully—from civil liability related to abuse, by arguing that bishops are not employees or officials of the Holy See. If the bishops are thus beholden not only to the Pope but to his central governing apparatus, it stands to reason that a lawyer might ask a court to take a closer look at the nuts and bolts of the bishops' relationship to Rome.

The US bishops' acquiescence to the Pope's "request" for a delay—it could be argued—is just the sort of thing that gets the camel's nose under the tent. Mitchell Garabedian, a Boston-based attorney who has been representing victims of clerical sexual abuse since the early 2000s, told *CWR*, "Even if the Holy See framed their order as a request, the key point is that the bishops abided by it. It tends to show a nexus of oversight." Garabedian also told *CWR*, "If the Holy See ordered the bishops not to vote on the policy measures, that would weaken the Holy See's claim that the bishops aren't agents of the Holy See." Here the legalities become complex, and depend largely on how judges decide to parse and apply standards of exception to sovereign immunity articulated in 28 USC 1605. Suffice it to say for the moment that the Holy See's action, and the US bishops' response, may have made the situation more complicated.

Bishop Christopher Coyne suggested the delay could have a salutary effect. "We in the U.S. can have a limited view of the worldwide church," Coyne told the *Washington Post*, also on Monday afternoon. "It would be difficult if we came up with [different] policies and procedures," the *Post* also quotes him as saying. Why that would be difficult at all, and why any eventual difficulties in that line should be insurmountable, are things Bishop Coyne left unexplored.

Ecclesial geometry

How that squares with Pope Francis's view of the Church as a polyhedron, is not entirely clear. "[O]ur model [for the Church] is not the sphere, which is no greater than its parts, where every point is equidistant from the center, and there are no differences between them," Pope Francis writes in paragraph 236 of Evangelii gaudium. "Instead," he continues, "it is the polyhedron, which reflects the convergence of all its parts, each of which preserves its distinctiveness."

We know Francis allowed the French bishops to vote on reform measures last week, which included an independent investigation of their conduct with respect to clerical abuse since 1950. We also know he allowed the Italian bishops to vote on their own safeguarding measures at an extraordinary plenary that took place at the Vatican and roughly in concurrence with the US bishops' gathering in Baltimore. Neither the Pope, nor the bishops, can have it both ways: which is it going to be?

Most of the drama played in the first ten working minutes of the first public session on Monday morning, when USCCB President Daniel Cardinal DiNardo—who faces his own difficulties in his See of Galveston-Houston—announced that Rome had "requested" the bishops not vote on measures designed to protect the young and the vulnerable from the predations of evil bishops and secure a measure of episcopal accountability with regard to their duties of oversight and governance.

Three days of mostly scripted theatre ensued. The various interventions made, and positions staked, are amply documented. They require no rehearsal here. They terminated in a vote on the following measure:

> Regarding the ongoing investigation of the Holy See into the case of Archbishop McCarrick, be it resolved that the bishops of the USCCB encourage the Holy See to release soon all documentation that can be released consistent with canon and civil law regarding the allegations of misconduct against Archbishop McCarrick.

In case the reader has not heard by now, the bishops punted. Perhaps more closely, but still in the sporting metaphor, they called a play on fourth down, then snapped the ball, and took a knee. The vote was 83-137, with three abstentions. They could not bring themselves to ask the Holy See to share the documents it uncovers during its unsupervised internal audit of its own McCarrick files. If the bishops cannot break their thrall to their umbrella organization, and their paralysis within the warped culture of cronyism that structure fosters from top to bottom, all under the more general rubric of collegiality, it will likely be their undoing. It may already have been.

Voices raised

It is true that, from the floor, a few bishops noted the cultural rot. Bishop Stephen Biegler of Cheyenne addressed what he called a culture of "toxic brotherhood" fostered under the guise of collegiality:

Some bishops fostered a "toxic brotherhood" which caused them to overlook questionable behavior, ignore rumors of problems, believe clerical denials and seek to preserve a cleric's ability to minister. At times, they acted to protect the reputation of the Church or clergy, while they shunned the victims/survivors of sexual abuse and their families. Bishops frequently ignored the voices of the laity who spoke up about sexual abuse and the mishandling of allegations; instead, they acted within institutional isolation.

That is all true. The problem with the statement is that it employed the wrong verb tense. There was plenty of each index of toxicity on display during the three days' deliberations in Baltimore. None was more egregious than the speech of the Archbishop-emeritus of Los Angeles, Roger Cardinal Mahony. It was beyond farcical to hear the bishops wonder aloud how they would have treated Uncle Ted if he had dared show his face at the meeting, when they welcomed Mahony and gave him a respectful hearing.

Bishop Shawn McKnight has received praise for some forceful words he spoke on the sidelines of the Baltimore meeting, and others he wrote in the wake of it. "At the time of this writing, there has not been one bishop, archbishop or cardinal in either the Holy See or the United States who has come forward on his own to repent publicly of his sins of omission or commission with regard to Archbishop McCarrick's series of promotions over decades," wrote McKnight—who was consecrated and installed in his See of Jefferson City, Missouri, only this past February—in a letter to the faithful of his diocese, which he posted to his diocesan website after returning from Baltimore.

"Please, be men, not cowards, and come clean on your own!" McKnight exhorted his brethren in a letter not addressed to them, a letter written from his own See, to which he had just returned after several days in the bishops' company. "There doesn't have to be a formal and long, drawn out investigation," McKnight also noted in the letter, "for a bishop to exercise a little compunction and concern for the well-being of the whole Church."

Lack of will

Awful as l'Affaire McCarrick doubtless is, McCarrick is only the worst of the lot—the worst we know of, at any rate. Bishop Richard Malone of Buffalo sat with the other bishops, and received not a single call from the floor to answer for himself, though he is credibly accused of grossly mishandling several cases in his diocese.

The head of the US Bishops' National Review Board, Francesco Cesareo—a layman and president of Assumption College in Worcester, Ma.—told the bishops, "While much of the guilt has been placed on priests, bishops have often escaped punishment." He went on to say, "As more information is publicized regarding the inappropriate handling of abuse by bishops, it remains clear that some bishops have escaped the consequences of their acts of omission regarding abuse, and that little is being done to address this injustice." The problem is not a want of information at this point, but a lack of will.

The Bishops of the Missouri Province wrote a blunt, direct letter to Bishop Timothy L. Doherty of Lafayette, Indiana, who is Chairman of the US Bishops' Committee for the Protection of Children and Young People. Their letter was dated October 6. They made it public on November 12, after the Holy See spiked the US Bishops' proposals. "The McCarrick scandal has shaken not only the confidence of Catholics," the Missouri bishops wrote, "but also of others who look to our Church for moral guidance." They went on to say, "It is our moral obligation to acknowledge the negative consequences of a pastoral strategy of silence and inaction in the face of such a horrific scandal that is so widely known."

"The very credibility of the Church has already been seriously damaged by a persistent silence and inaction over many decades," the Missouri bishops said—and they are not wrong.

Morality and monsters

Nevertheless, the almost exclusive focus on the corporate moral obligation of all the bishops together elides the duty of each bishop toward the same. So long as the bishops insist on acting only or even primarily as a body, the bishops deserve—in justice—to be judged according to the worst of their lot. The worst of their lot are monsters, though there is still a general clerical unwillingness to admit even that. The president of the University of Notre Dame, Fr. John Jenkins, CSC, drew significant flak last week for some comments he made regarding Uncle Ted McCarrick specifically, and the broad crisis, generally.

In an exclusive interview with *Crux*, he said, "There's a tendency, and I don't think it's a helpful tendency in this kind of situation, to turn the perpetrators into monsters." Jenkins went on to say, "[The tendency is] just to imagine that they are thoroughly corrupt people, but the problem is that it's not true. It's a part of their lives that is deeply problematic, but another part that is not."

"That's why it's so hard to identify the problem," Fr. Jenkins added, "and sometimes, that person doesn't seem to see the problem."

Fr. Jenkins's line reminded me of a conversation many years ago—a typical newsroom shop session—in which we were talking about the classification of Hamas as a terrorist organization. "Well, it seems pretty straightforward to me," I said roughly, "they kill civilians on purpose and break things to make a political point." One of my interlocutors responded, roughly, "It's more complicated than that," adding, "they run maternity clinics and distribute medicine, baby formula, and the like." I responded, "There's nothing complicated about that: Hamas are terrorists who run maternity clinics and distribute medicine, baby formula, and the like."

Many of us expect our devils to appear as great cloven-hoofed beasts: mouths dripping, tails lashing, pitchforks poised. In reality, the Devil appears most often and most dangerously as "a man of wealth and taste": a "lover" of exquisite things and a "friend" who is a fixer; a gregarious chap, at once familiar and powerful. The Devil, in short, looks like Uncle Ted McCarrick. When he finds himself up a tree, he will adopt all sorts of guises. Most often, though, he will feign ineptitude and attempt to lull those who have treed him into complacency, if not to elicit their pity.

The Devil, in short, often looks like Ted McCarrick—and when he's in a bind, he looks and acts like Verbal Kint.

"How ordinary Catholics can respond to the Church's crisis"

At risk of sounding like a scratched disc: the crisis in which the Catholic Church is embroiled at present is global, protracted, and persistent. The institutional interests driving it are also deeply entrenched. What the response of the laity ought to be in our circumstances is difficult to discern. Ultimately, there will be as many responses as there are lay people in the Church. What is certain is that we all have a role to play.

Broadly and generally, some outline of appropriate response—individual and corporate—is available: the corporal and spiritual Works of Mercy. The suggestion sounds trite. Consider it nonetheless. The Works of Mercy are duties to which each Christian is called by virtue of Baptism, hence they are the corporate responsibility of all the baptized faithful. As such, every Christian—including any group of Christians formed of set purpose—has *eo ipso* all the rights necessary and applicable to the discharge of the corresponding duties. We require neither the permission, nor the direction of bishops, when it comes to feeding the hungry, clothing the naked, sheltering the homeless, welcoming the stranger, visiting the imprisoned, caring for the sick, or even burying the dead (though clerics are especially useful when it comes to those last two).

Likewise, the instruction of the ignorant, counsel of the doubtful, admonishment of sinners, patience in bearing wrongs, forgiveness of offences, comfort of the afflicted, and prayer for the living and the dead, are all things to which every Christian is as such already called, and for which we are all basically prepared (though some of us have special preparation for specific kinds of work, and all of us will be better at some things than at others—and although the bishops' exercise of it often leaves us wanting, if not consternated, they do have authority to say what the Faith of the Church is).

There are also already existing structures and enterprises of charity, independent of the bishops though animated by Christian—indeed Catholic—zeal and sense of missionary purpose, which are not only prepared to receive our time and treasure, but anxious to receive them.

If this crisis is a struggle for the soul of the Church—and it is—it is also a power struggle: too much power over too many areas of life either not proper to the mission for which the bishops' office is given, nor directly applicable to the essential ends of their power, has been ceded to bishops with too much willingness and too little oversight over far too long a period of time. All this will be messy, for sure—and there will be missteps—but then, if it were necessary, we have been exhorted repeatedly by the highest authority in the Church to make a mess, and not to be afraid to get ourselves dirty. If the hierarchical leadership expect the laity to "pray, pay, and obey," then we might as well give them what they ask of us—only, they might be surprised, as often happens, when they get the things for which they asked. We are also told that ours is a God of surprises: it will be interesting to see what effect the surprise has, when the shoe is on the bishops' other foot.

In the meantime, we can—we must—tell our bishops what we want of them: transparency, justice, genuine pastoral solicitude, basic decency. We should make it clear that we demand these things as ours of right, not as favors. We should, in short, make it clear to them that they owe us an account of themselves, and that we are no more willing to suffer goats in shepherds' clothing than we are prepared to tolerate wolves in the same.

For the Catholic World Report, November 23, 2018

"The Vatican obfuscates even while preparing for February meeting on abuse"

The Vatican finally announced the members of the organizing committee responsible for preparing the meeting of the heads of the world's bishops' conferences this coming February 21-24. Most of the early reaction and attention has been on the membership of the organizing committee: Cardinal Blase "The Pope has a bigger agenda" Cupich of Chicago is a conspicuous presence, while Cardinal Seán O'Malley, OFM Cap, the President of the Pontifical Commission for the Protection of Minors and Vulnerable Adults, is rather conspicuous by his absence.

Cupich is a known Papal favorite, and at the center of controversy over the recent spiking of the US bishops' proposals, which were supposed to get a vote at the recent plenary meeting in Baltimore. O'Malley is a member of the C9 Council of Cardinal-Advisers, in addition to his role as President of the Commission for the Protection of Minors. He has criticized Pope Francis publicly for his treatment of abuse victims in Chile, and faced criticism for his inept handling of a letter detailing some of the strange proclivities of the depraved and now disgraced former Archbishop of Washington, Theodore Edgar "Uncle Ted" McCarrick.

A statement from Cardinal O'Malley issued early Friday afternoon in Boston essentially takes credit for the idea of holding the meeting, and made clear that he will, in some capacity, be taking part:

> The proposal for such a meeting was developed by the Pontifical Commission for the Protection of Minors, was reviewed by the Council of Cardinals and subsequently accepted by the Holy Father. I am pleased that this meeting has been convoked by the Holy Father and I look forward to participating.

It requires no stretch of the imagination to believe the idea for the February meeting did not originate with Pope Francis. The wording of the February meeting's announcement made it sound to this Vatican Watcher as though the C9—facing serious troubles of its own—had to twist the Pope's arm to get him to do anything at all.

The inclusion of Cupich is theater, but the real story is elsewhere: in the stated purpose of the meeting, and in the talking points Fr. Hans Zöllner hit in his interview with official Vatican media outlets, which was released in concert with the announcement from the Press Office of the Holy See on Friday. "As the Holy Father wrote in the letter to the People of God," Fr. Zöllner told Vatican News and *L'Osservatore Romano*:

> [W]e feel shame when we realize that our style of life has denied, and continues to deny, the words we recite. With shame and repentance, we acknowledge as an ecclesial community that we were not where

we should have been, that we did not act in a timely manner, realizing the magnitude and the gravity of the damage done to so many lives.

Neither the Vatican, nor the world's bishops, simply found themselves someplace else. The problem is not that the Vatican or the world's bishops "did not act in a timely manner," nor is it that they failed to realize "the magnitude and the gravity of the damage done to so many lives." Bishops—and evidence suggests Popes among the bishops—were not merely slow to cotton to the magnitude and gravity of the damage done. They were complicit in it.

What's more, the theme of the meeting is "the protection of minors in the Church"—a worthy cause and a needful thing—but what we most need from bishops is accountability, transparency, and readiness to foster a sane moral culture among the clergy, high and low. The whole reason we are in this unholy mess in the first place is that the bishops have proven themselves incapable of any of that.

There are also the promises and assurances, repeated *ad nauseam*—this time by Fr. Zöllner in the aforementioned interview with Vatican media—that the Pope is really serious about this:

> The Holy See reiterated this clearly: "Both abuse and its cover-up can no longer be tolerated and a different treatment for Bishops who have committed or covered up abuse, in fact represents a form of clericalism that is no longer acceptable."

If that is so, why did Pope Francis rehabilitate Cardinal Danneels? For that matter, why is Cardinal Ezzati still in his See? Or Bishop Malone in his?

Francis's handling of the lavender Mafia within the Vatican also begs to differ. One would have to be blind not to see the infiltration of clerical ranks—even in the episcopate, even in the Roman Curia—by active homosexuals for whom their collars are little more than cover. Such men are not abusers of children, in the main, though they do lead disorderly lives, and they do use their position within the clergy to fund their depraved purposes, shield their perverse proclivities, and recruit men into their nefarious ranks.

The Prefect of the Congregation for Bishops, Cardinal Marc Ouellet, admitted as much in his reply to the former Apostolic Nuncio to the United States, Archbishop Carlo Maria Vigano:

> [T]he fact that there may be persons in the Vatican who practice and support behavior contrary to Gospel values regarding sexuality, does not authorize us to generalize and declare this or that person as unworthy and as accomplices, even including the Holy Father himself. Should not the ministers of truth be the first to avoid calumny and defamation themselves?

Ministers of truth ought to be the first to avoid calumny and defamation. Truth, however, is a defense against slander. (So, why not try Viganò?) The accusations Archbishop Viganò leveled against the character and proclivities of men in the Curia may be misplaced. If they are, then true and genuine solicitude for their good names should compel the Holy

See to vindicate them with more than a nasty letter from an underling.

In any case, Cardinal Ouellet's riposte still not only concedes the broad point about the presence of a so-called "lavender Mafia" inside the Curia, but also demonstrates a rather cavalier attitude toward it and its members—as if it were no concern of the Vatican unless the hapless official in question gets himself convicted of a go-to-jail felony. In the case of Msgr. Pietro Amenta—erstwhile judge on the Roman Rota—that's what it took, and even then, he was allowed to resign shortly before copping a plea to escape jail time.

"Give him time," urged Archbishop Charles Scicluna of Malta, referring to Pope Francis, when asked on the sidelines of the October synod what the faithful ought to do in the face of burgeoning crisis and apparent paralysis at the highest echelons of Church governance. Francis has given himself until February.

"Cupich and Scicluna hit their talking points, but are silent on key problems"

Two significant interviews dropped late last week, in which key figures in the organization of the upcoming meeting of the heads of the world's bishops' conferences on the theme of child protection gave their views of the gathering, its scope, and their hopes for its outcomes. Cardinal Blase Cupich of Chicago spoke with *Crux*, while Archbishop Charles Scicluna of Malta—recently named adjunct secretary to the Congregation for the Doctrine of the Faith—spoke with *America*. Both sets of remarks are revealing, and merit close attention.

Both men hit all the talking points. "In addition to [its] being a crime," Cardinal Cupich told *Crux*, "sexual abuse of minors by clerics is about the corruption of our ministry." Archbishop Scicluna told *America*, "[S]exual abuse of minors is not only an egregious phenomenon in itself and a crime, but it is also a very grave symptom of something deeper, which is actually a crisis in the way we approach ministry." Scicluna went on to say, "Some call it clericalism, others call it a perversion of the ministry."

Tick one.

The problem is also global. "[T]his is a global issue, it is not a case of geographical or cultural criteria, rather it is a global issue which the church would want to approach with a united front, with respect for the different cultures but with a united resolve and with people being on the same page on it," Archbishop Scicluna said. "It's important to note that by calling a global meeting he understands this to be a global issue, and he wants to reinforce our shared commitment as a church to establishing responsiveness, accountability, and transparency," offered Cardinal Cupich.

Tick two.

Pope Francis understands the problem, too. "Time and again he has shown that he sees the protection of children and the accompaniment of those who have been harmed as a priority of the whole people of God and central to our mission," said Cardinal Cupich. "[H]e realizes that this issue," i.e. clergy sexual abuse of minors, "has to be top on the Church's agenda," offered Archbishop Scicluna.

Tick three.

They were also careful to manage expectations. "[T]his meeting has to be understood as part of a long-term commitment to reform, realizing that one meeting will not solve every issue," said Cardinal Cupich. "[I]t is a very important start of a global process which will take quite some time to perfect," offered Scicluna.

Tick four.

The approach to the "phenomenon" will be at once universal, and culture-appropriate, hence active at different levels of the Church. "[A] number of initiatives on a continental level will start to happen that will re-create the atmosphere of resolve, determination but also purpose which I hope will mark the Rome meeting," said Archbishop Scicluna, all in order, "to address the issues in a different number of cultures, that have their own restraints, their own important positive aspects but also deficits that have to be discussed on a continental but also local level." Cardinal Cupich offered, "Of course, assuring [mistakes] are not repeated will require all levels of the Church to take responsibility—local, regional, national, and universal."

Tick five.

Note also the mention of specific initiatives. Archbishop Scicluna more than hinted at what some of them might be. "[A] stronger role for the metropolitan bishops," was one— something for which Cardinal Cupich has advocated *in separata sede* and to which he strongly alluded in his remarks quoted above. "[A] bigger role for the victims in canonical penal processes," was another Archbishop Scicluna named, though he demurred on whether there would be any changes in these directions as a direct result of the February meeting.

Conspicuously absent from the conversation of both men, was any address of the secrecy of canonical process, for either priests or bishops accused of abuse, cover-up, negligence, or other involvement in criminal activity. Throughout both Cardinal Cupich's and Archbishop Scicluna's remarks, there is discernible a persistent attitude of denial regarding the role of the bishops in the ongoing crisis. Both Cardinal Cupich and Archbishop Scicluna assume—at least in the published remarks reviewed here—that the bishops are ready and willing to be part of the solution, while both Churchmen also consistently misidentify the nature and scope of the crisis, and significantly downplay the bishops' responsibility for getting us to where we are in it.

We hear several times from both men of the horror of sexual abuse of minors, but when we hear of cultural reform, it is in regard to macro-level questions in particular—though not better identified—geographical regions and the corresponding ecclesiastical jurisdictions. There is virtually no acknowledgment of the extent of the rot, much less of the bishops' active role in spreading it.

It is abundantly clear, however, that Pope Francis is very much in charge. "[W]e cannot avoid the important theological aspect that we bishops are stewards in a hierarchical communion together with the Holy Father," said Archbishop Scicluna to *America*, "and so there is a jurisdiction of the Holy Father over each and every one of us bishops that we have to respect when we talk of accountability within the context of the Roman Catholic Church." In his conversation with *Crux*, Cardinal Cupich said the meeting's organizing committee is, "committed to achieving specific outcomes from this meeting that reflect the mind of Pope Francis." Couched that way, the question becomes: if the Holy Father is ultimately responsible—and he is—and the purpose of the meeting is to reflect the mind of Pope Francis—and one supposes the chief organizer will know that—then, why hold it at all?

The meeting is being billed as the beginning of a global movement directed from the top to change hearts and minds among the hierarchical leadership, so they really can start to get their heads around how awful child sexual abuse really is—while it almost completely ignores—whether carefully, or downright blithely—the unspoken supposition on which the entire program rests: the world's bishops need to be convinced of this.

For all their talk of cultural change—and there is a good bit of it—there is next to no readily apparent recognition of the cultural problem that needs changing: the bishops, who are the overseers of the Church, are deeply invested in maintaining the untenable status quo, in which the bishops themselves exercise all the power, control all the money, and make all the decisions; while the lower ranks of the clergy are taught systematically, from their first day of seminary, to keep their heads down and their mouths shut, as the price of their portion in a system and a culture designed for corruption. After hearing these two leading Churchmen tell it, one gets the impression the February gathering is shaping up to be, at best, another one of those meetings that should have been an e-mail.

For the Catholic Herald, November 30, 2018

"Cardinal Müller seeks the middle ground between Viganò and the Vatican"

Cardinal Gerhard Müller may no longer be the Vatican's doctrinal chief, but since being relieved of his position he has become, if anything, more outspoken. In recent days he has given two in-depth interviews, one to *Life Site News* and one to *La Stampa*. Those publications are generally seen as coming from opposite "sides" of the Church, and the content of the interviews suggests that Cardinal Müller may be trying to chart a third way through the troubled waters in which the Church finds herself at present.

On the one hand, the cardinal in effect criticized Archbishop Carlo Maria Viganò, whose spectacular *J'Accuse!* in August called for the Pope's resignation. "No one has the right to indict the Pope or ask him to resign," Cardinal Müller told *La Stampa*, following and adopting the precise juridical language—*stato di accusa*—in which interviewer Andrea Tornielli's initial question was couched. For Müller, the Viganò dossier overstepped the bounds of submission to the Pope.

On the other hand, the cardinal's interview with *Life Site News* showed that Müller is ready to criticize the Pope over the McCarrick Affair, if only provisionally and indirectly.

Müller said the Vatican under John Paul II should have investigated the rumors against McCarrick, and should not have made him a cardinal and Archbishop of Washington, DC. But he also told *Life Site* that the "involved Church authorities" had questions to answer, if it is true that the Vatican knew of McCarrick's misdeeds and that he nevertheless became a papal counselor:

> [W]hen there even has already been paid some hush money—and with it, the admission of his sexual crimes with young men—then every reasonable person asks how such a person can be a counselor of the Pope with regard to episcopal appointments. I do not know whether this is true, but it would need to be clarified. The hireling helps in the search of good shepherds for God's fold—nobody can understand this. In such a case, there should very clearly come out a public explanation about these events and the personal connections, as well as the question as to how much the involved Church authorities knew at each step; such an explanation could very well include an admission of a wrong assessment of persons and situations.

Taken together, the two interviews tend toward a position which argues that Viganò overreached, while acknowledging the substantial concerns to which the McCarrick Affair gives rise—even epitomizes—and calls for a real inquiry into them and a public explanation.

Müller's interventions attempt to chart a course that will be acceptable both to those scandalized by what they see as Viganò's intemperance, and to the increasingly numerous ranks of faithful fed up with what they see as obfuscation from Church leadership. Perhaps Cardinal Müller's remarks intend his "third way" to take the wind out of the sails of the extreme wings of both camps, populated and controlled by Team Francis partisans and anti-Francis reactionaries respectively. This was suggested by another comment he made to *La Stampa*. "We must all work together to overcome this crisis, which harms the credibility of the Church," the cardinal said. "Unfortunately, we have these groups, these 'parties'—the so-called 'progressives' and 'conservatives'. We are all united in the revealed faith, and not by the prejudices of political ideologies. We are not a political entity."

CHAPTER 6

IN THE EYE OF
THE STORM

December 2018 – January 2019

For the Catholic World Report, December 11, 2018

"February meeting at the Vatican needs to address directly the crisis of leadership"

By refusing to assist the US bishops in their investigation of Archbishop McCarrick, and then ordering the US bishops to delay any corporate action to achieve a measure of accountability (and stop the massive hemorrhage of credibility with the faithful, civil authorities, and the public), until after the February 21-24 gathering of the heads of the world's bishops' conferences, the Vatican really has raised the stakes on the February meeting.

At the same time, the meeting's principal organizers have attempted to lower expectations. "[The February meeting] is a very important start of a global process which will take quite some time to perfect," Archbishop Charles Scicluna of Malta—recently named adjunct secretary to the Congregation for the Doctrine of the Faith and a leading organizer of the gathering in February—told *America* Magazine shortly after the Vatican announced he would lead the organizing committee.

By calling it the beginning of a process, one may also detect an attempt to escape, if not to erase the past, take back promises, or otherwise rewrite history, rife as it is with protestations to the effect that Church leaders—including

Pope Francis—really get it now, and replete with assurances
they're going to do better. As Phil Lawler pointed out in a
terse commentary on the announcement, "[A]ll those times
in the past, when we've been told that the all-out response
was underway, it actually hadn't even begun?"

The "process" has begun, in fits and starts, and with more
help from Caesar than anyone wants—in places ranging
from Chile to Ireland to the US, the Philippines, and now to
Germany, not to mention the Pope's own native Argentina.
Nor will it do for the Pope or his lieutenants to protest that
they need to get everyone on the same page, before letting
any bishops anywhere have any sort of go.

"Many [bishops from the developing world, particularly
the global south] are convinced that their cultures don't har-
bor the problem to the same extent, and they resent the way
that Western discussions of abuse scandals overshadow their
own concerns and priorities," Crux's editor-in-chief, John
Allen, wrote in an analysis piece this past Sunday. He's right.
"They question the need for their nations to make a priority
out of something many of them regard as a geographically
and culturally limited phenomenon," Allen continues, right
once more. Francis, however, should know how perception
in these regards does not always line up with reality. He was,
by his own admission, part of the problem.

It would be easy to get into the weeds at this point, especially if one were to indulge the temptation to explore even
a few of the ways in which the Pope's preferred polyhedral
(or prism) model of the Church could apply to the current
crisis, and his handling of it. Suffice it to say that uniformity

is not always to be desired, and almost never—to hear Pope Francis tell it, anyway—to be imposed:

> [N]ot all discussions of doctrinal, moral or pastoral issues need to be settled by interventions of the magisterium. Unity of teaching and practice is certainly necessary in the Church, but this does not preclude various ways of interpreting some aspects of that teaching or drawing certain consequences from it. (*Amoris laetitia*, 3)

In that passage, Pope Francis was primarily concerned with teaching. The crisis of leadership in the Catholic Church is a problem of governance. That is to say, with precisely those practical consequences of doctrine, over which there can and indeed must be plenty of room for legitimate difference.

Just how much difference is legitimate, will always be a matter of tension if not contention, and that is one of the reasons we have the authority of Peter in the Church. But to say that the Church in the United States, for example, ought not address the burning question of episcopal accountability at all, because bishops in other jurisdictions do not have the same problems to the same extent—or do not perceive that they do—ignores the bishops' duty to care. That is the fact of the matter, even as it flies in the face of the Pope's own statements on the proper mechanics of governance, betrays a callousness to the needs of the faithful, and frankly beggars common sense.

For one thing, anyone who needs a three days' meeting in Rome to learn that raping children is wrong and aiding and abetting it either before or after the fact is in many respects worse, should not only not be a bishop, but should not be in Orders at all. Indeed, anyone who doesn't get that is unfit for decent society. For another, the evils plaguing the US hierarchy are not limited to the capitally gruesome realities of child abuse and cover-up, but include entrenched networks of corrupt and morally bankrupt clerics, high and low, as well as endemic cowardice even among those not guilty of the worst crimes, or any crimes at all.

If there are bishops in some parts of the world, who do understand that these things are enormities, but have a hard time getting their heads around the extent to which the practice of them has affected the life of the Church in other places, then that's more reason not to insist on waiting where there is a need for action that has gone unmet for generations. Nevertheless, the idea that Catholics in some places plagued by these evils will just have to wait for bishops in other jurisdictions to be brought up to speed, is the message Catholics in the United States have received, and it is a message not lost on Catholics wherever the crisis has come to the attention of the faithful and the broad public. It is a message driven home for Catholics in the United States by the double blow of the Vatican's refusal to assist in the US bishops' attempt to fathom the depth and breadth of the rot spreading from McCarrick's forty years' malign presence, and the heavy-handed intrusion on the US bishops' recent business in Baltimore.

Neither Pope Francis nor his handlers and lieutenants in the Vatican can have it both ways. They cannot arrest responses already underway and announce they're taking the reins, and in the same breath announce they're pulling those reins in—let alone beg leave to tinker with their own takes on the crisis. That, however, is the path they have chosen. The upshot of all this, however, is that the US bishops have, indeed, been hamstrung: forced to wait more than three months before they can attempt to do what they were going to do anyway.

When they are finally let off the leash, they will be operating under strictures: tethered to an appraisal of the crisis designed for bishops, who either haven't the same skin in the game, or will have only very recently discovered how much they do have in it, or are working in very different sociopolitical and cultural environments.

"It is more important to start processes than to dominate spaces," Pope Francis advises parents in *Amoris laetitia*. Apparently unwilling to admit he's missed the chance to do the former, he seems now bent on the latter.

For the Catholic World Report, December 23, 2018

"Pope's remarks to Curia on abuse more of the same"

"To those who abuse minors I would say this: convert and hand yourself over to human justice, and prepare for divine justice." Those were the words upon which reporters rightly seized, and from which headline writers took to craft their hooks, when Pope Francis delivered his annual "state of the Church" address to senior officials of the Roman Curia on Friday. The words echoed Pope St. John Paul II's passionate denunciation of organized criminals delivered on May 9, 1993. "In the name of the crucified and risen Christ, who is the way, the truth and the life," Pope John Paul II intoned in remarks to the faithful gathered in the Sicilian city of Agrigento, "be converted, one day the judgment of God will come!"

One significant difference is that John Paul II's remarks were extemporaneous, turgid with genuine ire, delivered in the midst of a mafia terror campaign that had already claimed the lives of two high-profile anti-mafia prosecutors, Giovanni Falcone and Paolo Borsellino, and would see more attacks later that same year in Rome, Florence, and Milan. Pope Francis's remarks two days ago were studied, calculated, scripted. More to the point, Francis is rather better positioned to assist the clerics guilty of abuse in coming to face human justice, than was his sainted predecessor to help members of *la cosa nostra* come into the reach of the same. If Francis had given Friday's speech—at least that section of it—in 2013, and followed it with concrete action taken swiftly and transparently, things might be different.

Then again, he did say similar things in 2013. "Act decisively as far as cases of sexual abuse are concerned," Pope Francis urged then-Prefect of the Congregation for the Doctrine of the Faith, Cardinal Gerhard Müller, "promoting, above all, measures to protect minors, help for those who have suffered such violence in the past [and] the necessary procedures against those who are guilty."

Almost exactly a year later, in off-the-cuff remarks, Francis told the International Catholic Child Bureau, BICE, "I feel compelled to personally assume all the evil which some priests—really quite a number, but not in proportion to the total number—to assume the burden myself and to ask for forgiveness for the harm they have done for having sexually abused children."

"The Church is aware of this damage," Pope Francis continued. "It is a personal, moral damage carried out by men of the Church, and we will not take one step backward concerning the treatment of this problem and the sanctions that must be imposed," he said. "On the contrary, I believe that we have to be very strong. There is no messing around when it comes to children!"

In 2015, in Philadelphia, Pope Francis said, "The crimes and sins of sexual abuse of minors may no longer be kept secret." Francis went on to renew his promises of zealous watchfulness. "I commit myself to ensuring that the Church makes every effort to protect minors and I promise that those responsible will be held to account," he said.

2015 was also the year Pope Francis appointed Bishop Juan Barros to lead the Diocese of Osorno, Chile, against the counsel of the Chilean bishops and over the objections of the faithful, who suffered as a result of his obstinacy. "[The Church in] Osorno suffers, because she is stupid," Pope Francis explained to pilgrims on the sidelines of a General Audience in May of that year.

In 2016, Pope Francis made it clear that the most vocal member of his Commission for the Protection of Minors, the Australian abuse survivor and victim-advocate, Peter Saunders, would not be welcome on the body anymore. Stories like the one by papal biographer Paul Vallely in the *Guardian* under the headline, "Is the pope serious about confronting child abuse?" began to appear.

In 2017, frustrated with its lack of progress, another abuse survivor, Ireland's Marie Collins, quit the Commission for the Protection of Minors. It became apparent that the special court Pope Francis had established to prosecute wayward and negligent bishops and religious superiors would not be sitting, after all. A mere rehearsal of events in 2018 would run the length of a book.

Hearing Pope Francis say what he said last Friday, at the end of a week in which we learned the extent of his own Jesuit order's commitment to policies of foisting abusers on Native American populations and hiding abusers on a college campus (that last a policy of which Francis's hand-picked adviser and one of the principal organizers for the upcoming February meeting on child protection, Cardinal Blase Cupich of Chicago, knew and apparently failed to mention to his successor in his former see of Spokane): as well as of the egregious failure of Church leadership in Illinois to report the names of some five hundred accused priests, or even investigate many of the claims against them; on the very day we heard news of criticism from other of the Pope's closest collaborators over an appeals panel Francis established, which has reduced penalties imposed on priests found guilty of sexual abuse at canonical trial in the first instance; the words fall rather flat.

That so many miscarriages were a matter of policy makes other of Pope Francis's protestations in the "state of the Church" speech Friday simply incredible. "It is undeniable," Pope Francis said, "that some in the past, out of irresponsibility, disbelief, lack of training, inexperience, or spiritual and human short-sightedness, treated many cases without the seriousness and promptness that was due." Some, certainly, of the thousands of claims later deemed credible, were ones Church leaders mishandled out of irresponsibility, disbelief, lack of training, inexperience, or spiritual and human short-sightedness.

Even then, however, Church leaders did not simply treat cases without the seriousness and promptness they were due. Bishops actively sought to protect themselves and their priests—resorting even to intimidation, victim-blaming, and character-assassination. When they knew a man was guilty, they moved him, hid him, did almost anything to shield him from public authority and themselves from public scrutiny.

That self-regard and concern for "the institution" continues, poisonously, in the culture of the Church's hierarchical
leadership, along with a tendency to tout their achievements
in finally taking measures to prevent evils they never should
have allowed to occur in the first place. "The Charter is
working," the US bishops tell us, time and again. Except
when it doesn't. Those the charter is not designed to protect
are on their own. Ask Bishop Malone, in Buffalo. Ask the
sheep of his flock. Ask a seminarian, if you can find one of
the handful willing to talk.

"Let it be clear that before these abominations the Church
will spare no effort to do all that is necessary to bring to justice whosoever has committed such crimes," Pope Francis
also said. "The Church will never seek to hush up or not
take seriously any case," Pope Francis promised. He said this,
with a straight face, the very week it came to light that a
priest with settled allegations against him had been saying
Mass in New York and San Diego until the story of Archdiocesan payouts to his alleged victims was about to break.

This was the same week we learned of an auxiliary bishop
appointed during the reign of Pope St. John Paul II (and
during the tenure of the notorious Archbishop emeritus of
Los Angeles, Cardinal Roger Mahony). It turns out Bishop
Alexander Salazar had served for thirteen years with Vatican-
imposed "restrictions" on his ministry as a result of the allegations against him. If Francis thinks accepting Salazar's
resignation after the LA archdiocesan review board found
the allegation credible is sufficient proof of earnest, he is
mistaken.

The hard fact is, Pope Francis's talk is just that: talk. There has been a lot of it. There has been enough of it.

"2018 in review: the Church's annus horribilis"

2018 has been *annus horribilis* for the Catholic Church. There's no point mincing our words. The mere rehearsal of the major disasters would run the length of a volume. An exhaustive list of the missteps and failures starting or ending at the Vatican would require a hefty tome. From the explosion of the abuse-and-coverup crisis—in Pope Francis's face, at the end of January—the worldwide body of the faithful has been treated to a relentless succession of half-measures, publicity stunts, and increasingly incredible promises of earnest coming from the Pope and the Vatican. None has been minimally sufficient, let alone satisfactory.

The talk from the Pope and the Vatican regarding the abuse-and-coverup crisis has been equally relentless. It is boring, by now, and that is a problem on its own. The talk, however, is not the worst thing about the past year. The worst thing about the past year has been the double-talk.

Whether it concerns parsing of the difference between "proof" and "evidence"—a subtle distinction, to be sure—or the caviling of "pardon"—if Francis has not pardoned anyone guilty of abuse, he has previously reduced the sentences imposed and even restored men to the clerical state, who had been penally laicized—he has been artful, rather than frank and direct. Meanwhile, questions that arose when the generational crisis became a current scandal touching Pope Francis, remain unanswered.

There is the fate of the letter Juan Carlos Cruz wrote, supposedly hand-delivered to Pope Francis in 2015 by his hand-picked President of the Pontifical Council for the Protection of Minors, Cardinal Seán Patrick O'Malley, OFM. Francis publicly stated in 2018 that no witnesses had ever come forward to bring him evidence of Bishop Juan Barros's misdeeds in relation to his mentor, Fernando Karadima. An adequate explanation for the apparent discrepancy remains wanting.

There is the question of Francis's knowledge of the character and proclivities of the disgraced Archbishop McCarrick, and the date Francis became aware of them. Legitimate questions remain outstanding as to the extent of papal and curial involvement in promoting and protecting McCarrick and other churchmen. Francis has repeatedly promised to be transparent, and consistently failed to be forthright.

However, Pope Francis has taken several bold steps in other areas, the most significant of which is his rapprochement with China. He took a beating in the press over the agreement with the Chinese government, the precise terms of which have yet to be disclosed officially, but apparently involve significant involvement of Chinese authorities in the choice of bishops. Whether the arrangement will prove workable in the long run obviously remains to be seen, but the short-term cost has already been high.

The end of the year also saw major news on the diplomatic front: Pope Francis will be the first reigning pontiff to visit the Arabian Peninsula—and celebrate a public Mass—when he goes to the United Arab Emirates in January. He is well-regarded in the country, the population of which is overwhelmingly composed of foreign guest-workers, nearly a million of whom are Catholic. Whatever comes of the visit, the fact it is happening at all is a significant diplomatic achievement.

Pope Francis's calls for responsible care for creation have continued to be clarion, and his support of migrants' rights constant. The force of his advocacy in these and other regards, however, has been diminished by public perception of his ability and sometimes commitment to the cause of ridding the Church of clerical abusers and reforming the leadership culture that fed and fostered the crisis.

Several year-end analysis pieces have appeared, questioning whether Pope Francis's apparent inability to get his head around the nature and scope of the crisis—and get out of his own way when it comes to it—might not have permanently scarred his legacy already. "[D]amage to his moral authority on the issue has been done," wrote Nicole Winfield for the Associated Press. "Before his eyes were opened, Francis showed that he was a product of the very clerical culture he so often denounces, ever ready to take the word of the clerical class over victims."

If Francis is no longer willing to take the word of a cleric over that of an alleged victim, it remains to be seen whether he shall have the force of will to demand and direct real institutional and moral reform.

As we head into 2019, the eyes of the world will continue to be on Pope Francis. The question is whether the Church at the highest levels of governance will finally recognize what Church-watchers across the spectrum of theological and political opinion have understood for some time: that this crisis of leadership is the worst to hit the Church since the days of Martin Luther; that major reform is necessary and indeed long overdue; that not only Pope Francis's personal legacy is at stake, but the power of the papacy to be a moral voice in the world.

"2018: The year the Church's crisis was unmasked"

Whatever else 2018 was, it was the year in which the crisis of clerical sexual abuse and cover-up revealed itself to be a cancer within the leadership culture of the Catholic Church. Protracted, persistent, and systemic, the rot in the hierarchy reaches all the way up, and could reach all the way through the Roman Curia and more than one national conference of bishops.

The first major event of the year was also the one during which the global crisis of clerical sex abuse and cover-up became permanently attached to Pope Francis. While on a fence-mending visit to Chile—the first stop on a trip that would have its Peruvian leg almost completely overshadowed by the Chilean fallout—Pope Francis accused victims of the man who was then Chile's most notorious abuser-priest (Pope Francis would defrock him in September) of calumny against Bishop Juan Barros of Osorno. The victims—Juan Carlos Cruz, James Hamilton, and José Andres Murillo—said Barros turned a blind eye to the predations of Father Fernando Karadima.

Francis eventually apologized, ordered an investigation into the matter, summoned the entire Chilean hierarchy to

Rome for an unprecedented emergency meeting, obtained their resignations, and then sat on the lion's share of them (he has accepted seven of thirty-four resignations, and dismissed two retired Chilean bishops from the clerical state), while Chilean prosecutors began raiding chanceries and offices of the Chilean bishops' conference. There were hopes that what appeared to be a genuine falling of the scales and change of heart on the part of the Holy Father—who reportedly said he was "part of the problem" when he met with Karadima's victims in May—would lead to concrete and sustained efforts to address the crisis. Instead, there was a good deal more talk, and very little action.

As spring turned into summer, l'Affaire McCarrick exploded, opening a gruesome new chapter in the crisis that would dwarf anything that's touched the Church in the age of modern communication. By August, it was clear that the hierarchical leadership of the Church in the United States was thoroughly compromised, panicked, and almost totally paralyzed. The release of the Pennsylvania Grand Jury Report proved beyond doubt that the US bishops' Apalachin moment had arrived. That was before the former apostolic nuncio to the United States, Archbishop Carlo Maria Viganò, released the first of his "testimonies": a spectacular, 11-page *J'Accuse!* that deepened existing divisions and opened new rifts in the hierarchy, the professional Catholic chattering class, and the body of the faithful in the US and around the world.

If Viganò had limited himself to exposing the rot, his publications might have been more effective. His original brief was powerful, and could have been stronger, but lacked a measure of discipline. As it happened, he called for Pope Francis's resignation, exposing himself to accusations he is part of a *coup d'eglise* and turning the discussion away from the right means of remedy for a situation that had become untenable, and transforming it into a referendum on Pope Francis—who has his share of the blame for letting things come to that.

As summer gave way to autumn, unforced errors committed by Church leaders at every level continued to pile up, while the crisis deepened, and the scandal intensified. Stories broke in other countries, until every inhabited continent was dealing with some part of it. In September, Pope Francis called a meeting of the heads of the world's bishops' conferences to discuss the crisis—to take place over three days in February 2019.

The misrule revealed in Buffalo dominated Church news in the United States for a few weeks, but largely gave way to the run-up to the US Conference of Catholic Bishops' annual fall plenary in Baltimore. Prepared to vote on reform measures designed to achieve a measure of accountability and stanch the hemorrhage of public confidence, the bishops found themselves hamstrung by an order from Pope Francis—couched as a "request" from the Congregation for Bishops—to delay their vote until after the February meeting.

As Autumn turned to Winter, a series of stories broke, while others took ugly—if predictable—turns. A rehearsal of them all would run to significant length and quickly become a grotesque litany, though it would include the Vatican's campaign to lower expectations for the February meeting after it raised the stakes on the same exponentially.

It would also include the news that the Vatican allowed an auxiliary bishop of Los Angeles accused of sexual misconduct to continue to serve—with restrictions on his ministry secretly imposed by the Congregation for the Doctrine of the Faith—for 13 years, and that the archbishop of New York apparently allowed a man with multiple abuse allegations settled on his account by the New York Archdiocesan Reconciliation and Compensation Program to continue in ministry (and even sent a letter of suitability for the priest to a California Catholic college as recently as December 4).

The main reason we do not know how deep the rot runs or how wide it has spread, is the Pope's refusal to order the necessary investigations. At the turning of the year, civil authorities in several countries are poised to solve that problem in a way that cannot fail to devastate the Church's institutions. For Pope Francis, whose oft-delayed and much belated reform agenda was already on the rocks, 2018 was going to be a critical year:

> 2018 is likely to be the year in which Pope Francis will have to decide whether he will use his immense talents, charisma, and strength of personality to harness and direct the energies of the Curia and the Church in a manner consistent with the best angels of her tradition, or whether he will continue to channel his efforts into a project that appears to have as its only overarching vision the remaking of Rome into a sort of Buenos Aires-on-Tiber.

In a sense, Pope Francis never got to make that decision. Circumstance decided it for him, with the effective

disintegration of his principal reform organ, the "C9" Council of Cardinal Advisers, which became the "C6" in October
after Francis relieved three members and apparently chose
not to replace them.

To hear the Vatican tell it, the work of the C6 is essentially complete—their draft Apostolic Constitution, *Praed-
icate evangelium*, was apparently ready for Pope Francis in
June—so there is no need for fresh blood. Practically speaking, the reform is dead in the water. Even if Francis does
mark up the draft and send it for fine tuning, then get the
fine copy back, promulgate it, and begin to roll it out, the
reform will take years to implement. Bureaucracies are resistant to change, and the Roman Curia is well practiced in the
Fabian arts. Plus, institutional reforms are nothing without
personnel changes, and there are too many curial officials
with too much skin in the game to go quietly.

Two of the three members Pope Francis "thanked for their
service"—Cardinals Francisco Errázuriz and George Pell—
are embroiled in major sex abuse and cover-up scandals in
their home countries. Francis dismissed the three senior
churchmen in October, but only announced the change in
December, after the embattled Cardinal Errázuriz let slip
that he was no longer serving on the body. In a year characterized by a widening credibility gap, in which transparency has been declared the order of the day, the delay in the
announcement was perplexing, to say the least.

That Cardinal Errázuriz stayed as long as he did was surprising on its own. He skipped the meeting of the Chilean
bishops in May, already under intense scrutiny and facing
heavy criticism that included calls for his imprisonment

from Chilean victims of the man for whom Errázuriz allegedly covered. Francis promised those victims and the whole Church a hard line, but in Errázuriz's case went with a half-measure.

The scandal and the crisis. The crisis and the scandal. The two are no longer separable, but they are distinguishable: the crisis is of very long standing, rooted in the *mysterium iniquitatis*, and at its most basic level a disease of the spirit, a sickness caused by lust for power, which perverts everything it reaches even as it makes use of every perversion it encounters on the march through souls; the scandal is an effect, rather than a cause of the crisis, and may yet be harnessed to the good. "The crisis of clerical sexual abuse [and cover-up] is a crisis of clerical culture, and more specifically, a crisis of episcopal leadership," I wrote in July:

> The bishops have lost their way, and they have brought the whole Church with them into a quagmire. The only way out is through, and the only way through the filthy muck and slime of half-truth more devilish than outright mendacity, is veracity. The bishops—all of them and every one of them—must tell the whole, unvarnished truth.

All throughout the year, we have learned details of specific abuse cases, which the bishops kept hidden as long as they could. Some of the details regarded run-of-the-mill perversion. Other details bore the unmistakable mark of the Satanic. Others were in between. All of them were sickening—overwhelming at times, and permanently scarring to anyone who has become familiar with them—truly and in the strict sense of the word, wretched.

As 2018 turns into 2019, we realize that we are at the beginning of a generational struggle for the soul of the Church. Institutional reforms are needed at every level of ecclesial life. Likewise necessary is a renewal of basic Christian devotion to both charity and piety. There are more sickening, maddening, heartbreaking revelations to come. Individual bishops from whom we hope and deserve better will disappoint. The hierarchy will fail us again. This is going to get worse before it gets better. We need to be prepared for that. We also need not to lose sight of the good.

It seems paradoxical, but in spiritual warfare, the tiniest act of charity is a greater blow to hell than the most sweeping reform, and the surrender of the tiniest smidgen of bitterness in one human soul a mightier victory for heaven than a thousand searching exposés. Exposure of rot and sweeping reform are both necessary and urgent, and we all have a part to play in both. Nevertheless, the work of the Christian in fear and trembling for his soul's salvation is the first and perennial task, before which all must give way. It is work that requires community, though its working is often secret, even and especially to the one in which it is worked, and the principal worker is Christ.

The real challenge in 2019 will be to keep Paul's charge: "Rejoice always, pray without ceasing, give thanks in all circumstances."

For the Catholic World Report, January 4, 2019

"The Zanchetta situation is a microcosm of the current crisis"

The story of Bishop Gustavo Zanchetta, emeritus of Orán, Argentina—broken Friday by Nicole Winfield for the Associated Press—might be no more than just plain, run-of-the-mill bad. Or it could be the tip of a continent-sized iceberg of a scandal. It is certainly a world-in-a-nutshell instance of almost everything sick and broken within the Church.

Zanchetta is currently under investigation for alleged sexual misconduct. The investigation is being conducted by the current bishop of Orán, Luis Antonio Scozzina, and is in the preliminary stages. That we are only hearing of this now would be appalling on a good day. That it comes in the midst of a critical worldwide failure of leadership in the Church, with systematic occultation of abuse near the heart of the crisis, and in the wake of promises of transparency repeated ad nauseam, is beyond execration.

The allegations against Zanchetta apparently involve misrule, bad blood, and sexual impropriety connected with the seminary Zanchetta personally founded during his tenure in Orán. There are also reports of retaliation against the priests who brought the allegations, setting once again in high relief the conspicuous and intolerable absence of protections for whistleblowers in the Church.

The Press Office of the Holy See confirmed the bones of the report for the Associated Press, and released the interim Press Office Director, Alessandro Gisotti's remarks on the matter in an email blast to accredited journalists. When Pope Francis accepted Zanchetta's resignation from the See of Orán on August 1, 2017, the Press Office of the Holy See noted the development in the daily bulletin, but gave no reason for the move. Zanchetta issued his own statement citing health problems as his reason for resigning.

Now, the Press Office claims his resignation was over problems of governance. "The reason for [Zanchetta's] resignation is tied to his difficulty in managing relations with the diocesan clergy and to very tense relations with the priests of the diocese," Gisotti's statement reads. "At the time of his resignation, there had been accusations of authoritarianism against [Zanchetta], but there had been no accusation of sexual abuse against him," Gisotti's statement continued. "The problem that emerged then was linked to the inability to govern the clergy."

Those two things—serious governance problems and serious health problems—are not mutually exclusive, nor are they incompatible with a simmering moral crisis ready to become a scandal. There was no reason—no good one, anyway—not to say why Zanchetta was resigning at the time he resigned, along with as much detail as possible regarding the specific kinds of tension there were between him and the diocesan clergy.

Pope Francis appointed Zanchetta to the diocese of Oran early in the first year of his reign. When an early appointment in one's native country doesn't work out, it is an embarrassment, but everyone understands these things happen. Francis then created a special position for Zanchetta within the powerful department of the Roman Curia, the Administration of the Patrimony of the Apostolic See (APSA) that manages the Vatican's real estate and some of the Vatican's liquid assets—after a three months' convalescence in Spain.

The sudden and unexpected reappearance of the Argentinian prelate, so soon after his sudden and unexpected disappearance, and in a position created especially for him, did raise eyebrows at the time. Gisotti explained in his statement Friday that Pope Francis did not want Zanchetta's administrative talents to go to waste. "After the period in Spain, in consideration of his administrative management capacity, he was appointed Assessor of the APSA (a position for which no responsibility of governance in the dicastery is foreseen)."

So, Zanchetta was such a good administrator—albeit a poor governor—that Pope Francis could not spare him, even with his health in such a fragile state—and the job for which Francis needed him was a tailor-made sinecure in a department already dealing with several scandals. What if they'd just told the whole truth, right from the start?

For the Catholic World Report, January 13, 2019

"What Peter Steinfels got wrong about the Pennsylvania Grand Jury Report"

Veteran religion reporter Peter Steinfels's recent, lengthy essay in *Commonweal*, on the supposed faults and failings of the Pennsylvania Grand Jury Report and the media coverage of the Report, is the sort of piece that tempts a writer to respond point-by-point, and line-by-line. I will resist that temptation, but Steinfels's essay does call for a reply.

Steinfels raises some real and significant concerns, most of which regard the grand jury system in general. The specific case of the grand jury that investigated the Catholic bishops of Pennsylvania is at best an instance of those concerns.

Steinfels is right to note that grand juries are easily manipulated for political purposes, and their reports can be used to damage rivals or enemies. I share his concern. There is a risk to core principles of rule-of-law in free society—hence to free society itself—attendant on the use of grand juries, arguably illustrated in the kind of grandstanding the Pennsylvania Attorney General made of the Grand Jury empaneled to investigate the Church in Pennsylvania.

"Eternal vigilance, the price of liberty," is not just a slogan. If Attorney General Josh Shapiro was careless in the use he made of the instrument, bishops were counting on greater and more general carelessness when they covered up abuse and enabled abusers.

Steinfels is also deeply concerned with reporters and news outlets, which he says have given short shrift to the improvements bishops have made in crafting and implementing new and robust safeguarding measures. That may not be exactly wrong, but there are two problems with making it a central complaint in an essay like the one he wrote.

First, making that case might not take the column inches his essay did, but it would have to be backed by more real data than he brings to bear, and much more rigorous analysis of it than he offers. Second, the Pennsylvania Grand Jury Report was not about the bishops' progress in getting a handle on the noxious culture and nefarious dealings of clerical and hierarchical leadership over the past 15 years. It was about their failures—which were not mere failures of oversight, but included active coverup and enabling—for which only a few Catholic clerics have ever been charged and no bishop in Pennsylvania past or present has faced meaningful consequences.

Steinfels accuses the Pennsylvania Grand Jury of using its report "to be judge and jury, and to hand down convictions." The report itself explicitly disavows this role, however; in fact, it describes its work as simply the best that could be done under the circumstances, due to statute of limitations. "This Report is our only recourse," the Report reads. "We are going to name names and describe what they did—both the sex offenders and those who concealed them. We are going to shine a light on their conduct, because that is what the victims deserve."

There is room for doubt regarding some specific claims against individuals named, but the Pennsylvania system provides for responses, which are contained in the Report. But in the absence of the preferable public trial, the Report is the sole, admittedly inadequate, public remedy for a very unsatisfactory situation.

When it comes to the Report itself, the central theses of Steinfels's treatment are that the Report makes an "ugly, indiscriminate, and inflammatory charge," specifically that, "all of [the victims] were brushed aside, in every part of the state, by church leaders who preferred to protect the abusers and their institution above all," and that media coverage of the report was, "amenable to uncritically echoing this story without investigation," which led to, "[t]he prevalent story about Catholic clergy sex abuse as deeply entrenched, largely unabated, and uniquely Catholic," being, "now so embedded in the media as to make it resistant to evidence to the contrary." Steinfels concludes that the Report's charge against Church leadership in Pennsylvania was "unsubstantiated by the report's own evidence, to say nothing of the evidence the report ignores," and, "is truly unworthy of a judicial body responsible for impartial justice."

First of all, a grand jury is not, properly speaking, a judicial body—not, at any rate, the way a trial jury is—nor is its purpose to render impartial justice. As Steinfels himself notes, a grand jury is an investigative instrument, the purpose of which is to collect and weigh evidence of crime, and determine whether there is a prima facie case for criminal prosecution or sufficient grounds for other government action.

This is also why Steinfels's charge the Pennsylvania Grand Jury did not properly highlight, weigh, analyze, or otherwise take into account exculpatory evidence, is misplaced. That's not what a grand jury does. A trial jury does that—at trial. Steinfels consistently ignores this basic and key distinction, or misapplies it in his analysis. In the case of the investigating Grand Jury that issued its report last August, the Pennsylvania Attorney General needed to show evidence of such criminal activity sufficient to warrant the Grand Jury's empaneling in the first place. It was not a fishing expedition. Also, there was never any question of indicting the Catholic bishops of Pennsylvania—certainly not on the vast amount of evidence the Grand Jury collected, which pertained to crimes for which the statute of limitations had expired. Grand juries in Pennsylvania, however, are not limited to recommending judicial indictment. Here is how Pennsylvania defines a grand jury report in law:

> A report submitted by the investigating grand jury to the supervising judge regarding conditions relating to organized crime or public corruption or both; or proposing recommendations for legislative, executive, or administrative action in the public interest based upon stated findings. (Title 42, Chapter 45, Section 4542)

It is odd to hear anyone crying foul over the Pennsylvania Grand Jury Report on the grounds it denied the bishops due process, as Steinfels does. A great part of the reason the grand jury was convened, and its report came out the way it did, were the decades of episcopal machinations that, among their effects, made timely prosecution of individual crimes impossible.

Steinfels takes particular issue with the Grand Jury Report's claim that "all" of the victims were "brushed aside" when clearly, it wasn't "all" of the victims. It was only "most" of the victims. Steinfels concedes the report proves widespread abuse and systematic cover-up over decades. After his painstaking read of the document, Steinfels in essence discovers that the 40th Statewide Grand Jury of Pennsylvania did its job.

Though his essay runs to nearly 12 thousand words, Steinfels does not offer a systematic critique of the Pennsylvania Grand Jury Report. He does not even try to do so. He sets up a straw man: the inflated claim in the introduction to the report. He waves a red herring: the report doesn't do the work of the defense. He picks a couple of cherries from the low, low branches: the misattribution of the phrase "circle of secrecy" to then-Bishop Donald W. Wuerl was one cause for considerable hand-wringing (even though the Pennsylvania Grand Jury Report contained the Diocese of Pittsburgh's extended rejoinder).

Steinfels's protestations in that specific regard have a particular tin ring to them, as well: Cardinal Wuerl did not coin the phrase, "circle of secrecy," but he did participate in the thing. We now know he participated in the thing both in Pittsburgh and in Washington, DC, where he succeeded the disgraced Archbishop Theodore McCarrick.

We now know Cardinal Wuerl had at least one report of McCarrick's perverse conduct directly from one of McCarrick's victims in 2004, when Wuerl was still bishop of

Pittsburgh. One doubts whether Steinfels would have dedicated so much of his ink to this point, had he known then what we know now.

Steinfels's concern about how the Report downplayed the post-2002 drop in reported incidents of abuse and improvement in safeguarding minors is also misplaced. The Report is perhaps "begrudging" in that last regard, as Steinfels says. Then again, "There is no reason, of course, why a grand jury has to take such diocesan testimony at face value," he also writes. To do their job, the grand jury didn't need to mention this progress at all, and shouldn't be faulted for not doing so.

If reportage of the story of the Pennsylvania Grand Jury Report contributed to the reinforcement of public perception of the abuse crisis "as deeply entrenched, largely unabated, and uniquely Catholic," and to that public perception being "now so embedded in the media as to make it resistant to evidence to the contrary," there's a reason—and it isn't hasty or irresponsible reporting. Abuse is a societal problem, as is coverup, as are the facile irenicism and a false sense of camaraderie that lead to institutional thinking of the worst sort. Highlighting that in a critique of a report dealing with abuse and coverup in the Church can easily sound like whataboutism.

Steinfels's essay is, in short, a 12,000-word cavil of a single adjective ("all") in the introductory paragraph of a 1,300-page document that, imperfect as it was (such documents always are), did what it set out to do, in spades: show there is a prima facie case to make against the bishops of Pennsylvania, who covered up abuse and enabled abusers for more than seven decades.

For the Catholic Herald, January 21, 2019

"Report: Vatican already knew about Argentine bishop's sexual misconduct"

An AP Exclusive report published Sunday claims the Holy See received evidence of misconduct on the part of an Argentinian bishop with ties to Pope Francis years earlier than the Vatican had previously suggested. The claims tend to contradict the Vatican's earlier statements regarding what authorities in the Holy See knew about the bishop's behavior, and when they knew it.

The bishop in question is Gustavo Óscar Zanchetta, who was executive undersecretary to the Argentinian bishops' conference during the years then-Cardinal Jorge Mario Bergoglio of Buenos Aires was conference president. Pope Francis made Zanchetta a bishop in 2013, and appointed him to the Diocese of Orán in the far north of Argentina.

In August of 2017, Pope Francis accepted Zanchetta's resignation from the See of Orán, after Zanchetta complained of ill health. In December of 2017, Francis named Zanchetta "Assessor" to the Administration of the Patrimony of the Apostolic See—APSA—a position Francis created especially for Zanchetta within the powerful department, which oversees the Holy See's real-estate and significant other assets.

In January of this year, the Holy See confirmed that Zanchetta had been suspended from his position in the APSA, pending investigation into various accusations of misconduct, including the sexual abuse of seminarians in his former diocese. In a statement issued on January 3, the Director of the Press Office of the Holy See, Alessandro Gisotti, told reporters the Holy See only learned of the sexual misconduct complaints very recently.

"At the time of his resignation [in 2017]," Gisotti said in the statement, "there had been accusations of authoritarianism against [Zanchetta], but there had been no accusation of sexual abuse against him." On Sunday, the Associated Press quoted the former Vicar General for the Diocese of Orán, Argentina, Fr. Juan José Manzano, as saying he sent evidence of Bishop Zanchetta's strange and untoward behavior in 2015 and 2017.

"In 2015, we just sent a 'digital support' with selfie photos of the previous bishop [Zanchetta] in obscene or out of place behavior that seemed inappropriate and dangerous," Fr. Manzano told the AP. "It was an alarm that we made to the Holy See via some friendly bishops," Manzano went on to explain. "The nunciature didn't intervene directly, but the Holy Father summoned Zanchetta and he justified himself saying that his cellphone had been hacked, and that there were people who were out to damage the image of the Pope."

Fr. Manzano also told the AP he believes Pope Francis has handled the Zanchetta matter appropriately. "There was never any intent to hide anything. There was never any intent of the Holy Father to defend him against anything," Fr. Manzano told the AP. Quite apart from the question of intent, the Vatican said on January 4 there had been no accusation of sexual abuse against Zanchetta when he was named Assessor to APSA in December of 2017. AP reports Manzano as maintaining that statement could be technically true, as a report of ambiguous behavior is not a formal complaint. As of press time, the Press Office of the Holy See had not responded to repeated requests from the *Catholic Herald* for clarification.

For the Catholic World Report, January 22, 2019

"What the Bishop Zanchetta case tells us about Church leadership"

The Vatican has doubled down on its insistence it never received any accusation of sexual abuse against Bishop Gustavo Zanchetta until well after Zanchetta, the former bishop of Orán, Argentina, was ensconced in a position Pope Francis created for him inside a powerful and scandal-troubled dicastery of the Roman Curia.

The new statement came in the wake of claims from the former vicar general of Orán, Father Juan José Manzano, who told the Associated Press the Vatican had evidence of Bishop Zanchetta's moral turpitude in 2015—two years before Zanchetta resigned as bishop of Orán, citing illness, only to reappear a few months later in the Vatican post Pope Francis had made for him.

Fr. Manzano's claims are significant, because they would mean the Vatican received evidence of Bishop Zanchetta's questionable moral conduct before Francis named Zanchetta "assessor" to the Administration of the Patrimony of the Holy See (APSA), which manages the Vatican's considerable real-estate and other financial and liquid assets. Manzano's claims appear to fly in the face of declarations the Vatican made when word got out in early January that Zanchetta was under investigation after complaints of misrule, bad blood, and sexual impropriety with seminarians. The director of the Holy See Press Office, Alessandro Gisotti, issued a statement January 4 saying the Vatican did not receive any "accusation" of sexual abuse until sometime in the fall of 2018.

In an AP exclusive published on Monday, Fr. Manzano says the evidence he sent to the Vatican in 2015 contained "a 'digital support' with selfie photos of the previous bishop in obscene or out of place behavior that seemed inappropriate and dangerous." Manzano also says that in 2017, "when the situation was much more serious, not just because there had been a question about sexual abuses, but because the diocese was increasingly heading into the abyss," he and other diocesan officials complained a second time, to the apostolic nuncio in Buenos Aires.

Further complicating the optics of the matter is that Pope Francis's acquaintance with Bishop Zanchetta is an old one. They knew each other when Francis was archbishop of Buenos Aires and Zanchetta was a priest of the Diocese of Quilmes and executive undersecretary to the Argentinian bishops' conference, of which then-Cardinal Jorge Mario Bergoglio was president from 2005-2011. Fr. Manzano told the AP Bishop Zanchetta gave Pope Francis a line: "[T]he Holy Father summoned Zanchetta and he justified himself saying that his cellphone had been hacked, and that there were people who were out to damage the image of the pope."

There are three basic possibilities here (with multiple permutations): the images allegedly sent to the Vatican in 2015 were of Bishop Zanchetta and were compromising, or they were not of Zanchetta, or they were not compromising.

Then there are the alleged 2017 reports. They may not have been formal legal complaints, but a halfway competent governor gets to the bottom of that story before he makes Zanchetta dog-catcher, let alone an official in an important Vatican dicastery. Instead, Pope Francis used the power of his office to make sure Zanchetta had a place to land, apparently either before he assured himself of all the facts or in spite of what he knew.

Following the publication of Father Manzano's claims, Gisotti issued a second statement, forcefully reiterating the Holy See's position. "In reference to the articles published recently by several news sources, as well as to some misleading reconstructions," Gisotti told journalists, "I resolutely repeat what was stated this past 4 January." Gisotti went on to say, "In addition, I emphasize that the case is being studied and when this process is over, information will be forthcoming regarding the results."

The Vatican Press Office did not address Father Manzano's claims directly, nor did it offer anything in the way of clarification. A close reading of the original January 4 statement could show that it contains no falsehood; evidence of the sort Father Manzano says he delivered and the manner in which he says he delivered it may not be considered a formal complaint or "accusation" in the strict sense of the term.

One thing, however, is certain. We have learned over the course of the past year that high Churchmen are practiced in the art of telling it crooked without actually speaking a technically false word. We learned the lesson from the former archbishop of Washington, DC, Cardinal Donald W. Wuerl, who changed his story several times with regard to what he knew about the habits of his disgraced predecessor, Archbishop Theodore McCarrick, and then claimed he forgot about the report he received from one of McCarrick's adult victims.

We learned the lesson from all the prelates who were "shocked" and "saddened" when word got out that "Uncle Ted" McCarrick is a pervert and a criminal. We learned the lesson from Bishop Richard J. Malone of Buffalo, who tried to make himself a hero by publishing "all" the names of credibly accused priests of his diocese, only to find himself pilloried for releasing an incomplete register and forced to expand the list. Malone continues to face scrutiny for mismanagement of abuse cases, but has so far refused to resign.

We learned the lesson when the former nuncio to the United States, Archbishop Carlo Maria Viganò, took an iron-clad fact pattern and undermined his brief exposing three decades of curial rot by gilding the lily—"sanctions" was a stronger word than he needed, especially when "restrictions" would have sufficed—and by calling for Francis's resignation. If he'd stuck to the facts, it would have been much harder for the *coup d'eglise* narrative to gain traction and almost impossible for Francis to ignore him. The way Viganò glossed his role in the Nienstedt business was also unfortunate; if he'd simply added a memorandum to the file, it would have fixed the discrepancy he outlined in his post factum discussion—but ordering (or even requesting) a letter be pulled from the file was never going to play in Peoria, however it might have done in Rome.

We learned the lesson from Pope Francis himself, when he claimed never to have signed a pardon for a cleric guilty of sexual abuse, even though he had reduced the sentences of several guilty priests, including one—Italian Mauro Inzoli— who was later convicted in Italian criminal court for abusing five victims aged 12-16. The *Wall Street Journal* reported late last year that an appellate panel Francis established has also significantly reduced trial court sentences and even restored men to the clerical state who had been penally laicized.

We learned the lesson from Pope Francis again, when he claimed never to have received evidence of Bishop Barros's wrongdoing, even though he had a letter from abuse survivor Juan Carlos Cruz that told in harrowing detail how Barros watched his mentor, then-Father Fernando Karadima, work on the boys in his charge, only to turn a blind eye and later aid in covering up his mentor's predations. Pope Francis has yet to explain what happened to Cruz's letter.

In his recent letter to the US bishops, Pope Francis wrote, "The Church's credibility has been seriously undercut and diminished by these sins and crimes, but even more by the efforts made to deny or conceal them." Pope Francis is right. "This has led to a growing sense of uncertainty, distrust, and vulnerability among the faithful." Yes, it has. "As we know, the mentality that would cover things up, far from helping to resolve conflicts, enabled them to fester and cause even greater harm to the network of relationships that today we are called to heal and restore." Yes, it has, and yes, you are.

"Having raised the bar, Pope Francis now seeks to lower expectations"

Pope Francis says he perceives "inflated expectations" for the February 21-24 meeting of the heads of the world's bishops' conferences at the Vatican, on child protection. A good deal of ink has already been spilt in efforts to explain the provenance of those expectations—in a word, Francis's own acts of governance—and there's no point rehashing them here. The short version is that Pope Francis raised the stakes, and now Francis is trying to manage expectations.

That is what it is, but it isn't the only thing Pope Francis did—or tried to do—with his remarks to journalists on the global crisis of abuse and cover-up while en route to Rome from Panama after concluding World Youth Day celebrations. For example, Pope Francis also managed to plant a mention of "Metropolitan"—perhaps telegraphing his preference for something very much akin to a proposal variously described as "Wuerl's Plan," the "Cupich Plan," or the "Wuerl-Cupich Plan" when it does come to actual reform measures.

There was also a sizable dose of edulcorated whataboutery thrown in for measure. "[T]he problem of abuse will continue," Pope Francis said. "It's a human problem, but human everywhere." He went on to cite a statistic he says he read "the other day" saying only half of all abuse anywhere is ever reported, and only 20 percent of those reports are given any sort of heed, and of that 20 percent, only 5 percent is ever condemned. "Terrible. Terrible," he added.

"It's a human tragedy and we need to become aware," Pope Francis went on to say. "Also us, resolving the problem in the Church, but becoming aware will help to resolve it in society, in the families where shame covers everything, and the victim—in so many others—or in so many other societies. But first, we must become aware, have the protocols (in place) and move forward. This is the thing."

Pope Francis seems to want to help "society" and "families" deal with the scourge of sexual abuse by raising awareness, even as he does little to discourage the impression he has given to the faithful—and especially the US Catholics about whom he was asked specifically—of making every effort to avoid dealing with the issue root-and-branch within the Church, of which he is the supreme governor.

Pope Francis even joked about how "sneaky" reporter Junno Arocho of the Catholic News Service was in wedging a question about the crisis into the in-flight presser, which Francis apparently wanted to be about something else—anything else. "During her lunch with a group of young pilgrims," Arocho began, "a young American girl told us that she had been asked about the pain and indignation of so many Catholics, particularly of the United States, for the crisis of abuse." Arocho went on to say, "Many American Catholics pray for the Church, but many feel betrayed and downcast after recent reports of abuse and cover-up by some bishops and have lost faith in them."

"Holiness," Arocho asked, "what are your expectations or hopes for the meeting in February so that the Church can begin to rebuild trust between the faithful and their bishops?" Pope Francis responded, "This is sneaky, he [Arocho] left WYD and he arrived here. My compliments. No, but thank you for the question." Pope Francis's remark about Arocho "sneaking" in an abuse question was telling. Interim Press Office Director Alessandro Gisotti had asked journalists to keep their questions to the doings in Panama. Arocho didn't so much leave World Youth Day to ask his question as he used his question to remind the Pope that the crisis was there in Panama, too.

In his answer, Pope Francis explained that the February meeting has two goals: "The idea of this was born in the [C9] because we saw that some bishops did not understand well or did not know what to do or did something good or wrong and we felt the responsibility to give a 'catechesis,' [so to speak], on this problem to the episcopal conferences."

"First," Pope Francis said, "a catechesis: that we become aware of the tragedy, what is an abused boy, an abused girl. I regularly receive abused people (in audience). I remember one—40 years without being able to pray. It is terrible, the suffering is terrible. That first, [the bishops] become aware of this." Pope Francis went on to say, "Second: that they know what must be done, the procedure, because sometimes the bishop does not know what to do." The Pope added:

It is something that has grown very strong and has not arrived at all angles, so to speak. And then, let them make general programs, but they will come from all the episcopal conferences: what the bishop must do, what the archbishop who is the metropolitan must do, what the president of the episcopal conference must do. But it must be clear in that—that they are—let's say it in terms (that are) a little juridical—that there are protocols that are clear.

The bishops have had decades to get their heads around the thing. The thing to do with men in leadership positions who still have trouble getting their heads around how awful the sexual abuse of minors really is, is to replace them with men who do understand. The real question is how men who don't know how awful the sexual abuse of minors is ever got into seminary in the first place.

Right from the beginning of this latest chapter of the crisis—call it the "episcopal" phase—Pope Francis has shown himself reluctant to remove such men. On return from Lima in January of last year, he said, "The case of [Bishop Juan] Barros [*olim* of Osorno] was studied, it was re-studied, and there is no evidence. That is what I wanted to say. I have no evidence to condemn. And if I were to condemn without evidence or without moral certainty, I would commit the crime of a bad judge." We know how that turned out.

Thing is, Pope Francis's hang-up about being a "bad judge" is entirely misplaced. There was no reason—no good one, at any rate—to make Barros bishop of Osorno in the first place. When it comes to any bishop's removal at this stage in the crisis, there is no necessary reason for it to be a juridical decision.

There is no reason—again, no good reason, at any rate—not to say to a man like Richard Malone in Buffalo, that His Excellency's performance in the job has been poor, unacceptably poor for too long, in these particulars X, Y, and Z, and that His Excellency needs to resign for the good of the Church. There's a way to convey the message clearly—to say, in essence: There's the easy way and there's the hard way, but one way or another Bishop So-and-So is not going to be the Bishop of Such-and-Such any longer. The next step is to tell people why.

Pope Francis has proven his willingness to demand resignations of prelates who are careless with money. He has removed bishops who are heavy-handed with the clergy in their charge. He has treated those cases as what they are: personnel matters. He hasn't been perfect in those cases—far from it, really—especially as far as transparency is concerned. Protocols can help, especially when they are designed to be culture-changers—the sorts of things as make it easier, rather than harder, for clerics of every rank to stand up and do right—but they are no substitute for a real reform effort that gets at the root of the problem, which continues to be the rot in clerical culture, high and low.

Bishops who fail in their mission of oversight insofar as the protection of minors is concerned obviously need to go. So do those who fail to keep appropriate vigil over the moral culture of their clergy generally, and especially those who fail in their duty to foster healthy environments for the formation of new clerics.

Specifically, the reform of clerical culture needs to be ordered to the recovery of a sense of uprightness: we want men who are stiff-necked in the face not only of wrong-doing but of idiocy; patient with sinners but intolerant of wickedness; zealous for the Gospel and resigned—eyes wide open—to the lasting and inevitable effects of Original Sin this side of the celestial Jerusalem. We want men who understand viscerally that the only way to save the institution is through perfect service to the faithful and tireless watchfulness over their weal.

That is where the real problem is—or a big part of it, at any rate—and that is why the February meeting is, I think, destined to fail: it is fighting the wrong battle.

CHAPTER 7

EYE OF THE STORM

February 1 – 20, 2019

For the Catholic World Report, February 3, 2019

"Pope Francis misses the mark in focusing on clericalism and synodality"

Papal biographer Austen Ivereigh has written a piece for *Commonweal*, on the meeting of the heads of the world's bishops' conferences scheduled for February 21-24 to discuss "the protection of minors and vulnerable adults." Francis is right, Ivereigh contends, to urge us to deflate our expectations of the meeting—especially those who are expecting major reforms to come from the gathering.

The thing is, very few people are expecting major policy changes to come from the meeting, nor are there many people expecting the meeting to fail solely on the basis of their lack. The main concern of skeptics—of those, at least, who do not see the whole thing as a mere publicity stunt—is that the meeting is fighting the wrong battle, i.e., "child protection" narrowly construed, rather than the rot in Church leadership and leadership culture.

Ivereigh's framing of the business is therefore a strange hybrid: a cross between a straw man and a red herring. Ivereigh's central thesis regarding the crisis and Pope Francis's approach to it is not unsound: the Holy Father sees the crisis as a particularly sickening manifestation of the *libido dominandi*, the only Christian response to which is and must be radical conversion to Christ. The word Francis uses to convey his sense of the specific evil at the root of this crisis is "clericalism." Ivereigh is right on that and so is Pope Francis.

To say that clericalism is at the root of the crisis is true, but it doesn't get us very far. As long as there are clerics, there will be clericalism. We need clerics to do their work in the Church, with and against the forces of disorder in the soul that are themselves the cause of human broken-ness and of its peculiar manifestation in men of the clerical state. Still, this crisis will not pass without soul-reform: in a word, conversion—and more particularly—the conversion of the Church's hierarchical leadership. Ivereigh is also cor-rect when he says that institutional reform is insufficient. "New norms, guidelines, and mechanisms will be necessary," Ivereigh says, "but they are by themselves powerless to bring about the *metanoia* to which the Holy Spirit is calling the Church." That's right.

One of Pope Francis's major problems—and Ivereigh's, in his analysis—is that neither recognizes the pressing need to start with institutional reform. In fact, they both get it exactly backward. "Before talking about new protocols and procedures," Ivereigh accurately paraphrases Pope Francis's remarks to journalists traveling with him to Rome from Pan-ama last Sunday before quoting Francis directly, "we [the bishops] must become aware." The hierarchical leadership of the Church has had decades to become aware of the wick-edness plaguing the Church. The crisis has been on Rome's radar for more than half a century.

Even if that were not so, any man who does not under-stand immediately and viscerally how awful the sexual abuse of minors is, has no business exercising Orders. That anyone with difficulty wrapping his head around the awful enormity of such abuse should have been admitted to a discernment program, let alone to formation, is itself a scandal in both the colloquial and the technical senses of the term. On the individual or micro level, the only responsible thing to do with a bishop who doesn't get it is to deprive him of his see.

When it comes to the macro level of institutional reform, *pace* Francis and Ivereigh, history both sacred and secular is replete with examples of culture following law. Whether one looks to St. Gregory the Great, or the Cluniac reforms, or Trent, or the Second Vatican Council—or even further back, to King Josiah or David or Moses himself—one will find enlightened rulers using legal reform to drive the renewal of culture.

The US Supreme Court did not wait to strike down Plessy for fear the country just wasn't ready for racial integration. Ten years later, Congress passed the Civil Rights Act over and against the protests of citizens who urged "moderation" and "prudence" and not forcing people to give up their racist ways until they saw the error of them. In any case, the need to raise awareness in some quarters is no reason to truncate reform efforts in others.

Whether owing to a desire for everyone to be on the same page, or owing to specific concerns over the legalities of the reforms the US bishops prepared to adopt at their Fall Meeting, the Pope's decision to impede the US bishops was frankly indefensible. For one thing, the US bishops were not looking to strengthen their child protection protocols, but to achieve a measure of accountability for themselves in the wake of revelations incontrovertibly manifesting their failures of oversight. For another, there would have been ample opportunity to fine tune the measures in concert with the Roman bureaucracy after the bishops passed the measures.

Then, Ivereigh's treatment of the incident that sparked the current phase of this crisis ignores or elides certain pertinent details, which tend to vitiate his analysis. Ivereigh says, "When Francis stubbornly defended his nomination of Bishop Juan Barros to the Chilean diocese of Osorno, he was caught up in a web of institutional desolation." Again, Ivereigh is not wrong. What he ignores, or elides, is Francis's own role in creating and perpetuating that institutional desolation. "I was part of the problem," Francis reportedly told the victims he had repeatedly attacked in public as calumniators, before "new elements" came to light, which prompted his decision to send his crackerjack investigator, Archbishop Charles Scicluna, to look into things.

Ivereigh goes on to say, "[Francis] was presented by the local church with a false picture, one that concealed the truth not just about the abuser priest Fernando Karadima, but about the widespread corruption and cover-up in many dioceses." That is a very incomplete summary of the matter, and inaccurate in two crucial particulars.

First, the "local Church" did not present Pope Francis with a false picture—the bishops did. The Chilean faithful had been crying foul over the ineptitude, irresponsibility, and downright corruption of their hierarchical leaders for at least a decade. The faithful of Osorno were vocal and organized in their opposition to Barros's appointment. Francis's response to the suffering faithful of Osorno was to tell them their suffering owed itself to their own stupidity. "[The Church in] Osorno suffers," Pope Francis told pilgrims who had asked him about the situation in Osorno when they met him on the sidelines of a weekly General Audience in May of 2015, "because she is stupid, because she does not open her heart to what God says and she lets herself be carried away by the idiocies that all those people say."

Second, the "incomplete picture" line is more than merely evasive. Pope Francis reportedly received an eight-page letter from Juan Carlos Cruz no later than April 2015, detailing Barros's role in enabling then-Fr. Fernando Karadima's abusive behavior and in covering it up. If Francis did receive the letter, then he had evidence of Barros's wrongdoing, perhaps a month before he spoke with the pilgrims and years before he publicly accused Karadima's accusers of calumny.

The Chilean bishops also warned Pope Francis against the appointment of Barros to the See of Osorno. They likely knew which way the wind was blowing, and cannot be accused of having unalloyed motives. Nevertheless, Francis had fair warning from them, as well. In fact, a letter obtained by the Associated Press, which Pope Francis sent to the Chilean bishops in early 2015, shows that Francis wanted Barros and two other "Karadima bishops" to resign and take a sabbatical year before receiving any new posting—in essence, to send the tainted men into quiet ecclesiastical retirement. In the letter to the Chilean bishops, Francs alludes to something that happened to derail that plan, though what it was remains unclear to this day.

Ivereigh praises the genius of Pope Francis's approach to the crisis, and cites the Pope's newfound reliance on the faithful as evidence of his turnaround:

> New norms, guidelines, and mechanisms will be necessary, but they are by themselves powerless to bring about the metanoia to which the Holy Spirit is calling the church. Only God's grace and mercy can do this; and these are found in His people. Hence the pope's call in August to the whole people of God to pray and fast. The people of God is the "immune system" of the church, as he told Chile's Catholics. If that immune system isn't working, no amount of procedural reform will be sufficient. Clericalism is a problem that affects every member of the church in one way or another, and so we can expect its solution to involve every member.

That is textbook gaslighting. It might not be quite tantamount to saying that priests never would have abused the children and the bishops never would have covered it up if only the laity were better Christians, but it does share the blame for the crisis without even suggesting a real responsible role for the laity in the solution. For centuries, the clergy have expected the lay faithful to pray, pay, and obey. For all his talk, the closest thing Francis has offered in the way of a concrete remedy to the awful, untenable state of affairs into which we have fallen as a result of clerical chauvinism, is more of the same.

Ivereigh goes on to say that Francis's vision of a "synodal" Church is just what we need for these troubled times:

If clericalism is the disease, synodality is the cure. Only when the church embraces its identity as what the Second Vatican Council said it was, the people of God, can the clericalist mentality behind the crisis be expunged. This means clergy and the hierarchy serving Christ in the people rather than the people serving priests as if they were Christ. It means getting over the institutional self-involvement that has led to so much desolation and denial, and putting the poor, the hungry, and the abused back at the center of the church's attention, where they belong.

Just as Francis himself could not resist a sop to his favorite talking points in the closing lines of his Letter to the Faithful of Chile, Ivereigh—riffing on Francis's Chilean letter—cannot avoid trying to make the crisis about something else. This is the heart of the problem with reducing the crisis to "clericalism": in technical language, it is an inadequate heuristic. Said simply: it is a catch-all—a cartoon villain—a bogeyman.

For the Catholic World Report, February 11, 2019

"As a McCarrick verdict looms, the Vatican still faces rough waters"

The world waits on tenterhooks for the announcement—expected, according to some sources, as early as Tuesday—of a verdict (and presumably a penal sentence) in the case of the disgraced former archbishop of Washington, DC, Theodore Edgar McCarrick. That story will dominate headlines for a couple of days, at least, but the truth is: it doesn't matter very much what Pope Francis decides to do with Uncle Ted. Where and how and in what state of life an 88-year-old pervert lives out his last days are less significant than what happens next.

Will he carry his secrets to the grave, or will he unburden himself? Will there be an investigation worth the name, into who knew what about McCarrick, and when, and where, and at what level of governance in the Church? Or will McCarrick be sent out into the desert as a scapegoat?

Patient and disciplined voices have grown strained, and some, strident. Usually as unimpeachably civil as she is forthright, Irish abuse-survivor and victim-advocate Marie Collins took to social media to lambaste McCarrick's expected penal laicization, saying, "The Vatican believe [sic] it will be good publicity, convinced that 'zero tolerance' is being implemented when it is NOT and take the heat out of the questions about who knew and when—including the powers that be in the Vatican!" (the emphasis is Collins').

Collins made her statement on Twitter as she retweeted John Allen's latest analysis piece, in which the usually circumspect *Crux* editor bluntly stated, "If Francis and his advisers want the McCarrick case to be wrapped up before the summit later this month, therefore, just laicizing him won't do the trick." Allen went on to say, "They'll also need to explain how we got to a point where such a move is necessary—and, of course, offer some reason to believe we won't be here again." That essay followed one from February 7, which Allen closed by eviscerating the Pope's attempts to deflate expectations surrounding the meeting of the heads of the world's bishops' conferences, on child protection: "Reasonable people likely would agree that expecting the pope to uphold his own public commitments hardly seems 'inflated,'" Allen wrote. "In less than a month," he concluded, "we'll find out whether Francis thinks so too."

Allen's February 7 analysis was in one respect too generous to the powers at the Vatican. "Twice now," Allen wrote, "and with ascending levels of authority, we've been cautioned not to expect too much from the summit on clerical sexual abuse Pope Francis has called for Feb. 21-24 for the presidents of bishops' conferences around the world." That's true, as far as the explicit warnings against expecting too much are concerned. However, the work to manage expectations began months ago, and has been transparently coordinated. The fact is, the papal apparatchiks have been talking out of both sides of their mouths.

From one side, we hear, "[The February meeting] is a very important start of a global process which will take quite some time to perfect," as Archbishop Charles Scicluna put it in an interview with *America*. From the other, we hear, "[T]his is not a 'year-zero' in the fight against abuse, because in the last 16 years many significant and concrete steps have been taken," as Vatican Media's editorial director, Andrea Tornielli, stated in a January 10 editorial for Vatican News. "The rules on how to respond have been established and strengthened by the will of recent popes," Tornielli said.

"It's important to note that by calling a global meeting he understands this to be a global issue, and he wants to reinforce our shared commitment as a church to establishing responsiveness, accountability, and transparency," Cardinal Blase Cupich of Chicago—another senior member of the February meeting's steering committee—told Crux in a November 23 interview.

Just today, the director of the Centre for Child Protection at the Pontifical Gregorian University, Father Hans Zöllner, SJ, told *Crux*, "[T]here can be no one-size-fits-all guideline for the whole Church, because our languages do not translate certain concepts, the law systems are completely different, the political and social situations are very diverse." That may be an academic point, since Pope Francis has already let it be known that new policy is not on the agenda at all.

There is no clear statement—because there does not appear to be any clear vision—of the nature or the scope of the meeting. The approach of the Vatican—and the Pope—has been almost completely opaque; this state of affairs may well serve the short-term purpose of so lowering expectations as to make any movement in any direction look like progress and provide the Vatican with the thinnest of pretexts for declaring the meeting successful. Meanwhile, the reigning pontiff is personally implicated in the cover-up of gross immorality and other malfeasance—quite possibly criminal—allegedly committed by Gustavo Zanchetta, a man Francis made a bishop in his native Argentina. Francis quietly accepted Zanchetta's resignation and created a position for him in a powerful department of the Roman Curia; it has been alleged that he did so after having seen evidence of Zanchetta's misdeeds, which are said to include sexual impropriety with seminarians.

Before Pope Francis stands an ineluctable fact, with which he will have to reckon sooner or later: credibility—his own, and that of his office—is threatened not only by his heretofore disappointing record of leadership with regard to a crisis he largely inherited, but directly and immediately by his own involvement.

"Francis has shown confidence in Farrell long before new appointment"

Pope Francis named Cardinal Kevin Farrell to the post of Camerlengo of Holy Roman Church on Thursday. With the appointment, Pope Francis has filled a post that had been vacant since the death of Cardinal Jean Louis Tauran in July of last year. A 71-year-old native of Ireland and naturalized US citizen, Farrell served as Bishop of Dallas before becoming Prefect of the Dicastery for Laity, Family, and Life in 2016, a position he retains as he comes into the Camerlengo's office.

The position of Camerlengo was once one of great power. It remains one of a very few curial offices, the terms of which do not cease immediately upon the vacancy of the See of Rome. These days, however, the position is mostly—though not entirely—symbolic. There are some duties still attached to the office of Camerlengo, including the direction of Papal funeral arrangements if the vacancy of the See of Rome is due to the decease of the former Pope. The Camerlengo is also charged with the protection and administration of the rights and property of the Holy See during the interregnum, though his powers are minimal: he cannot make policy, but only makes sure the bureaucratic gears continue to turn until the new Pope is elected.

The Camerlengo is the president and linchpin of the "Particular Congregation" that has a revolving membership and manages day-to-day affairs. In consultation with the senior members of each of the Cardinalatial orders: Bishops, Priests, Deacons—which are orders of rank within the College of Cardinals, rather than an indication of degree of Holy Orders—the Camerlengo also establishes the date on which the meetings ahead of the Conclave—the General Congregations—are to begin.

The decision to name Cardinal Farrell to the post of Camerlengo has already raised a few eyebrows. Cardinal Farrell went through formation and was ordained to the priesthood as a member of the Legionaries of Christ, founded by the notorious Fr. Marcial Maciel, who used the priestly society to create and maintain both a respectable façade and a source of income for his perverse proclivities. Maciel allegedly abused scores of victims, including minors, seminarians, and his own illegitimate children, which he had with at least two different women, whom he seduced under assumed names and false pretenses.

Though rumors of Maciel's moral turpitude swirled for decades, and had certainly reached the Vatican by the late 1990s, Pope St. John Paul II never disciplined the priest, who enjoyed his favor for many years. Maciel was finally asked to step down as the head of the Legion in January of 2005, just months before John Paul II died. In 2006, Pope Benedict XVI prohibited Maciel from exercising any public ministry and ordered him to a life of prayer and penance.

In 2009, Benedict authorized a special investigation of the Legion, called an Apostolic Visitation. Maciel's forced retirement and penance had already led Vatican watchers to wonder whether the Legion might be suppressed. Benedict, however, decided against suppression.

Cardinal Farrell left the Legion before the mid-1980s. In 2016, Farrell told the *Irish Times*, "I left the Legionaries because I had intellectual differences with them." Farrell also told the *Irish Times* he never knew anything about Maciel's wickedness and duplicity. "I never knew anything back then," he said. "I worked in Monterrey," Farrell explained, "and maybe I would have met Maciel once or twice, but I never suspected anything."

In 1984, then-Fr. Farrell joined the clergy of the Archdiocese of Washington. In 2001, not a year after Theodore McCarrick became Archbishop of Washington, then-Msgr. Farrell—who was already appointed Vicar General—was chosen to become an auxiliary bishop for the DC archdiocese. Farrell served as Vicar General and Moderator of the Curia until 2007, when Pope Benedict XVI made him Bishop of Dallas.

When the McCarrick scandal hit the papers in June of 2018, Cardinal Farrell faced media scrutiny because of his record of service under the former Archbishop of Washington. Farrell repeatedly said he never suspected anything was amiss with his former principal. "What Cardinal McCarrick was doing here, there and everywhere and all over the world, didn't enter into my daily routine of running the archdiocese of Washington," Farrell told the AP in July of last year.

During his time in Washington, DC, Cardinal Farrell lived with McCarrick and other clerics of the archdiocese in a residential facility near Dupont Circle, though he told the AP, "Never once did I even suspect," McCarrick of anything untoward. "Now, people can say 'Well you must be a right fool that you didn't notice.' I must be a right fool," Farrell continued, "but I don't think I am—and that's why I feel angry."

Pope Francis had shown great confidence in Cardinal Farrell's abilities long before this most recent appointment. In his position as Prefect of the Dicastery for Laity, Family, and Life, Farrell not only filled the top billet in one of the "super-dicasteries" of Francis's signature curial reform, but spearheaded the Vatican-side organization efforts for the 2018 World Meeting of Families in Dublin. Francis also made him a key figure in the organization of the 2018 Ordinary General Assembly of the Synod of Bishops on Young People, Faith and Vocational Discernment. Farrell also took a lead role in World Youth Day celebrations, and got the nod to announce that Lisbon, Portugal, would be the venue for the next iteration of the event in 2022.

En route to Rome from Abu Dhabi earlier this month, Francis wondered aloud whether he'd be Pope next year. Asked about possible travel to other majority-Muslim countries, Francis replied, "[I]nvitations have arrived from other Muslim countries but there's not time this year. We'll see next year. [Whether] I or another Peter, someone will go." It isn't the first time he's engaged in similar speculation. *En route* to Rome from Krakow after World Youth Day 2016,

Francis told a reporter, "If I don't go, Peter will be there [in Panama]," all the same.

With the appointment of a new Cardinal Camerlengo, whose office only activates during an interregnum, that speculation is likely to increase—even though the filling of a Vatican post is about as run-of-the-mill as one can get, and hardly a reliable indicator of the papal frame-of-mind. In any case, Pope Francis has chosen Cardinal Farrell to manage things after he's gone.

For the Catholic World Report, February 16, 2019

"Questions remain about McCarrick, even as new scandals emerge"

The Vatican announced on Saturday that the disgraced former Archbishop of Washington, DC, Theodore Edgar McCarrick, has been dismissed from the clerical state after being found guilty of several different canonical crimes, including "sins against the Sixth Commandment with minors and with adults" and "solicitation in the Sacrament of Confession" with "abuse of power" as an aggravating factor.

The Director ad interim of the Press Office of the Holy See told journalists at noon Rome Time on Saturday that the proceedings against McCarrick had been "extra-judicial"— meaning an abbreviated administrative process—and assured reporters that the rights of the accused were nonetheless fully respected throughout the process. "McCarrick's lawyers played an active role in the course of some of the interrogations," interim Director Alessandro Gisotti explained, before reaffirming that the verdict and sentence are both final. "[N] o recourse is possible," Gisotti said.

The Archdiocese of Washington issued a statement in response to the news on Saturday morning, saying the penalty, "underscores the gravity of his actions." The statement went on to say, "Our hope and prayer is that this decision serves to help the healing process for survivors of abuse, as well as those who have experienced disappointment or disillusionment because of what former Archbishop McCarrick has done." It is remarkable that, in an age in which the supreme pastor and governor of the universal Church has insisted "clericalism" is the root cause of the leadership crisis in which the Church is currently embroiled, the worst punishment ecclesiastical authority can impose on a cleric is to make him a layman. Nevertheless, thus is Mr. McCarrick punished, neither too soon, nor too severely.

Church leaders in Rome and in the United States seem awfully anxious to put the dreadful business with "Uncle Ted" behind them, and let the healing begin. Before that can happen, however, several outstanding matters require address. Questions regarding who in the US hierarchy and in the Roman Curia knew what about McCarrick, and when, remain without satisfactory—or any—answer from the Vatican, while delivery on promises of transparency and "zero tolerance" continues to receive postponement. Gisotti on Saturday quoted a communiqué from the Press Office dated October 6, 2018, which reported the Holy Father's 2015 remark: "Both abuse and its cover-up can no longer be tolerated and a different treatment for Bishops who have committed or covered up abuse, in fact represents a form of clericalism that is no longer acceptable."

That same October 6 press release also promised, "We will follow the path of truth wherever it may lead," quoting Pope Francis's remarks in Philadelphia on September 27, 2015.

Most importantly, it was in the October 6 communiqué that Pope Francis promised:

> The Holy See will, in due course, make known the conclusions of the matter regarding Archbishop McCarrick. Moreover, with reference to other accusations brought against Archbishop McCarrick, the Holy Father has decided that information gathered during the preliminary investigation be combined with a further thorough study of the entire documentation present in the Archives of the Dicasteries and Offices of the Holy See regarding the former Cardinal McCarrick, in order to ascertain all the relevant facts, to place them in their historical context and to evaluate them objectively.

Insofar as the verdict and penal sentence announced Saturday constitute the conclusions of the matter regarding Mr. McCarrick, Pope Francis may say he has made good on his promise. We hope and expect more information will be forthcoming. If Pope Francis and his lieutenants in the Vatican had hoped to score even a qualified public relations victory with the announcement of the McCarrick verdict, news that broke heading into the weekend made that unlikely.

On Friday, there was a story out of France—first reported by *Le Monde*—where the Apostolic Nuncio, Bishop Luigi Ventura, is under investigation for allegedly engaging in inappropriate contact with a male staff member at City Hall in Paris, during a reception held there in late January. The Press Office of the Holy See issued a terse statement saying the Vatican had learned of the investigation in the papers, and is "awaiting the results of the investigation." That is surely a case of bad timing, and may be much ado about nothing. Neither of those can account for what *La Croix International* reported, however, also on Friday.

A high-ranking official of the Apostolic Signatura—the highest ordinary tribunal in the Church's justice system—Msgr. Joseph Punderson, was listed as "removed from ministry" by his home diocese of Trenton, New Jersey. Punderson appeared on the list of priests credibly accused of abuse, which the Trenton diocese published on Wednesday. *CWR* attempted to contact Msgr. Punderson at his last known address, the Villa Stritch on *via della nocetta*, a residence for US clerics working in Rome, but was told Punderson left the facility in September of last year. A spokesperson for the Diocese of Trenton said Msgr. Punderson "resigned his position" last November. The Press Office of the Holy See did not respond to requests for information.

On Thursday of last week, the *Wall Street Journal* reported that the President of Pope Francis's Commission for the Protection of Minors, Cardinal Sean O'Malley OFM of Boston, has been privately complaining at least since 2017 that the Holy See has not been keeping its promises of "zero tolerance" when it comes to abusive clerics. "An appeals panel set up by the pope had reduced the punishments of a number of Catholic priests found guilty of abusing minors," the *Journal* reported. "In some cases, the panel canceled their dismissal from the priesthood and gave them short suspensions instead." The *Journal* article quoted O'Malley as telling the Cardinal Secretary of State, Pietro Parolin, "If this gets out, it will cause a scandal."

A great many unanswered questions remain, meanwhile, in connection with the Bishop-emeritus of Orán, Gustavo Zanchetta, for whom Pope Francis created a tailor-made position in 2017, inside the powerful APSA—the Administration of the Patrimony of the Apostolic See—which looks after the Holy See's real estate and financial holdings. Zanchetta is currently under investigation in his home diocese for possibly criminal malfeasance, including the sexual abuse of seminarians. Despite repeated promises of zero tolerance and transparency, the Vatican has been even more laconic when it comes to what Pope Francis knew about Bishop Zanchetta and when he knew it, than about Mr. McCarrick.

For the Catholic Herald, February 17, 2019

"McCarrick will continue to live at Kansas friary"

Theodore McCarrick, the former Archbishop of Washington, DC, whom Pope Francis has dismissed from the clerical state as punishment for sexual abuse of minors and adults, will continue to live at the friary in Salina, Kansas, where he moved in September of last year. The Diocese of Salina released a statement on Saturday saying: "Mr. McCarrick will continue to reside at the St. Fidelis Friary in Victoria until a decision of permanent residence is finalized."

St. Fidelis is operated by the Capuchin Franciscans. The statement also says Salina's bishop, Bishop Gerald Vincke, "expresses his gratitude to the Capuchins at St. Fidelis Friary for their charity and compassion shown to all who seek refuge in the Church, as well as the remarkable people of Victoria for their mercy in this difficult situation." There is still no word on how the nearly 89-year-old former cleric will support himself, though he is reported to have independent financial means at his disposal. Significant questions remain regarding where McCarrick—an inveterate fundraiser—got his personal wealth, and how much of it he got during his more than six decades as a cleric.

Pope Francis reduced Mr. McCarrick to the lay state last week, after nearly two years of investigations and proceedings that began in New York—where McCarrick was ordained—and eventually made their way to the Vatican. A communiqué from the Congregation for the Doctrine of the Faith (CDF), which conducted the canonical proceedings against Mr. McCarrick, reported on Saturday morning that the CDF found the former Cardinal and Archbishop of Washington, DC, guilty of "sins against the Sixth Commandment"—against chastity—with both minors and adults, and of the crime of solicitation in the Sacrament of Confession.

The communique also stated the CDF found "abuse of power" to have been an aggravating factor in McCarrick's guilt. The CDF communiqué said Mr. McCarrick was first found guilty on January 11, and that he presented a recourse, which the Ordinary Session of the Congregation for the Doctrine of the Faith rejected on February 13, before officially notifying McCarrick of the decision on Friday, February 15. The CDF communiqué also said Pope Francis has ruled that decision final and unappealable.

At noon on Saturday, the interim Director of the Press Office of the Holy See, Alessandro Gisotti, appeared before reporters to read the CDF communiqué in several languages. Speaking in English, Gisotti also said: "I remind you that the penal process in the Congregation for the Doctrine of the Faith can be one of two forms: judicial or extrajudicial." Gisotti went on to say, "In this case of McCarrick it was the second form, in which all of his rights were respected."

"I can affirm that McCarrick's lawyers played an active role in the course of some of the interrogations," Gisotti also added. "I underline that after this decree of the Congregation [for the Doctrine of the Faith], no recourse is possible," he said. Gisotti also quoted—in English—from a October 6, 2018 communiqué from the Press Office of the Holy See, which stated: "Both abuse and its cover-up can no longer be tolerated and a different treatment for Bishops who have committed or covered up abuse, in fact represents a form of clericalism that is no longer acceptable."

Theodore Edgar McCarrick was ordained a priest of the Archdiocese of New York in 1958, by the late Francis Cardinal Spellman. McCarrick quickly rose through the ranks, becoming secretary to then-Archbishop of New York, Terence Cardinal Cooke, in 1971. One of the accusations against McCarrick—that he sexually assaulted a minor in St. Patrick's Cathedral—dates to his period of service as secretary to Cooke. Pope St. Paul VI made McCarrick an auxiliary bishop of New York in 1977. McCarrick went on to serve from 1981-1986 as the first bishop of the Diocese of Metuchen, New Jersey, and then as Archbishop of Newark, before Pope St. John Paul II made him Archbishop of Washington, DC, in 2001.

Rumors about McCarrick's behavior—especially with seminarians, whom he would "invite" to a now-notorious beach house for weekend getaways—were widespread. In November of the year 2000—after the announcement of McCarrick's appointment to Washington had been made, but before McCarrick had been installed—a professor at the Immaculate Conception Seminary of the Newark archdiocese, Fr. Boniface Ramsey, (then a priest of the Dominican order) made a report of McCarrick's behavior to the Apostolic Nuncio to the US at the time, Archbishop Gabriel Montalvo.

The rumors were known to the Vatican no later than 2000, and possibly as early as 1994. In that year, the man serving as the papal representative to the US at the time, Archbishop Agostino Cacciavillan (now 93 and a cardinal in retirement) received a call from a person concerned the scheduled visit of John Paul II to Newark could cause scandal, owing to the rumors surrounding then Archbishop McCarrick. Cacciavillan says he asked the then Archbishop of New York, Cardinal John O'Connor, to look into the matter. Cacciavillan told the Catholic News Service that O'Connor reported: "[T]here was no obstacle to the visit of the pope to Newark." The rumors regarding McCarrick persisted and spread for years. Benedict XVI accepted McCarrick's resignation when McCarrick turned 75—canon law requires a sitting bishop to tender his resignation upon reaching that age—and eventually imposed some restrictions on McCarrick in his retirement. The enforcement of those restrictions was spotty at best.

In June of last year, the Archdiocese of New York announced it had deemed "credible and substantiated" the aforementioned accusation against then Cardinal McCarrick—of abusing a minor in 1971—and had turned the matter over to the Vatican. Several further accusers then came forward, and it emerged that several US dioceses where McCarrick once served had been involved in settling civil complaints against him stemming from McCarrick's alleged misbehavior with adults.

One of the witnesses against McCarrick was James Grein, who testified that McCarrick abused him for nearly two decades, starting when Grein was 11 years old. Grein is the son of a man who had a close friendship with McCarrick. Then Fr. McCarrick baptized Grein in 1958, two weeks after receiving priestly ordination. Grein also testified that McCarrick abused him during the Sacrament of Confession.

A former priest of the Diocese of Metuchen, Robert Ciolek, also came forward as one of McCarrick's adult victims. "I trusted him, I confided in him, I admired him," Ciolek told the *New York Times* in July of 2018. "I couldn't imagine that he would have anything other than my best interests in mind." McCarrick's disgrace led to intense and persistent public scrutiny.

Questions regarding who knew about Mr. McCarrick's behavior—or suspected, or should have known or suspected McCarrick of moral turpitude—persist, even in the wake of repeated denials from high-ranking prelates. The faithful and reporters alike asked how a man whose reputation for perverse and lascivious wickedness was apparently so firmly established could have risen so high and so easily through the ranks. In the same communiqué of October 6, 2018, from which Gisotti read on Saturday, the Holy See promised it would:

> [I]n due course, make known the conclusions of the matter regarding Archbishop McCarrick. Moreover, with reference to other accusations brought against Archbishop McCarrick, the Holy Father has decided that information gathered during the preliminary investigation be combined with a further thorough study of the entire documentation present in the Archives of the Dicasteries and Offices of the Holy See

regarding the former Cardinal McCarrick, in order to ascertain all the relevant facts, to place them in their historical context and to evaluate them objectively.

That promise came after repeated requests from senior Church leadership in the United States, for papal and Vatican assistance in investigating McCarrick, who helped many clerics rise during the course of his 60-year career, even as he received help from others. In September of 2018, the President of the United States Conference of Catholic Bishops, Cardinal Daniel DiNardo, travelled to Rome to ask Pope Francis to authorize an Apostolic Visitation of the US hierarchy—a request Pope Francis rejected.

The promise also followed the publication of a spectacular 11-page dossier by the former Apostolic Nuncio to the United States, Carlo Maria Viganò, detailing a 30-year cover-up of McCarrick's behavior. That cover-up allegedly involved three popes, three secretaries of state, and dozens of other very senior Churchmen. Pope Francis may consider he has made good on the promise "to make known the conclusions of the matter," regarding the man who was styled "Archbishop McCarrick" when the promise was made. If so, the communication of those conclusions was rather short on detail. Questions regarding who knew what, and when they knew it—in the US hierarchy and at the Vatican—remain unanswered.

For the Catholic World Report, February 20, 2019

"Transparency biggest challenge for Vatican heading into abuse summit"

Responsibility. Accountability. Transparency. Those are the themes of the working days scheduled for the meeting on child protection, which opens tomorrow in the Vatican. Organizers and participants of the meeting have a long row to hoe before they can begin to convince anyone they are serious about any one of those three themes, which are not conversation-starters for shop sessions, but prerequisites for morally competent leadership of any organization of any size or scope, and basic requirements those who are ruled make—in justice—of their rulers.

Everyone you talk to has a theory—often a variation on a theme—regarding what's wrong, who's to blame, and how to fix it, but there are two points on which there is broad and deep agreement among Church-watchers across the spectrum of Catholic opinion: this crisis of leadership is the worst the Church has seen in at least five hundred years; Church leadership at the highest levels still is not close to serious about dealing with the crisis.

Responsibility and accountability sound easy, but really aren't. There needs to be lots of hard work to get those two right—and there are going to be missteps along the way.

Transparency, on the other hand, is a no-brainer. At least, it ought to be—and it ought to be the starting point: insisting on transparency is the first, the absolute, the *condicio sine qua non* of sincerity. Practicing transparency—especially when it hurts—is always the best and most powerful driver of cultural reform within institutions.

There was plenty of talk about transparency at the Holy See Press Office on Monday, during the press conference presenting the meeting, but it took two journalists—the *National Catholic Reporter*'s Joshua McElwee, and this writer—repeated questions to extract any sort of statement from interim Press Office Director Alessandro Gisotti regarding the status of Msgr. Joseph Punderson, a priest of the Diocese of Trenton and a long-serving official at the Apostolic Signatura, which is the highest ordinary tribunal in the Church's judicial system.

NCR's question at the presser on Monday was, in essence, whether the Vatican can expect to speak credibly in the fight against abuse, if it is unwilling to be responsible, accountable, and transparent when it comes to its own precincts and personnel. Msgr. Punderson was the case-in-point. Trenton listed Msgr. Punderson as "removed from ministry" last week, owing to a credible abuse allegation against him, but offered no information at that time about the exact nature of the allegation, or regarding when the alleged abuse took place. *La Croix International*—which broke the Punderson story last Friday—quoted a priest of the Trenton diocese, Fr. John Bambrick, as saying he'd heard from an alleged victim of Punderson some fifteen years ago.

"I knew [Punderson] to be an abuser," Fr. Bambrick told *La Croix*. "I have always known he was an abuser, but he was powerful and had a great deal of influence here and in Rome. He had many friends in our curia and the pope's curia," Bambrick also said. On Monday, February 18, the Vatican didn't want to say whether Msgr. Punderson has resigned, or was fired, or placed on leave pending an investigation. Under pressure, Gisotti offered, "Msgr. Punderson is not at the Tribunal of the Signatura in this moment," and directed journalists to the Diocese of Trenton.

On Wednesday, Feb. 20, the Catholic News Service reported that Punderson had been deemed credibly accused in 2003, of abuse that allegedly occurred 26 years earlier. Trenton's Director of Communications, Rayanne Bennett, issued a statement saying, "The allegation was also reported to the Holy See, and Msgr. Punderson submitted his resignation in 2004." The statement continued, "The Holy See, however, permitted him to continue in office but under specific restrictions regarding public acts of ministry initially imposed by the Diocese of Trenton in 2003." Bennett's statement also says it was Msgr. Punderson's bishop, who ordered him to resign from the Apostolic Signatura in the Fall of 2018.

The timeline of the case suggests that three Popes and as many as four Prefects of the Apostolic Signatura had oversight of Msgr. Punderson after the Vatican was informed of the allegations against him: Cardinals Agostino Vallini, Raymond Burke, Dominique Mamberti, and possibly Cardinal Mario Francesco Pompedda, who resigned in late May of 2004. Cardinal Burke and Msgr. Punderson served together in junior positions at the Signatura: Burke was Defender of the Bond when Punderson came to the Tribunal in 1993 as a deputy Promoter of Justice. It is still not clear who knew what, or when they came to know it. Other high-ranking Churchmen have served for years under secret restrictions, more or less officially imposed and spottily enforced. The case of Theodore McCarrick is one.

The better analogy, however, may be that of Bishop Alexander Salazar, auxiliary of Los Angeles, on whom the Congregation for the Doctrine of the Faith imposed secret restrictions sometime after Los Angeles reported an allegation against him in 2005. Salazar served as many as thirteen years under those restrictions—until last December, when Pope Francis accepted his resignation. The Press Office of the Holy See announced Bishop Salazar's resignation, but gave no reason for it. The Archdiocese of Los Angeles revealed the circumstances of the case in separate statements.

Also at the Monday presser, in answer to a question from CNN, Archbishop Charles Scicluna—adjunct secretary to the Congregation for the Doctrine of the Faith and a principal organizer of the child protection meeting—spoke of the need to escape and condemn the cultural and institutional structures that foster opacity and favor cover-up. CNN's Delia Gallagher asked a question regarding the hypothesis that some clerics' illicit behavior—Cardinals' and bishops' as well as priests'—might make them unwilling to denounce one another, and that such relationships in the hierarchy might enable cover-up.

Archbishop Scicluna said, "[T]he fact that we're going to insist on transparency is not something that's—you know—it's deliberate. Because, a system that ensures cover-up is a no-go. We have to move forward from that, and condemn it, and condemn it without any hesitation." Gallagher had put her question first to Cardinal Cupich, who responded, "You were right in saying it's a hypothesis, and hypotheses have to be proven—and I think that is something that has to remain at that level—of hypothesis." In the meeting opening Thursday at the Vatican, transparency is last on the list.

CHAPTER 8

CLIMAX AND DELUGE

February 21 – 24

"Abuse summit day one: Pope calls for 'concrete and effective' action"

The highly anticipated meeting on child protection opened at the Vatican on Thursday morning, with powerful testimony from victims, one of whom told the bishops flatly, "You are the physicians of the soul and yet, with rare exceptions, you have been transformed—in some cases—into murderers of the soul, into murderers of the faith."

The man who spoke those words was Juan Carlos Cruz, the Chilean victim Pope Francis had once accused of calumny. Cruz also had words of praise for Pope Francis's turnaround in addressing the crisis in his native country. "I ask you, please collaborate with justice, because you have a special care for the victims, so that what is happening in Chile, that is, what the Pope is doing in Chile, be repeated as a model in other countries of the world," Cruz said.

Not everyone takes so sanguine a view of Pope Francis's efforts in Chile, but that is another matter. The other victims chose to remain anonymous, but their stories are no less harrowing than Cruz's.

One story that participants heard was from a victim of a priest, who was abused from the age of fifteen. "I got pregnant three times and he made me have an abortion three times, quite simply because he did not want to use condoms or contraceptives," she said. "At first I trusted him so much that I did not know he could abuse me. I was afraid of him, and every time I refused to have sex with him, he would beat me."

The stories came from victims of different ages and sexes and states of life, from all around the world. "I was far more moved by what I heard this morning than I expected to be," the Archbishop of Brisbane, Mark Coleridge, told journalists at the press briefing that followed the morning sessions.

Pope Francis, for his part, presented the participants with an unexpected list of 21 "points for reflection." Francis distributed the list to the 190 participants from all around the world at the end of his own opening remarks. "The holy People of God look to us, and expect from us not simple and predictable condemnations, but concrete and effective measures to be undertaken," Pope Francis said. "We need to be concrete."

Though they were presented as conversation-starters, one journalist at the press briefing following the morning sessions noted that "reflection points" from the boss are rarely just that. Several of the suggestions are things that are already standard practice in the United States, Canada, Great Britain, and Ireland, as well as in many other places in the developed world.

"[These points for reflection] are a simple point of departure that came from you and now return to you," Pope Francis told participants on Thursday morning. "They are not meant to detract from the creativity needed in this meeting."

How they will affect the direction in which the meeting is to go, is something that remains to be seen. Day One, however, followed the program, which included presentations during the morning sessions from the Archbishop of Manila, Cardinal Luis Antonio Tagle, and from the adjunct secretary of the Congregation for the Doctrine of the Faith, Archbishop Charles Scicluna.

Archbishop Coleridge described Cardinal Tagle's presentation to journalists gathered for the daily press briefing as a "meditation" and "not what I expected, but, better for that." Archbishop Scicluna's was "very different" more practical. "What we had from the two men," Archbishop Coleridge explained, "was vision and tactics—and this was a way of saying that we need both."

Below, please find the 21 points for reflection Pope Francis distributed to participants on Thursday morning.

1. To prepare a practical handbook indicating the steps to be taken by authorities at key moments when a case emerges.

2. To equip oneself with listening structures that include trained and expert people who can initially discern the cases of the alleged victims.

3. Establish the criteria for the direct involvement of the Bishop or of the Religious Superior.

4. Implement shared procedures for the examination of the charges, the protection of the victims and the right of defense of the accused.

5. Inform the civil authorities and the higher ecclesiastical authorities in compliance with civil

and canonical norms.

6. Make a periodic review of protocols and norms to safeguard a protected environment for minors in all pastoral structures: protocols and norms based on the integrated principles of justice and charity so that the action of the Church in this matter is in conformity with her mission.

7. Establish specific protocols for handling accusations against Bishops.

8. Accompany, protect and treat victims, offering them all the necessary support for a complete recovery.

9. Increase awareness of the causes and consequences of sexual abuse through ongoing formation initiatives of Bishops, Religious Superiors, clerics and pastoral workers.

10. Prepare pathways of pastoral care for communities injured by abuses and penitential and recovery routes for the perpetrators.

11. To consolidate the collaboration with all people of good will and with the operators of mass media in order to recognize and discern real cases from false ones and accusations of slander, avoiding rancor and insinuations, rumors and defamation (cf. Pope Francis's address to the Roman Curia, 21 December 2018).

12. To raise the minimum age for marriage to sixteen years.

13. Establish provisions that regulate and facilitate the participation of lay experts in investigations and in the different degrees of judgment of canonical

processes concerning sexual and / or power abuse.

14. The right to defense: the principle of natural and canon law of presumption of innocence must also be safeguarded until the guilt of the accused is proven. Therefore, it is necessary to prevent the lists of the accused being published, even by the dioceses, before the preliminary investigation and the definitive condemnation.

15. Observe the traditional principle of proportionality of punishment with respect to the crime committed. To decide that priests and bishops guilty of sexual abuse of minors leave the public ministry.

16. Introduce rules concerning seminarians and candidates for the priesthood or religious life. Be sure that there are programs of initial and ongoing formation to help them develop their human, spiritual and psychosexual maturity, as well as their interpersonal relationships and their behavior.

17. Be sure to have psychological evaluations by qualified and accredited experts for candidates for the priesthood and consecrated life.

18. Establish norms governing the transfer of a seminarian or religious aspirant from one seminary to another; as well as a priest or religious from one diocese or congregation to another.

19. Formulate mandatory codes of conduct for all clerics, religious, service personnel and volunteers to outline appropriate boundaries in personal relationships. Be specific about the necessary requirements for staff and volunteers and check their criminal record.

20. Explain all information and data on the dangers of abuse and its effects, how to recognize signs of abuse and how to report suspected sexual abuse. All this must take place in collaboration with parents, teachers, professionals and civil authorities.

21. Where it has not yet been in place, establish a group easily accessible for victims who want to report any crimes. Such an organization should have a certain autonomy with respect to the local ecclesiastical authority and include expert persons (clerics and laity) who know how to express the Church's attention to those who have been offended by improper attitudes on the part of clerics.

"Abuse summit day two: How to hold bishops to account"

"Accountability": that was the theme chosen for Day 2 of the meeting for the protection of minors taking place this week at the Vatican. An address by the Archbishop of Mumbai, Cardinal Oswald Gracias, set the tone for the day. His Eminence focused primarily on bishops' accountability to each other—in the key of "collegiality"—and spoke of the bishops' need to engender and foster a sense of accountability to each other.

"Because we belong to the college of bishops in union with the Holy Father," Cardinal Gracias said, "we all share accountability and responsibility." He went on to say, "[D]o we really engage in an open conversation and point out honestly to our brother bishops or priests when we notice problematic behavior in them?"

"We should cultivate a culture of *correctio fraterna* (fraternal correction)," said Cardinal Gracias, "which enables this without offending each other." Whatever the merits of those concerns, they do not speak directly to the kind of accountability for which thousands of long-suffering and egregiously injured victims throughout the world, along with the sorely tried faithful insulted and aggrieved for their sake, are impatient. Cardinal Gracias—who has been accused of seriously mishandling a 2015 case—did not appear before journalists on Friday at the press briefing following the morning session.

The President of the Pontifical Commission for the Protection of Minors, Cardinal Sean O'Malley of Boston—who was not a member of the committee Pope Francis appointed to organize the meeting, and whose name is conspicuously absent from the roster of speakers over the three days of sessions—was on the dais Friday. Reminded by a journalist that Theodore McCarrick was the "reassuring face" of the US bishops in 2002, when they were summoned to Rome when the scandal of abuse exploded in that year, and asked what he could say to reassure the faithful that a similar episode could never repeat itself, Cardinal O'Malley said, "We are talking today about collegiality—about our obligation to each other—I would hope that any bishop, who is aware of this kind of misbehavior, would certainly make that known to the Holy See, and not feel that in any way we should try to cover it up or turn a blind eye to it." McCarrick was on the Holy See's radar as early as 1994.

Cardinal O'Malley's response to the question came after the Archbishop of Chicago, Cardinal Blase Cupich, spoke to the same question. "The only thing that I can tell you," said Cardinal Cupich, "is that I, and everyone else, has to be held accountable—and I've always believed that." Cardinal Cupich went on to say, "[T]his is a matter, first of all, of accountability on my part: that I am going to live my life this way," i.e. as a Christian disciple ought, "and then, to make sure that we are supportive of each other to live the Gospel."

Cardinal Cupich was the second speaker at the morning session, and presented an outline of his "metropolitan" proposal, i.e. to use the Metropolitan Archbishop in charge of the ecclesiastical province or "metropolis" to investigate, prosecute, and try a bishop accused of negligence, cover-up, or other malfeasance. Reminded by a journalist that Theodore McCarrick was a metropolitan, Cardinal Cupich directed his questioner to the footnotes of his text, where he discusses the possible alternatives in such an eventuality. That discussion, by the way, can be found in note 6 of Cardinal Cupich's text.

Another significant highlight during the press briefing was the discussion entertained over Point 15 of Pope Francis's "reflection points" for the meeting participants, which he distributed Thursday at the beginning of the meeting. The point reads:

> Observe the traditional principle of proportionality of punishment with respect to the crime committed. To decide that priests and bishops guilty of sexual abuse of minors leave the public ministry.

Journalists have noted the ambiguity of the text. It seems to call for prudential consideration of penalties according to the principle of proportionality—roughly, "let the punishment fit the crime." It might open the possibility of applying permanent removal as the penalty for every abuse offence, or not.

The second sentence seems to encourage bishops to apply the so-called "one strike policy," but does not propose that the rule—already in force in many Anglophone jurisdictions—become universal law. "I would advocate that," i.e. the one-strike policy, "for everyone," said Cardinal O'Malley. What the Pope meant in saying it remains unclear.

"If you read just one speech from the abuse summit, make it this one"

There's one speech you need to read from the Saturday sessions of the Vatican's child protection meeting—a day dedicated to the theme of transparency—and veteran Vaticanologist Valentina Alazraki of Mexico's *Noticieros Televisa* delivered it during the afternoon session. It was the last working session before Vespers and the special penitential liturgy, and it is not too much to say she nailed it. Alazraki's remarks were a frank challenge and a moral lesson that cut through the mystifying jargon that has dominated so much of the talk over the past three days, and she delivered them in words a child could understand.

"We journalists know that abuse is not limited to the Catholic Church," Alazraki said, "but you must understand that we have to be more rigorous with you than with others, by virtue of your moral role." In case it was needed, she illustrated the point. "Stealing, for example, is wrong, but if the one stealing is a police officer it seems more serious to us, because it is the opposite of what he or she should do, which is to protect the community from thieves."

Alazraki spoke of the right of the faithful—and the broad public—to know the truth, and to have it from those who are responsible for their safety and especially that of their children. "I would like you to leave this hall," Alazraki explained, "with the conviction that we journalists are neither those who abuse nor those who cover up. Our mission is to assert and defend a right, which is a right to information based on truth in order to obtain justice."

She explained the terms of the issue before the participants, and spelled out the stakes unsparingly:

> If you are against those who commit or cover up abuse, then we are on the same side. We can be allies, not enemies. We will help you to find the rotten apples and to overcome resistance in order to separate them from the healthy ones. But if you do not decide in a radical way to be on the side of the children, mothers, families, civil society, you are right to be afraid of us, because we journalists, who seek the common good, will be your worst enemies.

That wasn't a threat to the bishops, it was a promise: to them and to the public. Introducing Valentina Alazraki to the hall, Fr. Federico Lombardi SJ noted that she has been on this beat for many years. When she started, Paul VI was Pope, and she has hardly missed a single papal trip since Pope St. John Paul II's election (during whose pontificate she went to 100-104).

She's seen it all, and she knows the score. You can be sure she knew the room she was addressing, when she said, "Behind the silence, the lack of healthy, transparent communication, quite often there is not only the fear of scandal, concern for the institution's good name, but also money, compensation, gifts," and graft. That line appeared in the section of her speech concerning the notorious founder of the Legion of Christ, Fr. Marcial Maciel, who used the congregation he founded to create a veneer of respectability and provide a source of funding for the most grotesque immorality:

> One need not forget that in the Legion there was a fourth vow according to which if a Legionaries saw something he was uncertain of regarding a superior, he could neither criticize much less comment about it. Without this censure, without this total concealment, had there been transparency, Marcial Maciel would not have been able, for decades, to abuse seminarians and to have three or four lives, wives and children, who came to accuse him of having abused his own children.

"I assure you," she said, "that at the basis of that scandal, which did so much harm to thousands of people, to the point of tarnishing the memory of one who is now a saint, there was unhealthy communication."

"The faithful," Alazraki went on to say, "do not forgive the lack of transparency, because it is a new assault on the victims. Those who fail to inform encourage a climate of suspicion and incite anger and hatred against the institution." She told the bishops what they'd been doing wrong in concrete terms, frankly and forthrightly spoken, not in a spirit of condemnation, but of exhortation—and admonition. They needed to hear it. Here's hoping they take the message to heart. Now, they have no excuse.

For the Catholic Herald, February 24, 2019

"What was missing from the Pope's closing remarks at the abuse summit"

Pope Francis this morning delivered his concluding remarks to participants in the four-day meeting on child protection that began last Thursday here at the Vatican. It's a speech that makes interesting reading for several reasons, not least of which is the organization of its substance: Francis is a dozen paragraphs in—some of them short—before he mentions that sexual abuse occurs in the Church.

In paragraph 2—the first substantive paragraph of the address—Pope Francis told participants, "[T]he gravity of the scourge of the sexual abuse of minors is, and historically has been, a widespread phenomenon in all cultures and societies." Shortly thereafter, he reminded participants, that abusers "are primarily parents, relatives, husbands of child brides, coaches and teachers." He's not wrong, but the reason the patriarchs, presidents of bishops' conferences, religious superiors, and curial heads were here is because of the crisis of clerical sexual abuse of minors.

One could be forgiven for garnering the impression Francis wants to skip the part where the Church reforms herself in her laws and structures as a first step toward the cultural renewal that everyone within the Church and without agree is needed—what it should look like and how to get it are subjects on which there is and shall continue to be a good deal of disagreement, but that is inevitable and in any case another matter—and jump straight to the part where she is leading the world with her moral witness.

The question is whether Church leadership has the moral resolve to undertake the necessary reform: to take the "concrete, effective" measures for which Francis called. As the President of the Pontifical Commission for the Protection of Minors put it at the Friday briefing: "By addressing the problem, the Church is helping the broader society, but we have to begin by putting our house in order." Where the speech was not perfectly backwards, it was a jumble—a hodgepodge—a kitchen-sink collection of titbits and talking points that no one bothered to distill into a coherent statement of policy. All the promises were there, sure—but, as abuse survivor Marie Collins said, "We have heard these commitments to confront abuse many times before. When and how is what we need to hear: in detail."

Everyone was hoping Francis would knock this one out of the park, but proof of the meeting's effectiveness will come in the follow-through.

For the Catholic Herald, February 25, 2019

"As the abuse summit closes, what has changed?"

The Vatican's four-day "summit" on child protection ended on Sunday, with little to show. The three days of the meeting's working sessions began with a call from Pope Francis for "concrete, effective measures" to combat the clerical sexual abuse of minors, and ended with what essentially came to more promises.

Following Sunday Mass in the Sala Regia, which had Archbishop Mark Coleridge of Brisbane as the homilist and saw Pope Francis deliver a closing address that was not universally well-received, the Vatican announced three measures:

- An Apostolic Letter motu proprio on the protection of minors and vulnerable adults—which will accompany a new law for Vatican City and guidelines for the Vicariate of Vatican City (the ecclesiastical district responsible for the administration of the part of the Rome diocese that is inside Vatican City);
- A vademecum for bishops;
- A "task force" to assist bishops in combatting abuse.

The meeting's moderator, Fr. Federico Lombardi SJ, announced the new steps at the final press briefing that followed the meeting's close on Sunday. Fr. Lombardi did not say exactly when the new measures would come, but said the *motu proprio*, law, and guidelines are "mature" and awaiting final preparation for publication.

The adjunct secretary to the Congregation for the Doctrine of the Faith and the leading expert on the legal side of child protection in the Catholic Church, Archbishop Charles J. Scicluna of Malta, did offer news regarding one specific legal change that could be in the offing: modifying the canonical definition of "child pornography" to include any material involving anyone under the age of eighteen. At present, the pertinent law makes "the acquisition, possession, or distribution by a cleric of pornographic images of minors under the age of fourteen, for purposes of sexual gratification, by whatever means or using whatever technology" a very grave canonical crime (*delictum gravius*). In his final address on Sunday, Pope Francis said, "We now consider that this age limit should be raised in order to expand the protection of minors and to bring out the gravity of these deeds."

Regarding the handbook—which Fr. Lombardi described as a "very brief" guidebook prepared by the Congregation for the Doctrine of the Faith and intended "to help the world's bishops understand clearly their duties and their practical responsibilities [It. *compiti*, literally "tasks"]—Fr. Lombardi said he expected it to be ready "within a few weeks, maybe a month or two." If readers are surprised to learn that bishops should require such basic instruction—their mission, after all, is to govern the ecclesiastical jurisdictions in their charge—let them remember that Archbishop Scicluna told journalists at a briefing on Monday of this week, "[I]n recent months, the Congregation for Bishops, when they ask other bishops to comment on candidates for the mission of bishop, always include an explicit question on how the candidate has dealt with sexual abuse issues—whether [the candidate] has been criticized for not doing the right thing—that is also an important aspect, now, of discernment, before a person is presented to [the] mission of bishop."

Pope Francis has approved plans to prepare the program for the task forces, which are to include experts in various fields to help dioceses and episcopal conferences in difficulty for a lack of resources. Fr. Lombardi also issued a statement through the Press Office of the Holy See on Sunday, describing the promised measures as, "encouraging signs that will accompany us in our mission of preaching the Gospel and of serving all children throughout the world, in mutual solidarity with all people of goodwill who want to abolish every form of violence and abuse against minors." Also at the Sunday briefing, Archbishop Scicluna said, "At the end of the day, it's the change of heart that is important." Organizers and curial heads will meet to discuss the conference tomorrow. Organizers were to meet Sunday afternoon to discuss the Monday meeting.

For the Catholic Herald, February 25, 2019

"The Church needs transparency. These two cases show it has a long way to go"

Even before the thing began—whatever the thing was that happened over four days last week and into Sunday here in Rome—the pieces didn't quite fit. At the Monday presser presenting the three days of working sessions and two liturgies that were to serve as capstones to the event, several churchmen spoke about the need for concreteness in addressing the crisis and transparency in dealing with the public.

When journalists from two different outlets asked about the ongoing case of Msgr. Joseph Punderson (a priest of the Diocese of Trenton, who spent a quarter century as an official at the Apostolic Signatura—the Church's "Supreme Court"), recently listed by his home diocese as "removed from ministry" because of a credible allegation of sexual abuse against him, the response was that the specific question was beyond the purview of the briefing. Joshua McElwee reported the exchanges for the *National Catholic Reporter*:

"We are not now here to discuss single cases," said Vatican spokesman Alessandro Gisotti, responding to a question from *NCR* at the briefing, which also included three of the organizers of the upcoming summit: Chicago Cardinal Blase

Cupich, Maltese Archbishop Charles Scicluna and Jesuit Fr. Hans Zollner. Pressed again on the matter later in the briefing, Gisotti referred questions about Punderson's case to the Trenton diocese. The spokesman then said the priest "is not at the Tribunal of the Signatura at this moment," but did not specify if that response referred to the priest's physical location or his position within the Vatican.

In fact, the question the second journalist—this one, for the *Catholic Herald*—asked, was whether Msgr. Punderson was still an official at the Signatura. Trenton had described Punderson in an email to this journalist on Friday, February 15, as "formerly an official at the Apostolic Signatura" who had "resigned his position" in November 2018. The Press Office did not respond to our request for confirmation on Saturday. On the following Monday, the Holy See Press Office still wouldn't say if Punderson was still in his job.

On February 20, the Diocese of Trenton issued a statement saying Msgr. Punderson had been credibly accused of abusing a minor in 2003, and that he originally offered to resign his Vatican position in 2004. The Congregation for the Doctrine of the Faith put him under restrictions, but the Vatican allowed him to continue at the Signatura. Also on February 20, Gisotti finally confirmed that Punderson had resigned.

All throughout the three days of sessions, the senior churchmen called to speak on each day's overarching theme—Responsibility on Thursday, Accountability on Friday, Transparency on Saturday—largely interpreted or footnoted their issues into obscurity. The two great exceptions to the trend were the women—one a Nigerian religious superior and the other a Mexican laywoman and long-time Vaticanologist—who practiced the *parrhesia*—frank forthrightness—for which Pope Francis has repeatedly called. Sr. Veronica Openibo of the Society of the Holy Child Jesus told participants flatly, "This storm will not pass by." She also said, "At the present time, we are in a state of crisis and shame. We have seriously clouded the grace of the Christ-mission." Not rhetorically, but in earnest, she asked, "Is it possible for us to move from fear of scandal to truth? How do we remove the masks that hide our sinful neglect? What policies, programs and procedures will bring us to a new, revitalized starting point characterized by a transparency that lights up the world with God's hope for us in building the Reign of God?" At the end of the meeting, we are certainly no closer to answers for those questions as far as the hierarchical stewardship of the Church's fortunes on Earth is concerned.

Valentina Alazraki gave the final presentation on Saturday afternoon, before the participants ended their working sessions and moved to the Sala Regia for a penitential liturgy. Alazraki spoke on behalf of journalists everywhere, but especially as a representative of the Vatican press corps. The *Catholic Herald* described her remarks as the one speech people needed to read. "The faithful do not forgive the lack of transparency," she told the 190 participants, "because it is a new assault on the victims. Those who fail to inform encourage a climate of suspicion and incite anger and hatred against the institution."

The editor of South Africa's leading Catholic weekly, the *Southern Cross*, Günther Simmermacher, described Alazraki's words as, "Superb, prophetic stuff." He said, "[E]ven if these bishops go home and fail to do anything, none of them, no bishop, can still claim to be confused or uncertain about what's at stake."

"They have been told," Simmermacher said. Whether they have heard the message is another matter. In the last question at the last briefing on the last day of the meeting, *Crux's* Ines San Martin asked a question about another case of cover-up—one involving Pope Francis directly. Bishop Oscar Gustavo Zanchetta, emeritus of Orán, is under investigation for misrule in the diocese he formerly led, to which Pope Francis named him in 2013. The investigation is probing complaints including alleged sexual and financial misconduct.

Pope Francis created a position for Zanchetta—with whom he had a long-standing professional relationship dating at least to their days together in the Argentinian bishops' conference—in the Vatican, at the end of 2017, even though he had reportedly received evidence of Zanchetta's misbehavior as early as 2015. "We know that there was a bishop in Argentina, Zanchetta, who had gay porn in his phone, involving young people," San Martin said. "How can we believe that this is, in fact—you know—the last time we're going to hear 'No more coverup,' when, at the end of the day, Pope Francis covered up for someone in Argentina, who had gay porn?"

Archbishop Charles Scicluna of Malta, who is adjunct secretary to the Congregation for the Doctrine of the Faith, one of the principal organizers of the meeting, and the Church's leading expert on child protection law-enforcement, began to answer—San Martin had put the question directly to him—but the interim director of the Press Office of the Holy See, Alessandro Gisotti, interrupted him.

"[W]e have said that an investigation has been launched," Gisotti said, "it is ongoing, so we will inform you of the results once it has been completed. This is our position. This is all I can say at the moment. As you know, we had asked you not to focus on specific cases, and I think that generally speaking the meeting has provided extraordinary answers in this regard."

In reply, Archbishop Scicluna offered, "I don't have information about the case you mentioned, but if it's investigating—somebody's investigating a case—they're not covering it up. That's my take."

Shortly before 3pm Rome Time on Monday, the Press Office of the Holy See issued a statement from interim director, Alessandro Gisotti, on the first of the promised follow-up meetings involving organizers and the heads of Roman curial dicasteries. Gisotti reported that the participants promised to work toward "greater involvement of the laity on this front," i.e. the fight against clerical sexual abuse, "and the need to invest in training and prevention using reality with a consolidated experience in this field."

"Lastly," the statement reads, "it was stressed that the progress of the follow-up of the meeting should be verified with meetings of the curial department heads, in the name of synodality and synergy." In a word: more meetings. The "summit" on child protection in the Church ended as it began: with many pressing questions, and few answers, none of which are close to satisfactory.

AFTERWORD

It is now mid-October 2019. The Special Assembly of the Synod of Bishops for the Amazon is underway here in Rome. By the time the book you have just finished reading is printed and bound, another season will have come and gone. The crisis in the Church will still be with us. It is an essential feature of Catholic life now, and will be until such time as the hierarchical leadership of the Church should choose to reform itself, or until the secular arm decides to break the institution in its present form.

It is apparent that bishops will not reform of their own accord. Unsupported, public pressure is often only marginally effective, at best. It is apparent that, corporately, the bishops fear Caesar more than they love Christ or His faithful. Caesar's instruments are not surgical. His interests are not Christ's, nor are they those of Christ's Church. This is going to get worse before it gets better.

In his *Dissertatione on the Canon and Feudal Law*, the great American founder, John Adams, noted: "[The people] have a right: an indisputable, unalienable, indefeasible, divine right to that most dreaded and envied kind of knowledge," by which he meant, "of the characters and conduct of their rulers." Adams considered the Catholic Church an enemy of political liberty. I love him, but even today, I disagree. I do say that the Church is a polity. The right Adams asserted—to the characters and conduct of rulers—therefore inheres in all the members of the Church, who would be citizens of celestial Jerusalem.

An enlightened and energetic citizenry is truly the last bulwark against tyranny, whether temporal or spiritual. Thus, it continues to be important for Catholics—for people generally—to keep abreast of the doings at the center of power here in Rome and in their home dioceses and countries. Like it or not, every Catholic is a part of this story. There are many gifts, but one Spirit. Each of us must choose his part carefully.

The journalist's job is to tell the story as it unfolds. When a journalist is a Catholic, his professional responsibility elides perceptibly with his baptismal commitments, but is neither identical to nor co-extensive with those undertakings. The great twentieth-century political philosopher Eric Voegelin once noted that, when it comes to the things of the city, the philosopher has no questions to ask that are not those of the citizen. I have often wondered whether I am a journalist who covers Church politics, or a political philosopher who writes on a peculiar beat in the journalistic mode, but this is no time for navel-gazing. I will keep asking questions, the frames and answers to which may inform the public conversation in the Church and in society more broadly considered. Others have other, doubtless more important tasks, but this one is mine.

At this point, it is apparent that reform of the Church must come, one way or another. The necessary reform must somehow involve the sharing of power with all members of the Body, according to their state of life. One great object of the reform effort must be, therefore, to find a way to share governing power that does not violate the Church's hierarchical constitution. In the meantime, it is absolutely essential that we be about the works of mercy both corporal and spiritual: we must love each other and our enemies with renewed *élan* and great alacrity, for that is how the world will know we are Christians.